Developing the Globa

Developing the Global Student addresses the question of how students of higher education can emerge from their university life better equipped to dwell more effectively, ethically and comfortably amidst the turmoils of a globalizing world. It does this from a number of theoretical perspectives, illustrating the nature of the personal and educational challenges facing the individual student and the teaching professional.

The book explores the massive social changes wrought by the technologies and mobilities of globalization, particularly how present and future generations will relate to, work with and dwell alongside the global other. It outlines a range of social, psychological and intercultural perspectives on human tendencies to seek out comfort among communities of similitude, and illustrates how the experience of life in a global era requires us to transcend the limits of our own biographies and approach university education as a matter of knowledge deconstruction and identity reconstruction, rather than reproduction.

This book brings these considerations directly into the daily business of higher education by drawing out the implications for practice at a number of levels. It examines:

- the implications of a globally interconnected world and individual biographies for the design of the curriculum;
- a holistic view of learning in the context of the need to develop the global *self*;
- what the impact on non-academic practice will be if universities as institutions are to enable these changes;
- ways in which the broader student community can transform to offer an experience that is more supportive of the development of global *selves*.

Linking theoretical perspectives to present a model of learning as change, this book will be of great interest to those working in higher education, and particularly to anyone involved in policy design and the delivery of the student experience.

David Killick is Head of Academic Staff Development at Leeds Metropolitan University, UK, and has worked on institutional internationalization initiatives for several years.

Internationalization in Higher Education
Series Editor: Elspeth Jones

This series addresses key themes in the development of internationalization within Higher Education. Up to the minute and international in both appeal and scope, books in the series focus on delivering contributions from a wide range of contexts and provide both theoretical perspectives and practical examples. Written by some of the leading experts in the field, they are vital guides that discuss and build upon evidence-based practice and provide a clear evaluation of outcomes.

Titles in the series:

Tools for Teaching in an Educationally Mobile World
Jude Carroll

Developing the Global Student
Higher education in an era of globalization
David Killick

Governing Cross-Border Higher Education
Christopher Ziguras and Grant McBurnie

Developing the Global Student

Higher education in an era of globalization

David Killick

Routledge
Taylor & Francis Group

LONDON AND NEW YORK

First published 2015
by Routledge
2 Park Square, Milton Park, Abingdon, Oxon OX14 4RN

and by Routledge
711 Third Avenue, New York, NY 10017

Routledge is an imprint of the Taylor & Francis Group, an informa business

British Library Cataloguing in Publication Data
A catalogue record for this book is available from the British Library

Library of Congress Cataloging in Publication Data
Killick, David.
Developing the global student: higher education in an era of globalization /
David Killick.
pages cm.—(Internationalization in higher education series)
Includes bibliographical references and index.
1. Education, Higher. 2. College students. 3. Education and globalization.
I. Title.
LB2322.2.K55 2014
378—dc23
2014003295

ISBN: 978-0-415-72804-1 (hbk)
ISBN: 978-0-415-72805-8 (pbk)
ISBN: 978-1-315-76480-1 (ebk)

Typeset in Galliard
by Book Now Ltd, London

To Martin, whose years of challenge are woven through my lifeworld, though he has always known me to be right from my perspective.

Contents

List of illustrations   ix
Series editor's foreword   xi

Introduction   1

1   Questions of context   6

Introduction 6
Section 1: Global contexts 7
Section 2: Conceptions of higher education 12
*Section 3: Education for citizenship, social justice,
    and a better world? 16*
Section 4: Internationalization 19
Section 5: Internationalization of the curriculum 26
Section 6: The global self 29

2   Questions of alterity   35

Introduction 35
Section 1: Social consequences of globalization 36
Section 2: Social identity and ethnocentrism 45
Section 3: Intercultural competence and communication 54
Section 4: Contact and conflict theories 62

3   Questions of the lifeworld   66

Introduction 66
Section 1: A model of the lifeworld 68
Section 2: The habitus and the ready-to-hand 75
Section 3: Capital, capability and agency 78

Section 4: Cultural icebergs 83
Section 5: Schemata, scripts and types 87
Section 6: Attitudes and heuristics 91

4 Questions of learning 97

Introduction 97
Section 1: (Re)forming the lifeworld 98
Section 2: Holistic learning 105
Section 3: Learning triggers 111
Section 4: Situated learning and communities of practice 116
Section 5: Learning stages 119

5 Questions of practice 124

Introduction 124
Section 1: Shaping the environment – inclusivity and the hidden curriculum 129
Section 2: Shaping the curriculum – content and outcomes 138
Section 3: Shaping the delivery – learning experiences and communities 155
Section 4: Shaping broader institutional practice 170

Afterword 180

Appendix: Selected resources and links to support practice 183
Glossary 185
References 187
Index 206

Illustrations

Figures

0.1 Clines of major dichotomies around the role, purpose,
and defining features of higher education   3

1.1 Related dimensions to the global self – with self-in-the-world
identity having primacy   33

2.1 Simplified representation of Milton Bennett's stages of
ethnocentrism and ethnorelativism   51

2.2 Simplified diagram of communication with message sender,
message, and message recipient   58

3.1 Representation of the lifeworld with the self-world, the
socio-cultural-world, and the extended-world   74

3.2 Representation of the lifeworld and its horizons with
the self-world, the socio-cultural-world, and the extended-world   80

4.1 Learning as an iterative continuum between assimilative
and accommodative processes   100

4.2 Learning as an iterative continuum between assimilative and
accommodative processes with Mezirow's four types of
learning, including 'meaning perspective' transformation   102

4.3 Representation of the three dimensions of the lifeworld and
its horizons with self-, socio-cultural, and extended-worlds   106

4.4 Learning as an iterative continuum, perhaps with 'jump' points,
between assimilative and accommodative processes across the
affective, behavioural, and cognitive dimensions of being   109

5.1 Some characteristics which might be evidenced by more effective
intercultural communicators (in English)   136

Tables

4.1 Three-stage pattern of development from adolescent to adult   119

4.2 Baxter Magolda's 'four phases of the journey towards
self-authorship'   122

5.1 Reflective task: Curriculum review   144
5.2 Selected examples from the taxonomy of the affective domain   150
5.3 Reflective task: On learning outcomes to reflect aspects of
     the affective domain   151
5.4 Examples of intended learning outcome modifications to
     embed aspects of the graduate attribute of having a global outlook   153

Series editor's foreword

This series addresses the rapidly changing and highly topical field of internationalization in higher education. Arising from the notion of international education, which had essentially a curricular focus on international themes such as development studies and comparative education, use of the term 'internationalization' began more recently, during the latter part of the twentieth century. Since that time attention to the international dimension of higher education has become increasingly visible in institutional strategies as well as national and international agendas. Early distinctions were established between, on the one hand, market-driven interests in the recruitment of international students and, on the other, practitioners who see transformational potential through internationalization activities as a means of enhancing personal and professional development.

While those themes continue to be of importance, the intervening years have seen a more nuanced range of interests bridging that divide. Informed by diverse disciplines including anthropology, languages and communication, business and marketing, environmental studies, strategic leadership and pedagogy, internationalization is now high on the priority list for universities around the world. This is, in part, as a response to changing global environments but also in reaction to globalization itself with its potential for homogenization if taken to extremes. The many dimensions of contemporary internationalization require institutions to adjust and define the concept for their own purposes, adding to the richness of our understanding of the 'meta-discipline' in practice. This is perhaps most evident in countries where institutional and curricular internationalization is a more recent development, and traditional 'Western' internationalization practice requires further exploration for appropriacy in local contexts. Development and implementation of the concept in such new environments will add to our understanding of the benefits and challenges of internationalization practice over the coming years.

The answer to the question 'what is internationalization?' will thus vary from one university to another and indeed by subject discipline within that institution. Reframing the question as 'what is internationalization for this university, in this particular context, and for this discipline within it?' begins to reflect more accurately the diversity and complexity of this growing field.

Today there are compelling drivers for university leaders to adopt an integrated rather than a unidimensional approach to internationalization. Intensifying competition for talent, changes in global student flows, international branch campuses and growing complexity in cross-border activity, along with the rising influence of institutional rankings, all provide economic impetus and reputational consequences of success or failure. Meanwhile additional incentive is provided by growing awareness that the intercultural competence required for global contexts is equally important for living and working in today's increasingly diverse and multicultural societies. Research indicates a rising demand by employers for university graduates with enhanced global perspectives and intercultural competence, and students themselves are showing increased interest in international and intercultural experience. Internationalization thus has both global and more local intercultural interests at its heart.

Internationalization can facilitate an inclusive, intercultural dimension to the teaching, research, service and the commercial and entrepreneurial pursuits of a contemporary university. It is most successful when seen as an enabling factor in the achievement of wider corporate goals rather than as an aim in itself. Embedding internationalization through changing institutional language, culture and attitudes into standard university practice is more likely to achieve this than if seen as a separate goal in itself.

Internationalization as a powerful force for change is an underlying theme of this series, in contrast to economic or brand-enhancing aspects of international engagement. It seeks to address these complex topics as internationalization matures into its next phase. It aims to reflect contemporary concerns, with volumes geared to the major questions of our time. Written or edited by leading thinkers and authors from around the world, while giving a voice to emerging researchers, the series will offer theoretical perspectives with practical applications, focusing on some of the critical issues in this developing field for higher education leaders and practitioners alike.

This volume considers students in a globalizing world, addressing the question of how they can emerge from university life equipped to dwell effectively, ethically, and comfortably in changing environments. It considers a range of theoretical perspectives, illustrating the nature of the personal and educational challenges facing the individual student and the teaching professional.

The book explores the social consequences of globalization, particularly how present and future generations will respond to the global other, both personally and professionally. It considers a range of social, psychological and intercultural perspectives on cultural similarity and difference and the implications of these for higher education.

Key topics include:

- the implications of a globally interconnected world and individual biographies for the design of the curriculum;
- a holistic view of learning and development of the global *self*;

- the impact on practice if universities are to enable these changes;
- transformation of the broader student community in the development of global *selves*.

Linking several theoretical perspectives to present a model of learning as change, this book will offer thought-provoking reflections on personal development and ideas for inclusive practice. It responds to the implications of internationalization if we wish to encourage all students to consider alternative global perspectives from domestic as well as international standpoints.

Elspeth Jones
Emerita Professor of the Internationalisation of Higher Education,
Leeds Metropolitan University

Introduction

It's coming yet for all that
That Man to Man, the world over
Shall brothers be for all that.
(Robert Burns, *A Man's a Man For All That*, 1795,
Standard English translation)

Any situation in which some individuals prevent others from engaging in
the process of inquiry is one of violence.
(Freire 1970: 85)

This book presents university internationalization as a process aimed at transforming the student experience in response to changes in the wider world. The
contexts derive principally from my own experience in Anglophone 'Western'
institutions, and concern most directly students within 'taught' rather than
research provision. However, all universities have students who need and deserve
to have an appropriate curriculum, which is well-constructed, well-taught, and
situated within a supportive environment. This begs the questions:

- Where do we see the boundaries of what constitutes the *curriculum*?
- What is *appropriate* curriculum?
- What does it mean to be *well*-constructed and *well*-taught? And,
- What would constitute a *supportive* learning environment?

Through looking, albeit necessarily briefly, at key dimensions to the current
and emerging global context, and at psychological and sociological perspectives
on 'being' (how students come to their university life partly 'formed' through
their biographies, how they are to make their way, get by) within that context,
and then at learning theory perspectives on their 'becoming' (finding/creating
themselves, their learning and development through their university lives *and
beyond*), the book offers theoretical frames for those questions, and provides backgrounds to inform the shaping of the university experience *for all our students*.

Although I contextualize the discussion by reference to institutional responsibilities, constraining policy drivers, and the wider international contexts in which internationalization is enacted, this book is primarily about our students, about the challenges they face in their journeys through university and across their early adult years, and about the challenges we, as academic staff, must respond to if we are to support our students appropriately through and for these turbulent and uncertain times. Importantly, the book is about *all* our students. Although I will refer frequently to the domestic–international student nexus, the issue really is one of equitable, respectful and inclusive educational practices and spaces which every student has a right to, and which form the bedrock of the development of the global student as set out in the book.

In coming to examine internationalization as it is understood in this book, we are necessarily drawn into some fundamental questions, such as:

> What kind of education is required in the 21st century to face the challenges of globalisation? How can internationalisation contribute to developing educational programs adequate for the needs of this century? What are the characteristics and elements of an internationalised curriculum to educate global and multicultural citizens? What types of policies and institutional strategies must institutions of higher education follow to internationalise their main functions? ... What role should education play in international cooperation and international relations to foster a world citizenry?
>
> (Gacel-Ávila 2005: 123–124)

My philosophy is that higher education should be a process of empowerment, and that in these liquid times this requires in particular building capabilities to recognize, withstand and challenge the defensive fundamentalisms arising when identities are threatened. I propose this requires that we enable our students to gain a sense of how they stand in the world which rests upon the will, the confidence, and the capabilities to seek out the perspectives of others and to adopt critical stances to their own established thoughts and behaviours. This requires a holistic interpretation of learning, of individual agency, and therefore of the educational process.

These concerns underpin my own understanding of the internationalization agenda. The perspectives I present in the opening chapters in support of this agenda may be contentious, they are after all based in *theories* of self and world, and are presented with a sceptical bent. I sincerely hope that readers who find themselves in disagreement will be willing, nonetheless, to critically engage with the questions in the remaining chapters concerning what may drive, inhibit and frame our students' learning experiences.

The formulation of internationalization which I present also sits within my personal broader views of the current situation of higher education. I believe that we are at a rather crucial point in the development of higher education

Should higher education primarily seek:

to be for public good	or	to be for private good

←————————————————————————————————→

to bolster the status quo of existing social norms	or	to encourage a critical stance towards existing social norms

←————————————————————————————————→

to give primary support to national development and security	or	to give primary support to global development and security

←————————————————————————————————→

to be a process of knowledge transmission	or	to be a process of individual empowerment

←————————————————————————————————→

to be about the development of capabilities to 'do' something		to be about the development of capabilities to 'be' someone

←————————————————————————————————→

to support the needs of global capitalism	or	to support the needs of global humanity

←————————————————————————————————→

to be a legitimate field for generating shareholder wealth	or	to be primarily a not-for-profit enterprise

←————————————————————————————————→

to be exclusive and excluding	or	to be inclusive and including

←————————————————————————————————→

or

←————————————————————————————————→

or

←————————————————————————————————→

or

←————————————————————————————————→

Figure 0.1 Clines of major dichotomies around the role, purpose, and defining features of higher education

globally – a period of turbulence when many and varied stakeholders are vying to lay claim to their stakes in ways which pose challenges to the soul of our enterprise. It is a point at which each of us with responsibilities within higher education need to consider some fundamental questions. Those which seem to me to be most pressing are set out in Figure 0.1.

First reflective questions

- Where would you position yourself with regard to each of the clines in Figure 0.1? Mark a dot on each row to represent your position.
- Are there other important dichotomies which I have failed to include?

I find great sympathies with Paulo Freire's notion of education as a process of empowerment, rather than a route to domestication – a road to freedom through raising ourselves and our circumstances to consciousness rather than a process of 'banking' whatever is the dominant/dominating knowledge of our time/place (Freire 1970, 1972), and with the movement for critical pedagogies as disruptive, counter-hegemonic forces (Giroux and McLaren 1989; Giroux and Purpel 1983). These share with John Dewey (Dewey 1916/1966, 1938/1963) and with con-structivist interpretations of education (Lave and Wenger 1998; Vygotsky 1978) a strong sense of education/learning as individually constructed through socially enacted experience and reflection. Much in our globalizing world, and much in the current practice of higher education, I suggest, militates against individuals engaging equitably in the process of critical inquiry; in the terms of Freire's open-ing quote, we may be complicit in doing violence to others. These underpinnings will surface throughout the book.

Whatever our views on the objectives of (higher) education, the processes col-lectively termed globalization have 'increased contacts between people and their values, ideas and ways of life in unprecedented ways' (United Nations 2004: 85) and require 'universities to rethink what type of new knowledge and what type of graduates our future societies need' (Gregersen-Hermans 2012: 24). This, then, frames internationalization as *embedded within* globalization, but distinct from globalization. In this book, internationalization is conceptualized as *a complex series of processes which an institution adopts in response to on-going change across the global–local nexus*. Higher education, itself, is framed as a *transformative* process through which our students *become* more than they could have become without it. Such significant and lasting change to the individuals we are entrusted to edu-cate demands to be taken very seriously.

Internationalization, then, is about changes to the change process – changes in terms of what comprises the curriculum, changes to how university life is expe-rienced, and ultimately changes to what our students might be empowered to become as a result. These changes, I argue, are necessary in part because the pre-sent and future worlds present different challenges to the (student) self, and in part because much current practice in higher education actually does not operate equitably or appropriately – either for the needs of its diverse local populations or for the needs of a globally interconnected world. So, it is really a book about change for our students and change for ourselves as those who guide their learning, and change demands a willingness to learn on the part of everybody. To learn to 'move with the times' perhaps, but also to learn to be secure enough to resist the times – otherwise we and our students risk becoming only the *objects* of the changes which contribute to globalization; stripped of agency, devoid of the freedom to lead a life we have reason to value (Sen 1999). Considering the considerable on-going changes within Anglophone higher education, at least, we may wonder how much of it do we still have reason to value, and what more can *we* do to enhance or resurrect its value. I hope that some of the contents of the book will help empower individual readers to make changes in directions *you* have reason to value.

To help contextualize and think critically about our role and purpose as professionals in higher education in a globalizing world, about the social and personal challenges facing ourselves and our students, and about the processes which may be involved in developing the capabilities to meet some of those challenges, we will look (very briefly – and possibly too simplistically for specialists in these fields) at theoretical and philosophical perspectives from psychology, sociology, cultural theory, and learning theory. What we draw from these in the opening chapters of the book will be brought together in the final chapter, along with several perspectives on good practice from higher education learning and teaching literature, to ask how we might better shape our professional practice.

There are a few notes to make here about the use of terminology in this book. The specific meanings attached to a few of the key terms within some of the discipline areas which I draw on may not be familiar to all readers, so a brief glossary is provided in addition to explanations within the text itself. The title of the book refers to the global *student;* however, the aspirations set out here include that our students will take their learning and development forward as they make their way in life beyond their university life as global *selves,* and you will find both terms used throughout the book. My students are both male and female, and you will find *he/his* and *she/her* used more or less interchangeably throughout. Finally, and in recognition of the importance which I go on to attribute to the notion of *conversation,* I have chosen often to refer to *you* rather than in more formal terms such as *the reader.*

You will have already noted that I believe in a reflective approach to learning, so each section in the book is followed by a number of reflective questions which I hope will help you to critically review the content of the section and to ground it in your own professional values, contexts, and practices. Ideally, as I believe in learning as a social enterprise, you would get into 'real' conversations with colleagues around these questions rather than reflecting about them in isolation. But, in any case, these reflective questions are a way of formalizing the dialogic relationship between writer and reader. If you wish to take the trouble to continue our conversation by feeding back your thoughts, I would be delighted.

I hope you enjoy the book.

Chapter 1

Questions of context

You who celebrate bygones,
Who have explored the outward, the surfaces of the races, the life that has
exhibited itself,
Who have treated of men as the creatures of politics, aggregates, rulers
and priests,
I, habitan of the Alleghanies, treating of him as he is in himself in his own
rights,
Pressing the pulse of life that has seldom exhibited itself, (the great pride
of man himself,)
Chanter of Personality, outlining what is yet to be,
I project the history of the future.

(Walt Whitman, *To a Historian*)

Introduction

Recognizing the importance of values to human action, it might be reasonable
to expect that one of the outcomes of higher education is that a highly educated person will have a highly educated set of values.

(Harland and Pickering 2011: 14)

In this opening chapter, I describe a set of matryoshka, Russian dolls sitting one
inside the other, starting with the largest – the global contexts in which the others
are nested. Opening our dolls reveals in turn: current and future interpretations
or, more holistically, *envisionings* of higher education; the internationalization
'movement'; internationalization of the curriculum specifically; and, finally, the
global self of the global student. The descriptions are, of course, based upon
how I see each doll from where I am standing, in the available light filtered by
my own technical, social and aesthetic worldviews, forged through my unique
biography. The assumptions I go on to make in 'outlining what is yet to be' with
regard to the future lives of our students, and so the role higher education may
seek to play, are meant sincerely, but might reasonably be taken with a touch of
irony given that *unpredictability* is predicted to feature strongly in their worlds.

The matryoshka metaphor seems particularly apt, in the sense that the form of the smallest determines the form of the largest – and/or, the form of the largest determines the form of the smallest. A recurrent theme of this book is the ambiguity within relationships which shape self and other and self and world, and ambiguity also (as hinted at in the dichotomies presented in the Introduction to the book) within the role which higher education, itself situated among the matryoshka, can and should play in shaping either. Internationalization itself is a process or set of processes also taking place within and giving shape to these nested worlds, and this chapter contextualizes that process within those worlds.

Section 1: Global contexts

It is probably not necessary to rehearse the defining features of our globalizing world to the readers of this book. However, 'key to addressing the challenges for higher education today is the need to recognize the global reality within which learning takes place' (Bourn 2011: 559), and since it is many of the features of the transformations in our present and future worlds which drive the version of internationalization and the notion of the global self which underpin this book, a brief review of some of the territory will helpfully frame what follows.

That this territory is still a work in progress, 'radically incomplete' (Marginson 1999: 26) is of course one of its most salient features.

We have created and continue to tolerate a world with a vastly unequal distribution of wealth, typically graphically illustrated by Zygmunt Bauman:

> ... forty-nine poorest countries, inhabited by 11 per cent of the world population, receive among them but one-half of 1 per cent of the global product – an amount just about equal to the combined income of the three wealthiest men on the planet. Ninety per cent of the total wealth of the planet remains in the hands of just 1 per cent of the planet's inhabitants.
>
> Tanzania earns 2.2 billion dollars a year, which it divides among 25 million inhabitants. The Goldman Sachs Bank earns 2.6 billion dollars a year, which is then divided among 161 stockholders.
>
> (Bauman 2008: Loc 2572 and 2631)

In terms of the ethics of international education this demands a particular reflection, since the overwhelmingly predominant flow of for-profit international students which features in many institutional and national internationalization strategies is from poorer to richer countries. Many of these individual students do go on to contribute to their home economies significantly through remittances, but they do so only by remaining as primarily contributors to the economy of their new host. Of those who return home with their 'Western' degree, in many of cases there is little evidence that much more than personal gain flows from the investment made in them. More current practices in establishing branch campuses, franchises and other varieties of off-shore higher education are also predominantly built upon the flow of economic capital from poorer to richer countries. Furthermore, even where the institution-at-home is a public one, in most cases 'as soon as they cross a border they functionally become a private entity' (UNESCO 2004: 12). Additionally, the intellectual capital built, for example by international PhD students, tends also to accrue to their hosting countries. Recent authors even assert that, as currently enacted, education is far from being a force to help right the wrongs of the world. Indeed, we academics are 'complicit' in a practice 'of social closure – of making opportunity unequal' (Brighouse 2010: 287), education 'does more to contribute to the underlying causes of conflict than it does to contribute to peace' and we need to ask ourselves what can be done so people 'emerge from educational institutions more inclined to challenge injustice and violence' (Davies 2003/2006: 1029 and 1030).

A self-identity which might frame such an inclination lies at the heart of the notion of the *global self* set out in this book. In the aspirations for the global student, be they 'home' or 'international', coming to experience and critique their personal interconnectivities and those of their discipline will be argued to increase the likelihood of a capability to recognize their own relationships to global others, and through those, perhaps, their relationships with global tensions, and global inequities.

That this unequal world, almost regardless of where we sit (North–South, wealthy–impoverished, emerging–receding, etc.) is undergoing change on many fronts at a remarkable pace is incontestable. Specifics, such as climate change and human contributions to it; the tensions between cultural homogenization and strengthening identifications of difference across ethnicities, religions, and other groupings; the calls for universal rights versus the demands for us to recognize differentiated conceptions of the good life; and whether human migration (immigration or emigration) is to be celebrated or resisted, are of course highly contested. But changes wrought by generating greater connectivities, expanding populations, increasing demands on resources, and movements in economic and political power are felt *by all*. They are not, however, felt equally, and who feels what to what degree is itself changing with the rapidity at which emerging economies are, indeed, emerging; and possibly even more than might have been imaged at the end of the twentieth century, there are 'more voices talking back to the West' (Featherstone 1995: 10) and, listening or not, the clamour has its impacts.

Despite these shifting balances of political and economic power, the majority of our home (domestic) students in the UK, the USA, and Australia at least are not accustomed *even to the idea* that finding their futures may well *necessitate* migrations beyond their national borders. Far less are they equipped to undertake the challenge. Helping them find their way, or even see that they may have a way to find, in these changing global spaces, hardly features in a higher education landscape dominated by reductive notions of employability and a persisting academic narcissism.

In setting out the precepts for what is being called 'comprehensive internationalization', in the USA, Green was able to confidently assert that:

> It is now a truism that American college graduates will live and work in a world in which national borders are permeable; information and ideas flow at lightening speed; and communities and workplaces reflect a growing diversity of culture, languages, attitudes, and values.
>
> (Green 2002: 7)

Can we equally confidently assert that those same graduates will have been adequately prepared to flow through those permeable borders, to deal effectively with the new ideas, and to participate fully in the diverse spaces and communities which will make up their world(s)?

That many of the world's political communities throughout history have been ethnically diverse, 'a testament to the ubiquity of both conquest and long-distance trade in human affairs,' may not have been given due prominence in our writing and reading of history, as Kymlicka (1995: 2) claims. However, this does not diminish the fact that diversities of many kinds are now a greater part of the lived-experience of a greater spread of the population than has hitherto been the general case. In terms of many individuals' lived-experience, I think it is something of an exaggeration to assert that '[i]n very few countries can the citizens be said to share the same language, or belong to the same ethnonational group' (Kymlicka, op. cit.: 1), in the sense that many people, including many of our students, do still experience *their* corners of *their* countries precisely as predominantly or even exclusively mono-lingual and mono-cultural. Many in such communities are so unaccustomed to finding 'others at the gate' that any potential for cultural 'dilution' is greeted with fear and hostility. These lived-realities, like all lived-realities, depend as much upon the perceptions of the individual concerned as they do upon the world surrounding him. But the shutters cannot stay closed against the world for ever – as we shall explore further in Chapter 2. Even when others are not yet at the gate, they are beamed into our living rooms, dropped through our letterboxes, encountered as we tour their holiday worlds. They are impacting on our laws, taking ownership of our soccer clubs, and – yes – marrying our daughters. I happen to think all this to be a 'good thing' – but even if you do not, you must still concede that enabling our students to make their ways amongst the diversity which flows all around us is a better option than allowing them to find themselves incapable of doing so. While we rarely give attention to this in our university 'celebrations' of diversity, it remains true that many of our students, home and international, may be encountering alterity for the first time when they join their freshman classes. How much (how little) responsibility do we take for enabling them to make those encounters successful learning experiences?

To further complicate the local–global situation which is framing our students' world, many commentators point towards the dissolution, or 'deterritorialization'

(Scholte 2000) of the nation-state and our sense of home within it as part of the globalization process. Not only has the nation-state been our primary political organization for over two hundred years (though not for much longer than that), but with that it has also developed into the primary identity marker for many. Of course, we know of places where this is not the case – very many of which illustrate starkly, and violently, how political map lines cannot erase more deeply held affiliations. You personally might also not recognize nationality as a strong identity marker for yourself, but that should not mean you do not see how strongly it plays out as such for many people. Through a process of internationalization, we can, and in my own view must, enable our students to establish for themselves more global envisionings of home.

If visions of the demise of the nation-state appear fanciful, the realm of dystopian social scientists, this is a hard line conclusion from the US National Intelligence Council:

> By 2025, nation-states will no longer be the only – and often not the most important – actors on the world stage and the 'international system' will have morphed to accommodate the new reality. But the transformation will be incomplete and uneven. Although states will not disappear from the international scene, the relative power of various nonstate actors – including businesses, tribes, religious organizations, and even criminal networks – will grow as these groups influence decisions on a widening range of social, economic, and political issues.
>
> (National Intelligence Council 2008: 81)

It is not only the nation-state which may be losing its salience for our students, Giddens points also to the 'shell' institutions of the family, work, and our traditions, each of which has 'become inadequate to the tasks they are called upon to perform' (Giddens 2002: Loc 445). Of course, this analysis also may be mistaken – but even the fact that such matters are posited as serious possibilities throws much uncertainty around what kind of identities will most readily enable our students to make their way in the world.

Other commentators point to our lack of identification with/sense of responsibility towards the future. Case (1993: 324) referred to this chauvinistic 'presentism' as 'a preoccupation with the interests and well-being of current generations to the exclusion of the interests of persons yet to be born into the world.' For Bindé, as we claim 'rights over the citizens of tomorrow' and shun our responsibilities, 'modern man is rejecting his status as a conscious, temporal being' (Bindé 2001: 90 and 93). And, indeed, since these future generations include our own gene-carrying offspring, it is difficult not to see his point. The quality of life available to the next generation is our responsibility, and how we educate them will shape how they accept or shun their own responsibilities to future generations.

So, while it has always been the case that '[w]hether we like it or not our behaviours (informed by our value systems, etc.) interfere with those of others' (Crossley 2001: 42), in this globalizing, interconnected world those interferences can reach far more quickly and more distantly beyond our immediate community – and, of course, they reach back into our immediate community from afar with equal alacrity. Future generations cannot reach back, so we need the capabilities and the *will* to imagine the impacts of our actions and to hear how their voices would speak back to us. The dissolutions of what for most of us is the only established world order we have known, including possibly the demise of the nation-state, the nuclear family, and our traditions which offer much of the framing of our identities, will be revisited when we look in more detail at the impacts of socio-cultural change associated with globalization upon the individual student in Chapter 2.

It would not, though, be appropriate to leave this section with nothing but a vision of challenge. There is also much to celebrate about the world today when set beside that of previous generations. There are enormous journeys still to make, but, for example:

- while human trafficking continues, it is no longer openly state-sponsored;
- while racism remains a force, it does so against laws and regulations;
- while we continue to exploit child labour, consumers challenge companies caught in the act;
- while we strip the planet of its resources and natural habitats, there is a growing consciousness about the rights of other communities and species;
- while there remain enormous gulfs between the capabilities of citizens in different continents to lead lives of value to themselves, individuals in their millions protest and donate in order to express solidarity and empathy with unknown others;
- many societies have taken huge steps to equalize their citizens' rights;
- corporal punishment and torture are outlawed in many countries – and where authorities are caught transgressing those laws, much of the public is willing to seek redress; and it would seem,
- contrary to our media-driven interpretations of the present, in relative terms, genocide, murder, state-sanctioned death and deaths through war have significantly and consistently decreased over generations (Pinker 2011).

These, and other shifts, are important not only in themselves, but for what they each say about human society and human sensibilities. We most certainly are not perfect, but this evidence would suggest that we are capable of becoming better than we are. Furthermore, whether as 'global' citizens or simply as human beings, we must hold with the belief that 'individuals can make a difference, especially if they co-operate' (Dower 2003: 45), otherwise what's an education for?

Reflective questions for Section 1

- What are some of the implications for our curricula which arise from the idea that globalization is 'radically incomplete'?
- Does your experience of your own domestic students suggest I am right to assert that most 'are not accustomed *even to the idea* that finding their futures may well necessitate migrations beyond their national borders'? If so, does higher education come too late in their biographies to make a difference?
- To what extent do you experience the world as a place where it is 'normal' to live alongside or among alterity? (How) has this changed for you over the course of your life?
- If you have children, do you seek to make provision for them by way of some form of 'inheritance'? Does the part you play in consuming the resources and depleting the environment they will inherit play *any* part in the life choices you make? Do any of your considerations in this respect extend to more distant future generations – and/or to people in those generations who are not related to you?
- On balance, do you agree that 'evidence would suggest that we are capable of becoming better than we are'?

Section 2: Conceptions of higher education

We shall not live long, in any case, if we do not replace the anachronism of national sovereignty, industrial autarchy and cultural narcissism – which are combined into a stew of leftovers by the schools.

(Illich 1973: 108)

Central to the goal of adult education in democratic societies is the process of helping learners become more aware of the context of their problematic understandings and beliefs, more critically reflective on their assumptions and those of others, mournfully and freely engaged in discourse, and more effective in taking action on their reflective judgements.

(Mezirow 2000: 31)

... how internationalisation is framed and defined has important implications for how society interprets the role of universities in contemporary society; the overarching mission and management of particular establishments, and how departmental and individual practices are then steered, resourced and supported.

(Peel and Frank 2008: 104)

In the Introduction to this book you were invited to consider where you positioned your own vision of higher education along a number of clines. In this section we briefly survey some of the dominant conceptions of higher education today, leading us into the following section which considers how internationalization sits within this landscape.

That higher education has experienced, and continues to experience, discomforting change is to say nothing more than that it, too, sits in the globalizing world. Higher education has expanded rapidly ('massification'), both in terms of absolute numbers and in terms of the percentage of the population it serves. While those of us who believe in the value of education should celebrate this growth, we cannot deny the challenges this expansion has brought, most notably to the academic community who have found themselves needing to respond to larger classes populated by individuals with a greater diversity of experience, expectation and aspiration. This expansion has more or less coincided with the rise in educational technologies. Again, these more sophisticated and exciting tools of the trade should largely be a cause for celebration, but they too bring their own challenges as academics struggle to keep up, to compete with more cutting-edge social communication and gaming technologies, and to balance concomitant drivers for glitz and speed with cautions concerning equity, standards, and academic rigor. The trends of massification and technological delivery 'solutions' are now coming together as various players (private, public, for-profit, etc.) experiment with massive online open courses (MOOCs). Whether, in the push for monetization, these will remain open for long is doubtful, and so MOOCs (or, when delivered to fee-paying audiences, presumably MOCs) may well be a highly significant feature of future marketization efforts. Expansion in student numbers and advances in technology have been accompanied by a third major change – an increasing focus on good practice, the 'professionalization' of learning and teaching. Once again, something which we can only believe a good thing in principle, but which brings with it new pressures as subject expertise (and so for many, their academic *identity*) is reduced in stature, and professional competence is made more complex as familiarity with *educational* fields becomes a demonstrable requirement for tenure and career advancement across the disciplines. Challenging though these changes are, however, they are not what many would see as the major disruptions to higher education. There are more deep-rooted shifts concerned with managerialism, marketization, and the 'terrors of performativity' (Ball 2003: 216). They manifest themselves in a 'crisis of identity for the university' resulting from the 'increasingly porous boundaries' of public sector and private sector (Lapworth 2008: 163 and 172). Robinson and Katalushi identify 'increased professionalization, in search of efficiency and accountability', 'contract, market and choice', and 'commercialization' (alongside massification) as three of the 'four riders of the apocalypse who have challenged the seemingly "settled values" of the university' (Robinson and Katulushi 2005: 244). While they recognize a certain persistence in several underlying values, the *threat* to the values of the enterprise itself is more fundamental than the (not inconsiderable) struggles to keep up with numbers, technologies, and capabilities to 'deliver'. Clifford points out the irony that the focus on 'servicing the needs of the economy' and an 'ethic of individual advancement', 'will not serve the future needs of our local or global societies' (Clifford, V.A. 2011: 556). These are not trends which leave much scope for the aspirations for higher education set out in this series of books; they are, though, trends which make the kind of work which internationalization seeks to engage us in all the more urgent.

The marketization of higher education has two facets, that which is concerned with selling itself to prospective students (and sponsors) in the competitive arenas of both national and international marketplaces, and that which is concerned with defining its purpose around meeting the needs of the employer (the market for its graduates). With respect to the second, 'universities seem to have accepted a role as servants of the economic machine and the existing order' (Haigh and Clifford 2011: 580). The 'key' discourse in higher education has become that of 'market fundamentalism – the doctrine that market exchange is an ethic in itself and a guide for all human action' (Walker 2010: 219). Corporate interests, not society at large or the students themselves, have become a significant definer of the purposes which drive higher education (Morley, 2001), a situation which Jarvis (2008: 90) would extend beyond the university to the whole framing of education: '... the dominance that global capitalism has means that it strongly influences what knowledge is regarded as important, relevant and is taught and other forms of knowledge are regarded as out of date and irrelevant.' And:

> [Global capitalism] needs an educated but compliant and flexible workforce that will work hard and efficiently for low wages and so it needs education to be vocationally orientated. In fact, it needs a type of learning society which we have in the West today.

Framing the debate around ethics in the university, co-editors Strain and Barnett along with other contributors to the same volume present generally more optimistic visions than that of universities having *yet* been 'colonised by the global capitalist system' (Jarvis 2009a: 13), but all see mounting challenges to academic practice. While traditionally higher education may set itself up as broadly in tune with Freire's (1970, 1972) opposition to a 'domestication' model, the employability drive threatens a more invidious form of subjugating education if interpreted as an agenda to develop denizens of global capitalism, or fodder for advancing national economic interests:

> ... universities, as the pre-eminent knowledge organisations, have become the focus of much state interest, activity and the exercise of power and can be characterised as performing three functions. First, they can produce the knowledge that underpins economic growth. Second, universities can effectively produce the worker/consumer citizens that Foucault (1977) would refer to as 'docile bodies' on which such growth depends. And third, they represent important areas of profitable business opportunity in a globalised HE environment.
>
> (Boden and Nedeva 2010: 40)

National statements and policies strongly evidence this agenda. In the USA, for example, even the Obama administration's statement on higher education begins: 'Earning a post-secondary degree or credential ... is a prerequisite for the growing jobs of the new economy' (White House 2013).

In the UK and Australia, higher education sits under their respective government ministries with responsibility for growing national industry and skills, not those responsible for education. In addition to shifts in the objectives of higher education, have been shifts in the relationships between the academy/institution and the student. For example, '... the 1994 Group of UK-based universities has adopted the idea that the customer is always right and that flattering them is the way forward' (Furedi 2011: 3); adding significantly to the 'dislocations of identity' (Di Napoli and Barnett 2008: 5) among the academy.

Finally in this section – whether as a result of managerialist and performativity agendas, or as a result of (mis)understandings concerning what drives learning is unclear, but there has been a wholesale shift in how higher education learning is packaged (into unitized 'modules' [UK] or 'courses' [USA, Australia]) and its outcomes delineated as discrete and measurable learning outcomes. This 'commodification' of higher education is argued to cast the student as 'inert' consumer of credits 'given for safe banking' through which 'personal transformation is precluded' (Barnett, R. 1997: 173). As will be seen when we come to discussions on the formal curriculum in Chapter 5, I advocate harnessing the force of the learning outcome to the internationalization agenda. However, in doing so I am not out of sympathy with the feeling that this increasing structuring to unitized and constrained programs of study represents a process whereby higher education 'appears to be gravitating to the factory ideal as opposed to the academy' (Arthur 2005: 11). In the Introduction to this book I referred to my own 'sceptical bent' in the framing of several of the issues under consideration. Arguably, *higher* education has traditionally been precisely about encouraging a sceptical bent among students – but this sits uncomfortably in objectives for *employable* students and always-measurable outcomes, and in this perspective internationalization as presented here can be seen as a counter-hegemonic process. Doug Bourn (2011) calls for a move from 'internationalisation' to a global perspectives approach as the route to just such a counter-hegemonic enterprise, but I suggest that this is unnecessary and represents a misunderstanding of the internationalization agenda as framed by many of its advocates. Ron Barnett later frames the problem within higher education as a fundamental conflict in the 'grand narratives' which contest for the soul of the modern university, a clash between the university 'as a set of production processes' and 'as a site of undistorted critical dialogue' (Barnett, R. 2000: 57). Rhoads and Szelényi (2011a: 28 and 42) capture a sense of the fissure between these dystopian views of higher education in the twenty-first century, and the more utopian views which I seek to frame in the next sections: 'The problem is that the university itself has become a central target of the neoliberal assault.' And, 'We see the university as one of the last frontiers of hope of a more globally aware populace.'

So what of our grander purposes?

Reflective questions for Section 2

- Do you share any of the 'apocalyptic' interpretations of the 'neoliberal assault' which is disrupting the 'settled values' of the university'?
- Do you think it reasonable to cast the employability agenda for higher education as evidencing that it is becoming an instrument of global capitalism?
- Is the commodification of learning principally driven by managerialism and marketization, or by notions of good practice in enabling student learning?
- If universities are increasingly 'serving the needs of the economy' are they thereby failing local and global societies?
- Is a sceptical bent a proper outcome of higher education?

Section 3: Education for citizenship, social justice, and a better world?

> There is no such thing as a neutral educational process. Education either functions as an instrument that is used to facilitate the integration of the younger generation into the logic of the present system and bring about conformity to it, or it becomes the 'practice of freedom', the means by which men and women deal critically and creatively with reality and discover how to participate in the transformation of their world.
>
> (Shaull 1972: 13–14)

As indicated at several points already, and implicit in the title of this book, I am advocating a form of higher education which seeks to develop students who are *alert to* their own and others' entanglement in issues of (global) social justice, and *inclined* to act on the basis of informed and ethical choices. However, I must acknowledge that an education which seeks to formulate 'inclinations' of any kind will seem anathema to many. Arthur sets out an argument for university education playing a role (albeit a late one in terms of prior socialization) in 'character development', and his notion of character as a bestower of freedoms might do something to allay fears of indoctrination:

> Character development is about the kind of person we become in a particular kind of community. It is also about the kind of ethical understandings and commitments that are possible for us in that community. Character implies that we are free to make ethical decisions – it is not merely about controlled behaviour.
>
> (Arthur 2005: 11)

Rather than 'character', Barnett argues that insisting upon 'authenticity in the student' is the 'key concept within the deep structure of higher education' (2007: 40). The authentic self is not identical to Arthur's framing of character, but shares associated ideas of 'agency, of ownership of one's experiences, of self-meaning, of being free of undue restrictions and of particularity' (Barnett, R., op. cit.: 41).

However, in considering either of these formulations we need to remain alert to the fact that the character or the authentic being is situated in a social milieu. Barnett, perhaps more extremely than many other commentators on higher education in postmodernity, and as further discussed in Chapter 2, sees the dynamic complexity of this milieu as posing significant challenges to shaping and holding onto any established sense of authenticity. Nonetheless, we can only *be* authentic in the context of other beings, and our freedoms are always only definable in terms of other beings. George Herbert Mead (1967) proposed that we become who we are through our interactions in society. In his modelling, becoming conscious of oneself is only possible by taking an outsider's view of oneself – by imagining oneself as looking in from another's perspective. Whether we are doing this from a generic perspective of our societal context (the *generalized* other) or from the perspective of a specific (and perhaps 'significant') other, this process of assuming an imagined other to view the self requires a level of understanding of that/those other(s). While Mead's notion of the generalized other (and its ties to 'my' society, cultural group, etc.) may appear particularly problematic for the notion of a *global* self proposed in this book – the *extension* of that generalization from the local to the global, taking Mead's wider proposition that understanding self and other requires seeking to understand any situation from the perspective of both (all) actors, is really what I am arguing as the fundamental necessary step for successful global being. Enabling our students through their learning to experience positive and affirming relationships with individual others is suggested as a key mechanism for this to take place. If higher education is about a student's personal development it cannot avoid also being about how they are in relation to the other. It is not possible, therefore, for higher education to avoid an ethical stance towards the other as part of its purview. The shaping of that ethical stance, and in particular its 'reach' in terms of which others, are critical questions.

In 1916, John Dewey claimed that education in nineteenth-century Europe had shifted to a 'civic function' as it became harnessed to the nation-state. So the '"state" was substituted for humanity; cosmopolitanism gave way to nationalism. To form the citizen, not the "man" became the aim of education' (Dewey 1916/1966: 93). In Europe, this citizenship development function for education has been reasserted in recent agendas. In the UK, the Crick report resulted in a renewal of compulsory citizenship teaching in schools (Crick 1998), and the influential Dearing Report (Dearing 1997) set the agenda for higher education as making a contribution to democratic society in the UK. While on the face of it, less narrowly nationalistic in its interpretation of the location of our citizenship, the whole European Union agenda for higher education remains premised on notions of the *European* citizen, rather than a world citizen. Citizenship education in Australia 'entails knowledge and understanding of Australia's democratic heritage and traditions, its political and legal institutions and the shared values of freedom, tolerance, respect, responsibility and inclusion' (DEEWR 2013).

Education of this kind, whether for national or European citizenship, risks being limited to a form of socialization to established (or aspirational) norms rather than a reaching for authenticity; education for domestication rather than for freedom (Freire 1972).

More encouragingly, perhaps, the recent 'Crucible Moment' report of The Global Perspective Institute and the Association of American Colleges and Universities (GPI and AAC&U 2011) sets out a strongly worded, urgent case for the advancement of 'civic learning' and 'democratic engagement' across college education, and emphasizes the need to prepare 'students with knowledge and for action'. Pertinent to our focus, this report is clear that such 'education for democracy' in today's world

> needs to be informed by deep engagement with the values of liberty, equality, individual worth, open mindedness, and the willingness to collaborate with people of differing views and backgrounds towards common solutions for the public good.
>
> (GPI and AAC&U 2011: 10)

Moreover, it echoes much of the approach proposed in Chapter 5 regarding experiential learning and the value of successful intercultural contact: '... democratic knowledge and capabilities are honed through hands-on, face-to-face, active engagement in the midst of differing perspectives about how to address common problems that affect the well-being of the nation and the world' (GPI and AAC&U, op. cit.: 11).

The point of raising these matters here, though, is mainly as a reminder that promoting and developing values are necessarily part of the process of education. Even if some higher education practitioners may seek to claim that they are opposed to any values agenda, it is likely that their practice is underpinned by values which they hold as legitimate for themselves and their students. Why would you/how could you work in a Western university and not hold notions such as academic integrity, evidence-informed argument, personal responsibility, respectful discourse, and the like as necessary values? The UK Professional Standards Framework (HEA 2013) explicitly lays out the Professional Values which academics in higher education are required to evidence in order to gain professional recognition. As Case succinctly put it, the issue we need to grapple with in education is 'not *whether* but *which* values ought to be promoted' (Case 1993: 320). The view in this book, the underpinning rationale of the version of internationalization which I advocate for, is that in our globally connected and somewhat fluid world the values we promote (whatever they are) must needs extend beyond national or even supra-national boundaries, must equip our students with the ethical foundations for action among diverse peoples and in diverse contexts, and must contain some notion of making our way in the world in ways which do not make it a better place for me/us at the expense of you/them.

I would argue that it is in locating education in and for (global) society, with an underpinning commitment to personal transformation in order to advance broad aims of social justice which situates internationalization firmly in the critical pedagogy tradition alluded to in the Introduction (Freire 1970; Giroux and McLaren 1989).

Reflective questions for Section 3

- Do you agree that there is 'no such thing as a neutral educational process'?
- Is it possible to seek to develop 'character' without leaning towards a form of education as indoctrination?
- Is citizenship education a mechanism for state suppression and the denial of individuality – or a legitimate attempt to harness education as a force for the public good?
- What values underpin you own educational practice? How do these impact upon your students?

Section 4: Internationalization

The concept of internationalization itself appears too broad and means too many things to different people. Conceptualizations of the internationalization process are still hotly contested and might remain so for a considerable time to come, although internationalization has come to be widely seen as an integral part of the educational process.

(Schuerholz-Lehr 2007: 182)

... the literature on international education is either timid or silent about the field's complexity; international education is multidimensional and multidisciplinary because its concepts and theories have come from many disciplines and cultures and because it has several levels of analysis. Furthermore, its variables come in elementary, intermediate, and advanced levels of conceptualization.

(Mestenhauser 1998: 4)

Even though internationalization has become part of the mainstream discourse, and a 'key element of the future' (Altbach and Teichler 2001: 10) of higher education, there remain 'major misconceptions' (De Wit 2012: 12) about its complexity and the profound questions it raises. In this book, internationalization broadly is taken to be a university's response to the various, and locally highly differentiated developments which make up the construct and the experience of globalization, some of which we have touched upon above. It also must be recognized that as well as a *response* to globalization, aspects of internationalization *contribute to* globalization (Beerkens 2003). Examples would be, as already noted, through its global trading and off-shore adventuring, but also, through 'the hegemony exerted by universities in the USA and Western Europe and the advent of global league tables' (Naido 2010:79), the more invidious export of western models of higher education, notions of scholarship, the privileging of utilitarian forms of knowledge, and the pervasive spread of native-speaker varieties of English as *the* language of academic discourse across the disciplines. However, these manifestations and interpretations of internationalization, each of which is increasingly under threat, are not the focus of this book.

Given how the changes of globalization play out differently in different global contexts, we should not be surprised to find that there are probably as many models of internationalization as there are institutions of higher education. As a simple illustration, we can consider how considerably the contexts within which internationalization is given shape differ between Anglophone countries and those for whom one *fundamental* aspect of internationalization may be large, small, or wholesale conversion to English-medium delivery – the exporters and the importers of English as a lingua franca (ELF) (see perspectives on this in Preisler *et al.* 2011). Another example would be the massive differentiation between those institutions who sit within a national context of large-scale (predominantly for-profit) international student recruitment and those whose context is one in which many of their potential domestic students are instead lured away to study, and perhaps then to remain, overseas. Given such variety, it should not be surprising that universities find different priorities, perhaps with their locus of attention and activity also changing over relatively short timescales as local and global circumstances shift around them. The emergence of different models of internationalization is also driven by the very varied institutional constructs of their own identities, role, student bodies, and approaches to practice. Even within the apparently more homogeneous contexts of the Western Anglophone university, there are highly polarized forms of internationalization. These will be explored in different ways in several volumes in this series, and I will do so only briefly here to form the backdrop for the *particular version* of internationalization which I advocate.

Early iterations of internationalization in the UK, the USA and Australia placed a strong (often an exclusive) focus on international student recruitment. Apart from effectively divorcing internationalization from the interests and engagement of academic staff, this focus at times positively alienated those concerned with providing a quality learning experience to their students, as 'floods' of international students appeared in classrooms with no attention having been given to the impacts this 'radical change in campus cultural demographics, interactional and educational dynamics' (Luke 2010: 48) might have on academic practice, cohesion, retention, workloads, and the like. Within many European and South-East Asian contexts, it is also a focus on for-profit international student recruitment which has led to the continuing shifts towards English-medium delivery. As already noted, in much of Europe beyond the UK, an additional strong political motive for encouraging international student mobility has been that of supporting European Union policy around *Europeanization* in the form of European citizen identity formation. In the USA, financial drivers have often run parallel to drivers around bolstering national reputation and/or national security (Johnson and Mulholland 2006; US Department of Education 2012). For this book, however, it would be most helpful if readers could detach such political and economic drivers from the construct of *internationalization,* and recognize them as parts of other agendas instead. Universities need to attract income and achieve viable cohorts to survive; they have various mechanisms through which to do this, and diversifying their markets, taking additional students beyond those permitted by government/ funding council quotas or beyond those which can be attracted from the local population is one such mechanism. Nation-states and supra-national 'unions' have an interest in advancing citizenship identity and enhancing citizen security, and so seek to harness educational energies to these ends. Recruiting international students, developing transnational provision and encouraging outbound student mobility then become *means to these ends.* But they have little to do with the ration-ale for internationalization as presented here; these, at best, 'thin' understandings of internationalization (Schweisfurth and Gu 2009: 465), and the discourse which surrounds them 'prompts negative dispositions [towards internationalization] by association with the process of globalization and its impact on HE' (Caruana and Ploner 2010: 98). De Wit (2012) points also to a tendency to confuse or conflate the *means* with the *ends* of internationalization, and lists nine 'myths' in which this confusion is manifest. In these myths, internationalization means:

- education in the English language;
- studying or staying abroad;
- an international subject [i.e. international content];
- having many international students;
- few international students guarantees success;
- no need to test intercultural and international competencies;
- the more partnerships the more international;
- higher education is international by nature;
- internationalization as a precise goal [meaning that internationalization is, itself, only a *means* to achieve our ambitions for a higher education fit for purpose in the twenty-first century].

This is not to say many of these means might not be appropriate mechanisms to advance the goals of internationalization; for example, the presence of international students on campus can *potentially* contribute enormously to more educationally driven versions of internationalization, as can opportunities *potentially* offered by linking on-shore and off-shore cohorts. It is clear, though, from the paucity of resources and the general absence of key performance indicators (KPIs) and the like surrounding matters such as home–international student integration (i.e. what hap-pens beyond recruitment), or structured student exchanges with peers on off-shore campuses (i.e. what happens beyond recruitment), that in the main these potential mechanisms to support internationalization objectives fall way below the objectives of income generation or cohort viability in most institutional priorities. In general (and there are exceptions), the business of internationalizing *the student experience* on *educational grounds* has been non-strategic, under-resourced, and left to the commitment and enthusiasm of individual academic and administrative staff. Not ideal, since for successful internationalization, institutions need to clearly articulate 'a broad spectrum of activities' in a vision which itself is 'underpinned by an institutional ethos' (Jones and Lee 2008: 26). Nonetheless, this work has been doggedly advancing on many fronts. This book sets out to support those advances, and to present one model of what a values-driven form of internationalization, informed by broadly educational theory, might be, and how it might be advanced through the ways in which all our students experience their university lives.

Of the many definitions of internationalization, the most commonly cited come from Jane Knight: 'the process of integrating an international and intercultural dimension into the teaching, research and service functions of the institution' (Knight 1994: 7), subsequently 'updated' to 'the process of integrating an international, intercultural or global dimension into the purpose, functions or delivery of post-secondary education' (Knight 2003: 2). Knight sought to defend those who felt her definitions too generic by arguing that 'a definition needs to be objective enough that it can be used to describe a phenomenon that is in fact, universal, but which has different purposes and outcomes, depending on the actor or stakeholder' (Knight 2009: 115).

This seems to me a little disingenuous, perhaps worthy of the King at the trial in Lewis Carroll's ironic fantasy *Alice's Adventures in Wonderland* (Carroll 2005: 48): 'If there's no meaning in it, that saves a world of trouble, you know, as we needn't try to find any', and other definitions are more specific. However, Knight's definition is helpful in illustrating that internationalization is to be taken as a complex and comprehensive process, and one which it is not possible to delegate to any individual area of the institution. Of the many institutional functions which do need to be involved in the internationalization process, our attention in this book is upon those which impact most directly on the student *learning* experience. To locate that more generally within the discourse of internationalization, however, we'll first review a few perspectives upon how the broader internationalization endeavour can be framed.

Leask provided an illustrative list of the different **layers** within an institution (Leask 2003: 4–6) which are impacted/implicated in the process of internationalization [UK equivalents in brackets]:

Policy layer

Programme [course or programme] layer

Course [module] layer

Teacher layer

Student layer.

In this book, the major focus lies upon what happens to/with/for the student as a result of the interactions between cognitive, affective and behavioural dimensions of her self and what she encounters in terms of the curriculum (formal, extended, and hidden), its delivery, and its environment. This comes, though, with the recognition that policy in all domains can shape highly significant enablers and inhibitors. To explore these areas subsequent chapters set out to explore the global student; the socio-cultural context she inhabits; the enablers and inhibitors she embodies; and the processes which might give shape and direction to her development.

Qiang (2003: 250–251) offered a typology of **approaches** to internationalization as presented within the literature at the time; these can be summarized as:

1   The *activity approach*: 'promotes activities such as curriculum. Student/ faculty exchange, technical assistance, and international students'.
2   The *competency approach*: 'emphasizes the development of skills, knowledge, attitudes and values in students, faculty and staff ... the development of internationalized curricula and programs is not an end in itself but a means towards developing the appropriate competencies in the students, staff and faculty'.
3   The *ethos approach*: 'emphasizes creating a culture or climate that values and supports international/intercultural perspectives and initiatives ... This approach acknowledges that the international dimension is fundamental to the definition of a university or any other institutions of higher learning'.
4   The *process approach*: 'stresses integration or infusion of an international/intercultural dimension into teaching, research and service ... A major concern in this approach is to address the sustainability of the international dimension'.

In this book, internationalization is seen to be *driven by an ethos* which is based upon enabling students to make their way in a globalizing world – both as students in a discipline and as graduates enacting social and professional lives. This involves the growth of identities and the development of personal capabilities through the processes and activities encountered within their university experience.

Following an extensive literature review, Caruana found a 'consensus emerging' around **principles** of internationalization:

- Awareness that internationalisation entails a shift in thinking and attitudes to recreate globalisation in the form of social practices that confront homogenisation;
- Recognition that internationalisation is about more than simply the presence of international students on UK campuses and sending UK students overseas;
- Recognition that internationalisation is a long term process of 'becoming international' or developing a willingness to teach and learn from other nations and cultures as distinct from traditional definitions of 'involving more than one country';
- Awareness that internationalisation in the context of higher learning and pedagogy has social, cultural, moral and ethical dimensions that both transcend the narrow economic focus and establish a synergy with other agenda.

(Caruana 2007: 13)

This book recognizes each of these principles, and gives a particularly strong focus to the area of 'willingness' to offer and accept learning which derives from cultures beyond those of the individual student and traditional/Western interpretations of the discipline under study. Within this, confronting homogenization is both a driver and a consequence, but *underlying* this is the principle that the student experience should prepare them for the globalizing world. So, rather than a political objective, a will and a capability to confront homogenization are seen as personal attributes to enable students to make their way in a world where homogenization may threaten their own and others' individual ways of being.

Middlehurst and Woodfield (2007: 32) present an overview of **rationales** found in institutional internationalization strategies:

- Teaching and learning – curriculum design, approach to teaching, opportunities for overseas study, collaborative programmes and research;
- Research – capacity building (e.g. staff and student recruitment), developing an international knowledge base, joint programmes, and new funding opportunities;
- Cultural – intercultural understanding, diversity, respect, communication (languages), global citizenship;
- Reputational – securing international standing and branding (e.g. 'research leader', rankings in world lists);
- Economic/market-led – fees income from overseas student recruitment, generating research funds and consultancy income;
- Managerial – an emphasis on organizational efficiency, co-ordination and centralization to avoid duplication of activity and to maximize viability;
- Developmental – capacity building (research and teaching) and assistance in developing countries.

I would suggest that not all of these are *rationales*, but more aspects of activity/ focus. That said, this book is fundamentally about teaching and learning, and within that it sees those areas listed under 'cultural' above to be highly relevant. This can be facilitated in part through dimensions of the research activity listed, since those designing and delivering curricula need to develop/update their own international knowledge base, and as noted earlier, joint activities with partner institutions offer the *potential* for bringing international/intercultural encounters into the student experience. Other areas in the list are largely outside the understanding of internationalization presented here, though an institutional ethos and related activity around a capacity building approach to its international activities is a good example of how an institution might support student learning by itself exhibiting in its behaviours what it espouses in its objectives ('walking-the-talk'), and such activities can have a significant impact upon the capacity and inclination of academic staff to engage with the process.

Although coming a little belatedly to the picture, some now draw specific links between internationalization, multiculturalism and equality and diversity work (Caruana and Ploner 2010). Reporting on roundtable discussions with colleagues in the USA, Olson *et al.* (2007: 1) summarize areas of synergy:

Working at the intersection of internationalisation and multicultural education provides creative opportunities for faculty, staff, and administrators to:

- Help students understand multiculturalism and social justice in a global context.
- Develop intercultural skills.
- Broaden attitudes to appreciate the complexity of the world.
- Examine values, attitudes, and responsibilities for local/global leadership.
- Disrupt silence and make visible hidden issues not explicit in networks of relationships.
- See how power and privilege are shifting in the local/global context.
- Experience conflicts and develop skills to work together.
- Prepare students to cooperate and compete in a multicultural and global workplace.

A review of these 'creative opportunities' sheds light upon how the dimensions of inclusivity and global relevance framed in Section 5 come together in the formal curriculum through objectives, content, delivery, learning outcomes, and assessment mechanisms. However, as our focus on learning processes in Chapter 4 will illustrate, all aspects of the student experience impact on their journeys of becoming, and so we will also pay attention to the informal and hidden curricula as features in the internationalization endeavour. I conclude this brief survey of the internationalization landscape with a proposed model for objectives for the internationalization of the curriculum (IOC), something we will return to when we look at Practice in Chapter 5. See the volume by Leask in this series for a much more detailed examination of IOC.

Reflective questions for Section 4

- Do you agree that (for-profit) international student recruitment and the opening up of off-shore campus and franchised provision are not in themselves part of the internationalization agenda?
- To what extent do you think these activities, in the context of your own courses and students, contribute as means to help achieve the internationalization agenda?
- To what extent does your own institution clearly articulate 'a broad spectrum of activities' in a vision which itself is 'underpinned by an institutional ethos'?
- I characterize internationalization as being concerned with the 'growth of identities and the development of personal capabilities through the processes and activities encountered within their university experience'. Which processes and activities do you have some measure of control over?
- What synergies do you identify between internationalization (as being presented in this book) and those seeking to embed an equality and diversity agenda in higher education?

Section 5: Internationalization of the curriculum

> Isolation of subject matter from a social context is the chief obstruction in current practice to securing a general training of mind.
>
> (Dewey 1916/1966: 67)

Many advocates for the internationalization of the curriculum (IOC) would recognize the validity of Dewey's assertion, contextualizing it, of course, to the *global* social context of our times, and noting that the 'training of the mind' needs framing as a more holistic development process if we are to ensure we can equip students for that same global context. Many advocates of IOC would also wish to argue that for the kind of learning which is envisioned to be meaningful, it must also not be isolated from the disciplinary context of the student's area of study.

In a review of Canadian tertiary institutions, Bond (2003) identified three characteristic approaches to IOC. In ascending order of embeddedness these are: the add-on approach, the infusion approach, and the transformative approach. The infusion approach was found to be the most common in Bond's research in Canada, and it seems likely that either an add-on or an infusion approach is most common in the UK, the USA and Australia. If we look at approaches to internationalization presented in Section 4, and consider what has been claimed with regard to rationales thus far, the kind of IOC which will be advocated for here sits most closely within the 'transformative' approach:

> The transformational approach produces reform, which requires a shift in the ways in which we understand the world. As an approach to curriculum reform ... [it] has the potential to involve many more people, and change, in fundamental ways how faculty and students think about the world and their place in it.
>
> (Bond 2003: 8)

Transformative learning of this kind requires considerable attention to the content of the curriculum. But also (and many would say more so) it requires attention to the learning experience; what it is that students *do*, and the challenges which they face as they construct and enact their learning.

Taking as our starting point the position that internationalization is a response to globalization, we can ask questions about what kinds of change to the student experience globalization should cause us to consider. Gacel-Ávila proposes:

> In this new global environment, one of the basic and fundamental functions of a university should then be the fostering of a global consciousness among students, to make them understand the relation of interdependence between peoples and societies, to develop in students an understanding of their own and other cultures and respect for pluralism. All these aspects are the foundations of solidarity and peaceful coexistence among nations and of true global citizenship.
>
> (Gacel-Ávila 2005: 123)

Looking at IOC, I propose that aspirations such as these can helpfully be represented as comprising two dimensions – *inclusivity* and *global relevance*, broadly as portrayed in my own university's construct of a *global outlook* (Killick 2011).

Inclusivity

Globalization directly impacts upon the make-up of our university populations. The home campus is more diverse in both the student and the staff body; students enter, live and study beside, compete and cooperate with, search out their own identities among, make life plans surrounded by, and graduate alongside a range of cultural (national, ethnic, socio-economic, etc.) diversity all but unimaginable fifty years ago. Some of this arises from obvious outcomes of globalization alluded to earlier such as greater diversity and engagement in migration and so an expansion of local cultural ranges, and the global marketization of higher education. Some may be more tangentially connected – the 'massification' of access to universities, for example, may be driven by a view that to compete globally, we need a wider base of graduates to feed into employment and enterprise activities. This policy has been supported by widening participation initiatives, and has led also to a (slightly) more diverse local population on the home campus. The inclusivity strand of this model of IOC, then, surrounds attempts to make the student experience more *inclusive*; that is – more appropriate for and more equitable towards/among this diverse group of individuals. Our responses to this diversity across home and international students (should) knit together internationalization and equality and diversity activities (Caruana and Ploner 2010). This inclusivity dimension is of relevance to all aspects of the student experience from finance, through academic regulations or the availability of appropriate food services, to what happens during tutorials. Crucially, inclusivity needs to be understood as central also to how we seek to engender more inclusive attitudes and practices *among* our students as well as *towards* them. As will be picked up in Chapter 5, campus diversity can offer sites of significant learning related to inclusivity and to our second dimension of an internationalized curriculum, global relevance.

Global relevance

Globalization impacts directly upon how students need to be able to understand and apply their disciplinary knowledge. There are many facets to this, some of which play out more significantly in some disciplines than others. The interconnected nature of many world systems requires abilities to understand problems and to research and implement solutions which take account of these connections. The impacts of individual decisions have the potential to be felt by people in other global settings, requiring abilities to predict, evaluate, and apply ethical judgements to personal and professional actions informed by a global perspective. As noted above with regard to the campus, most of the contexts in which students and graduates (and colleagues) enact their working and their social lives involve direct or indirect contact with 'others', those whose ontologies, norms, rituals, and motivations may differ significantly from our own – requiring not only the confidence and competencies to engage successfully with alterity, but also the will and inclination to do so.

While both dimensions to internationalization play out most strongly in the *design* and *delivery* of the curriculum, the university experience in its entirety should be one where inclusivity and global relevance are evidenced through policies and processes. A very obvious example highlighted in earlier discussions is how the university might see its own responsibilities towards the societies from which it attracts (or extracts) its international students or in which it establishes its off-shore campuses and franchises.

While I find it is helpful to model internationalization as encompassing the two dimensions of inclusivity and global relevance, there are significant synergies between them. This will be apparent in the next section, which proposes a picture of the global self; it will also be clear when we look at aspects of learning theory which can inform the development of that global self in Chapter 4. Fortunately for practitioners and students alike, these synergies also play out in the ways in which curricula, learning activities, and the broader university experience can be shaped.

We have seen that IOC is a complex task, and it is relevant to note here that it requires of the academy an on-going quest to 'understand the future needs of our students' and an attitude of openness to 'new knowledges and ways of working' (Clifford 2011: 556). For this to happen, of course, our institutions need to ensure that their 'human capital' is supported to 'make that transition on a personal and professional level' (Van der Werf 2012: 101). I will briefly return to this when we look at practice questions in Chapter 5.

Having now briefly outlined dimensions to an internationalized curriculum, the final section of this chapter briefly presents a model of the global student – and the global self – as the aspirational 'outcome' of an internationalized higher education experience: The person capable of making their way in the new, emerging and uncertain flows of our globalizing world. This model will be expanded upon throughout the book as we look at questions of our 'being' and our 'becoming' in Chapters 2, 3 and 4.

Reflective questions for Section 5

- Do you see any place for curriculum internationalization – defined around inclusivity and global relevance – within the construction of your own courses?
- If you believe that inclusivity and/or global relevance are already included in your curriculum – can you think of examples where they are made explicit to students and to wider stakeholders?
- Is 'global' relevance the same as 'international' relevance?
- Do you feel personally equipped (developed and supported) to make the kinds of changes to your own curriculum and its delivery which are being advocated in this section?

Section 6: The global self

> Education not only has a role to play in the development of the functional knowledge and skills within and beyond the immediate educational subject area ..., but must also enable [students] to develop a set of values that transform them, both now and in the future.
>
> (Otter 2007: 42)

Many commentators, and several universities, argue the need for a response to the various facets of globalization based upon the development of 'global citizens'. I propose instead the notion of the 'global self'. This is not prompted by a lack of sympathy with many of the calls for global citizenship education, (I have used the term myself in previous publications), but rather because the term is highly contested and confused – and in many cases is presented as a set of performative activities, is tied in with disputes about universal 'rights' and cultural relativism, or depends upon somewhat utopian forms of global governance. The expansion in our connections and impacts upon each other across global communities would clearly suggest that a citizenship construct which is confined within a nation-state 'no longer holds good, if it ever did' (Elliot 2001: 48). Cogan (2000: 6) points to an increasing literature arguing for 'a global conception of citizenship in which people will identify less with their own nations and more with the planet as a single entity'. McIntosh tells us that 'The 21st century requires us to think about citizenship as extending far beyond the "city" from which the word derives, and the state and the nation to which is has also been associated' (McIntosh 2005: 22).

Some commentators, recognizing the ambiguities and contestations which 'citizenship' conjures, take pains to redefine the term, Dower for example asserts that 'the word 'citizen' may of course be used in a metaphorical sense to indicate, for instance, no more than the idea of membership of a community in which the legal and political aspects of standard citizenship are discarded' (Dower 2003: 36).

Others have composed typologies of different formulations of the global citizen. Urry (Urry 2000: 172–173) for example, building from earlier works, cites seven potential types of global citizen. In summary:

1 'global capitalists' who seek to unite the world around global corporate interests;
2 'global reformers' who use large-scale international organisations to moderate and regulate global capitalism;
3 those working within such organisations as 'global managers';
4 'global networkers' ... who set up and sustain work, professional or leisure networks constituted across national boundaries through imagined or virtual travel;
5 'earth citizens' who seek to take responsibility for the globe through an ethic of often highly localised care;

6   'global cosmopolitans' who develop a stance and an openness towards certain 'other' cultures, peoples and environments, often resulting from extensive corporeal travel; and

7   'the green global backlash' that … uses 'environmentalists' and believers in 'political correctness' as the new global scapegoats which can be critiqued and attacked.

Most of these bear limited relationship to what many advocates for global citizenship understand by the term, and they illustrate clearly the sets of confusions it generates.

It may be that 'the socio-spatial context within which people can imagine themselves as being fellow citizens may be partly shifting from the nation to the globe' (Urry 2000: 186) such that we will at some time come to dissociate our construct of the 'citizen' from the nation-state as we have succeeded in dissociating it from the city-state. Perhaps with the dissolution of nation-states alluded to in Section 1, we will have no choice. But that time is not here now, and even if it were/when it is, we will still need to agree what it means to be a citizen, and whether that is the same as being a 'good' citizen, and how our citizenship rights and responsibilities play out, and how our wider citizen status impacts upon the way we respond as individuals to others with whom we share that citizenship. Even the United Nations, arguably the closest we have to a body for global governance, noted in the foreword to its report on cultural liberty (United Nations 2004: v) that while legislation and institutions might be helpful, 'unless citizens come to think, feel and act in ways that genuinely accommodate the needs and aspirations of others – real change will not happen'.

I suggest that how we 'think, feel and act' constitute the *person* (John Dewey's 'man') rather than simply the citizen. But for its rather grating cadence, I might well have borrowed from Soysal's (1994) notion of post-national 'personhood' to capture what I am instead referring to as the global self, developed and enacted in their university years by the global student.

How a student envisions herself is a matter of her identity, something which is dear to her, forged through her biography – her culture, her education, her friendships, her family, and so forth. Forged, then, in her relationships with the others who make up her world. The forces at work within those relationships as experienced by most of our students prior to university life may tend to push them away from the inclusive relationship to the global other (their sense of *self-in-the-world* discussed below) which I am advocating here, and that is what gives the university experience a particularly important role to play. It is not at all simple to shift our identities, to re-imagine ourselves differently – even when much in the world seems to demand it.

Self-identity will be described in Chapter 3 as part of the *lifeworld* (Husserl 1936/1970), each individual's total construction of 'reality' for them. Martin Heidegger (1962/1998) set out a view of our *being-in-the-world* as a very largely unexamined flow among objects/experiences which are so familiar to us ('ready-to-hand') that our interactions with them/within them rarely rise to the level of consciousness. Emerging from this unexamined flow is forced upon us when something we encounter/experience fails to conform to the ready-to-hand expectations of our lifeworld. (Re)-learning is required, lifeworld change is called for – processes explored in depth in Chapter 4. The unready-to-hand complexities of the globalizing world are argued in Chapter 2 to present our students with situations of disjuncture, and the conflicting needs for on-going security and for change. Such change is rarely a simple matter. But this fact need not make the *objective* of that change also complex; what we set out to help out students to become may be as simple as Appiah's version of cosmopolitanism: '... it begins with the simple idea that in human community, as in national communities, we need to develop habits of coexistence: conversation in its older meaning, of living together, association' (Appiah 2006: xix). I will propose enabling conversations and communities to be key to practice in our work with/for the global student in Chapter 5.

I suggest that these habits of coexistence are founded upon one fundamental sense of, what I shall refer to as, *self-in-the-world*, namely, that the others with whom I coexist are equally human. Once again, this is not proposed to be the *ready-to-hand* formulation of self-identity for most of us or for most of our students. However, I am proposing this sense of *self-in-the-world*, my identification of self–other, as the *primary* dimension to the global self – and precisely because this may not come to us naturally, it is the primary objective of internationalization in my terms. That another is 'equally human' does not demand that I like her, or that I agree with her – any more so than it would for a close neighbour or family member. What it does entail, though, is that I am prepared to interrogate my reactions to her, my relationships with her, my responsibilities toward her with as much ethical and practical diligence as I would any other 'other'. This might not be easy, I'm likely often to get it wrong; important, though, is my preparedness for making the attempt, and my preparedness to make the attempt flows from the starting point of 'equally human'. I do not believe this throws us into a mire of relativism or any tyranny of universalism. It is about global *selves* not *citizens;* connections between individuals. It is also about adopting a sceptical stance to the world, not an uncritical acceptance of it; crucially, though, global students and global selves need an equally sceptical stance towards their own ways of being as they have towards those of others.

The secondary dimension to the global self is comprised of the knowledge, skills, and values which enable me to *act-in-the-world*; by which I mean, the capabilities to take deliberative action with appropriate reference to the contexts and participants implicated in the action. Typologies of such capabilities have been presented by many of the advocates of global citizenship education. I quote at length from one source which offers a quite comprehensive picture:

> I associate global citizenship first with several capacities of mind: 1) the
> ability to observe oneself and the world around one, 2) the ability to make
> comparisons and contrasts, 3) the ability to see 'plurality' as a result, 4) the

ability to understand that both 'reality' and language come in versions, 5) the ability to see power relations and understand them systematically, and 6) the ability to balance awareness of one's own realities with the realities of entities outside the perceived self.

I also associate global citizenship with several capacities of heart: 1) the ability to respect one's own feelings and delve deeply into them, 2) the ability to become aware of others' feelings and to believe in the validity of those feelings, 3) the ability to experience in oneself a mixture of conflicting feelings without losing a sense of integrity, 4) the ability to experience affective worlds plurally while keeping a gyroscopic sense of one's core orientations, 5) the capacity to wish competing parties well, 6) the ability to observe and understand how the 'politics of location' affect one's own and others' positions and power in the world, 7) the ability to balance being heartfelt with a felt knowledge of how culture is embedded in the hearts of ourselves and others.

I further associate global citizenship with related capacities of the physical body and spiritual soul.

(McIntosh 2005: 23)

Something like these may be seen to offer objectives for curriculum design and learning outcomes in an education for the global student. They are the kinds of capabilities which offer our students agency in a globalizing world. But, to reiterate, without a sense of *self-in-the-world* founded upon the other as equally human, such *act-in-the-world* agency does not make for a global self.

In short, then, I suggest that to make their way in the increasingly interconnected and diverse globalizing world, and to do so in ways which are commensurate within a broad agenda of social justice, our students need opportunities to experience being global students in order to develop their capabilities as global selves. Such selves are founded upon a sense of *self-in-the world*, and supported through and stimulating capabilities to *act-in-the-world*. Although I have presented these formulations of identity and agency as separate dimensions of the global self, they are intimately interwoven in our lifeworlds, and need also therefore to be intimately interwoven in the experiences which internationalization creates for the global student. If the vision I hold of myself is that I am someone who *can*, that impacts upon how I envision what I *am*, and *vice versa*. As a simple example, the student who sees herself as someone who *can* engage in respectful dialogue with someone from another culture is more likely to be able to visualize herself as someone who *does* engage in respectful dialogue with someone from another culture than the student who does not recognize herself as having that capability.

The unfolding of this interrelationship is akin to what Baxter Magolda has identified as moving through the *crossroads* of young adulthood to become *authors of our own lives* (Baxter Magolda 2001, 2009). This has always been an objective of *higher* education (at least until the more recent agendas outlined

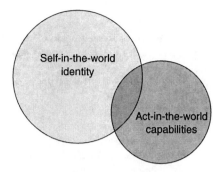

Figure 1.1 Related dimensions to the global self – with self-in-the-world identity having primacy

earlier in this chapter); the changing times 'simply' require that self-authorship needs to be framed in an extended notion of the 'we' in the lifeworld of the global self. For the global student, this means experiencing university life and learning in inclusive and equitable spaces which allow for and enable interactions across cultural borders and beyond narrow conceptualizations of us and them.

Much of the foregoing discussion can be summarized into a definition of internationalization as it is understood/advocated for in this book. Coelen ties internationalization to the 'provision of an [university] environment containing such elements that a learner is given the opportunity to attain achieved learning outcomes associated with intercultural awareness and intercultural competence' (Coelen 2013: 25). He also notes the importance of tying in what happens at university with other 'life-long' learning experiences. The focus on both learning outcomes and upon the continuing transformation of the individual are important, but I would wish for a more expansive aspiration in terms of the outcomes themselves, a more robust response than offering 'opportunities', and a greater recognition that life-long learning is the responsibility of the learner. The proposed definition of internationalization which guides this book, then, is:

> *The internationalization of higher education constitutes a complex set of processes which are identified by and incorporated into the activities of an individual institution through which all its students experience their subject as globally situated, their peers as equals, and perspectives as always challengeable, and graduate as global selves, with the confidence and the capabilities to make their way among diverse others on the basis of a critical awareness of the impacts of their actions.*

The main activities we will focus on concern the learning environments and experiences we create in order to support the development of the global student and her transformation to a global self.

Reflective questions for Section 6

- Would you agree that the term 'global citizen' is confusing because of its links to constructs such as citizenship 'rights' and legal and governance structures which do not (yet) exist at the global level?
- Does it seem reasonable to assert that our capabilities to *act* demand an underpinning sense of our *identity vis-à-vis* the global other?
- Do you see any validity in the construct of the global *self-in-the-world* as one who sees others as 'equally human'?
- Should the university be concerning itself with enabling students to become *authors of their own lives*? And if so, does that necessarily involve us in enabling a more globally situated authorship than has hitherto been the case?
- Before moving on the next chapter, has anything which you have read so far led you to reconsider where you would position yourself with regards to any of the dichotomies presented in the Introduction?

Chapter 2

Questions of alterity

Men grow habituated each to each,
Like jewels thread upon a single cord;
Succour each other in the war of life
In mutual bond, like workmen bound upon a common task.

(Omar Khayyam, *Iqbal*)

How shall I talk of the sea to the frog,
if it has never left his pond?
How shall I talk of the frost to the bird of the summerland,
if it has never left the land of its birth?
How shall I talk of life with the sage,
if he is prisoner of his doctrine?

(Chung Tsu, 4th century BC, quoted in Fantini 2000)

Introduction

Chapter 1 explored some of the general contexts in which higher education is being shaped/shaping itself, and I proposed that internationalization, as understood in this book, is a set of responses to the complexities of globalization. With a focus on internationalization as *means not ends*, I proposed a legitimate end would be the development of the global self – modelled primarily as a sense of *self-in-the-world* and secondarily as the capabilities to *act-in-the-world*. In this chapter we look in some detail at aspects of the relationships between our selves and alterity, *Otherness*, which seem to present barriers to the 'natural', unfacilitated development of such a global self among our students (and ourselves). Like the Yin-Yang symbol there seems to be a complex relationship between self and other, somehow detached, but also formulating the frame for our development and understandings. We begin by looking more specifically at the social implications of aspects of globalization, and see how it may be fracturing that frame. In that light we return to the notion of the global self through an examination of communication and other competencies which help shape our flow amongst alterity, and through considerations of what general conditions might better support the development of the global student. This last area will become particularly important when we look in more detail at *practice* in Chapter 5.

Section 1: Social consequences of globalization

What to do? How to act? Who to be?

(Giddens 1991: 70)

As already discussed, there is no doubt that some of the *conditions* to bring us into closer contact with each other are among the defining features of globalization. We have reminded ourselves how communications technologies, global media, business travel, tourism and migration, multinational/multicultural workforces, complexly networked global economics whirl us into daily contact with the other. Experiencing life surrounded by and in interaction with alterity is becoming a social norm for many, and is set to become so for many more. For our purposes, this deserves particular attention because the personal and social *consequences* of so much greater connectivity are anything but clear, and in the ambiguities of this interconnected world lie many of the roots of postmodern nihilism. In those ambiguities also lie the rationales for envisioning the growth of a global self, and for exploring an education better suited to its development. We have also explored in brief how higher education and internationalization sit within the globalization procession. In this section I will look further into some of the consequences of globalization in so far as they are theorized to impact upon individual identity and agency, and therefore upon the capabilities of our students to make their way in the world.

Zygmunt Bauman's 'liquid modernity' (1998, 2000, 2005) offers a resonant encapsulation of the ebbing and flowing of confidence, individual identity, agency, and certainty as once clear conceptual, ethical and procedural understandings of the world and the self are challenged. These challenges may arise through the puncturing of hitherto relatively closed systems of societal norms and rituals as we flow among those whose own ways of being appear strange to us. They may arise, for example, through an erosion of religious certainties for those shifting (or being shifted) into an advancing secularism, or from a (re)assertion of a religious 'fundamentalism' within hitherto more secular societies, or from the tension-spaces between societies or between communities within societies. They may arise through living in a political world where relatively stable notions of national friends and foes, or of rulers and ruled shift unpredictably, or where, as noted, the nation state itself 'is on its last legs' (Appadurai 1997: 19), facing the 'deterritorialization' of its salience (Scholte 2000), and siting us at a point of 'unanchored and free-floating' sovereignty (Bauman 2012: 50) – an 'interregnum' in which we have yet to imagine effective future structures for power and politics. And also a site of personal identity threat, since our nationalities offer easy safe-havens in which to anchor our identity. Easy, because as Kymlicka (1995: 89) points out, national identity is 'based on belonging, not accomplishment'; we *are* it, we don't have to earn it, or find it, or create it. At the same time, though, the nationhood we belong within is only as 'real' as we choose to make it; as Webb *et al.* (2002) comment on Bourdieu's (1984) representation (explored in Chapter 3), our communities and our nations are neither 'natural or coherent', but rather 'stitched together as effects of [their] stories, discourses, practices and authorized values', existing 'only in the stories and collective beliefs of groups of people' (Webb *et al.* 2002: 90). In this section I largely represent a world where the stitching is unravelling. Among the strongest threads binding our national and community identities are those of our traditions, and these too are seen to be failing us in our 'detraditionalising' world (Giddens 2002: Loc 1038).

Lauder characterizes globalization's impact on the nation-state and on education as '[t]he central question of the age' (Lauder *et al.* 2006: 189). In fact, to the extent that deterritorialization is realized, these two are inextricable interwoven, and reassert for our interrogation all of the questions raised in the Introduction to this book around the dichotomies upon which our views of higher education rest. What *can* a dissolving nation-state with confused, fused and de-fused traditions actually do for its citizens in terms of their education – almost regardless of what it might *aspire* to do? And, what can education do for its students regardless of who might be setting its agenda in lieu of the state? If we are doubtful of the demise of the nation-state we might reflect upon the degree to which 'the markets' are now the active agents driving the rise and fall of national economies. We might expect, at the very least, that a nation-state, if it is not a failing state, would be capable of setting and ensuring broad adherence to expectations for the payment of taxes, but the realities of global capitalism have rendered even this rather fundamental task an unreality. Consider the situation in the UK in 2012 where several multinational enterprises were 'outed' for employing devious (though technically legal) means to avoid paying taxes. The government was unable to take any action within the existing law, but more significantly it was *unwilling/unable* to change the law for fear of driving the businesses offshore. In such 'modern times', perhaps, the ensuing citizen-boycott of at least one company's products was the only political action which could be taken to encourage (not enforce) such global enterprises to play their part in the citizenship game. But, this particular collective consumer act, while not an isolated example, does not reflect dominant ascriptions in the identification of the consumer, as we discuss later in this section – and was in any case rather short-lived. In terms of its more insidious impact upon our students, the erosion in the perceived capacity of *her* national government to set its own rules and determine its own future can only add to any diminishing sense of personal agency. This erosion of personal agency has always been one of the many tyrannies of colonialism. A further personal consequence is likely to be a disengagement from participation in the political process. After all, why vote when whoever is elected is powerless to act? Postmodernists have been signalling the withering of the 'grand narratives' or 'metanarratives' and their associated values which framed modernization for some time. The loss of intelligible and relatively permanent stories (even if they are conflicted and conflictual) of how the world is, might be personally liberating in the sense that I can now 'elaborate a "self-culture"' (Archer 2007: 32) rather than be defined within those narratives. Elliot encapsulates this as a personalized 'heightened self-understanding of imagination and desire in the fabrication of meaning in daily life' which may evolve for us

> the capacity to proceed in personal and cultural life without absolute guidelines – in short, an increased toleration of ambivalence and contingency [but with the considerable risk that] there is no guarantee that the reflexive scanning of the imagination will prove solid enough to sustain interpersonal relationships.
>
> (Elliot 2001: 50)

To me, at least, this seems a risk we have an urgent responsibility to minimize, for the sake of the individual student and her world.

If the loss of the grand narratives and their associated values strips me of something to define myself against or within, and of the capacity to engage with others, and if the grand narrative of the nation-state itself is now withering, and with it the grander-yet narrative of participatory democracy with its associated sense of personal agency, what will fill the voids?

To draw a picture of how we imagine our world and ourselves within it, Arjun Appadurai (1966/2006, 1997) introduces the evocative metaphor of the *'scape'*, five of which form a 'framework for exploring [the] disjunctures' which encapsulate his 'theory of rupture'. A theory that 'takes media and migration as its two major, and interconnected diacritics and explores their joint effect on the *work of the imagination* as a constitutive feature of modern subjectivity' (Appadurai 1997: 33 and 3).

Just as there is nowhere so lonely as a crowded room, we are each, ironically, increasingly isolated amid advancing global connectivities as we imagine ourselves and our world through encounters with instantiations of the global other (our ethnoscapes); of the technologies we utilize or are denied access to within continuing/advancing global inequalities (our technoscapes); of the highly differential ways in which global money, untethered from any national hitching posts, exploits or rewards us (our financescapes); and of the images and narratives which flood our daily existence through television, newspapers, tweets and RSS feeds (our mediascapes). The increasing diversity of our ethnoscapes might be cast as an inevitable force for good, a lived-reality which will draw us into greater understanding and tolerance of the others we encounter. It might also

> equally lead to a disturbing sense of engulfment and immersion. This may result in a retreat from the threat of cultural disorder into the security of ethnicity, traditionalism or fundamentalism, or the active assertion of the integrity of the national culture in global culture prestige contests.
>
> (Featherstone 1995: 91)

Perhaps also indicating the decline in the nation-state is the diminishing *national* posturing within the dominant fundamentalisms of our times (times which have of course since Featherstone made his commentary witnessed the collapse of soviet communism and the evaporation of the cold war, the globalization of terrorism, and the surge of new axes of economic power in China and India). Giddens notes that fundamentalism is not defined by *what* people believe, but by *why* they believe it and *how* they justify it; 'it is a refusal of dialogue in a world whose peace and continuity depend on it' (Giddens 2002: Loc 786 and 789) and 'an assertion of formulaic truth without regard to consequences' (Giddens 1994: 100). I will argue that enabling our students to dialogue and encouraging them to challenge formulaic truths are key to the practice of education for the global self.

Outside temptations to the violent retreats to fundamentalism which most of us may hope to resist, there are less aggressive responses to our encounters with global others which are still unhelpful in terms of advancing dialogue or developing the global self. Martha Nussbaum (1997) models one such set, proposing that typically our individual responses to difference will either be characterized by *descriptive chauvinism*, whereby others are recreated in our own image – we imagine them as essentially the same as we are – or by *descriptive romanticism* which sees in the other culture only positives which contrast to deficiencies in one's own – and so highlights difference and denies complexities. A particular instantiation of physical encounters within our more diverse ethnoscapes arises through the massive growth in international tourism, which has been explored in depth by John Urry. Urry (1995: 165) proposes that as people tour, they reconstruct their envisionings of 'home', and, in their imaginations at least, their *rights* as citizens 'increasingly involve claims to consume other cultures and places throughout the world'. Our wealthier students, at least, are likely to have accrued some experience of international touring, gap years, volunteering, and the like; how this has impacted upon their sense of their individual rights or *responsibilities* towards those other cultures is a moot point. Apart from the very significant ethical questions this raises, the rabid 'consumption of the exotic' (de Jong and Teekens 2003: 48) which typifies the enactment of any such rights claims further constrains any humanizing of the other within our ethnoscapes. Tourism, of course, implicates not only the tourist but also the toured, and can radically restructure the *physical* as well as the imagined homes of those who are the objects of consumption. A particular way in which internationalization might exacerbate rather than challenge the impacts *of* the 'touring' student *on* the 'toured' global other is through its efforts to promote study abroad, international volunteering and foreign work placements.

We noted earlier one example of consumer action in the UK, and suggested how this was something of an exceptional response when set within the dominant enactment of consumerism. Rather than seeing our consumer worlds as a field for action, or a way of expressing a relatively enduring sense of self, our students may find asserting either individual agency or identity significantly challenged amidst a rampaging consumerism which drives us all to proclaim ourselves to the world, and to take our measure of our neighbours, of our heroes, and actually of ourselves, through its transient symbols. The transience of its symbols are seen by some commentators to be the core defining feature of the consumerist society, in which our 'pursuit of happiness' is shifted from acquiring things to 'disposing of them', and:

> For expectations to be kept alive and for new hopes to promptly fill the voids left by the hopes already discredited and discarded, the road from the shop to the garbage bin needs to be short and the passage swift.
>
> (Bauman 2008: Loc 1665 and 1811–1813)

And so, in this perspective, as soon as we purchase a symbol by which to define/proclaim ourselves, we are already formulating a want for something other. When we thus cast consumption as the 'building blocks of life worlds', the 'means of creating an identity' (Friedman 1994: 115 and 151) and the 'increasing aestheticization of everyday life where consumption has become a constitutive aspect of identity formation' (Isin and Wood 1999: 14), it is not at all as simple as craving the next iteration of a mobile phone, it is craving the next iteration of the bit of personal identity which it brings with it. Consumerism evokes a process which constantly destabilizes the self. If only things with monetary value have value, the rest are 'ignored and marginalized' and '[t]he meaning of life slips through our fingers' (Rutherford 2007: 10). The very growth of such types of consumerism in Western societies may itself add to the distancing between students socialized into its culture and those who are more typically the producers rather than the consumers of its artefacts. As noted in the previous chapter, also, the university itself is in danger of becoming another consumable object and/or becoming an adjunct to the consumerist ethic.

If we recognize the validity of the proposal in Chapter 1 that fitting students for 'employability' reveals how education is now about satisfying the needs of global capitalism, we might see in this consumerist orientation another side of its project – a socialization designed to ensure the continued consumption of capitalism's outputs by depriving our students of any more reliable sense of self. As long ago as 1984, Eric Fromm felt able to assert that 'modern man lives under the illusion that he knows what he wants, while he actually wants what he is supposed to want' (Fromm 1984: 218). If you do not 'buy' the notion of education being subverted to the ends of global capital, it does not significantly weaken the picture of how consumerism acts as a pernicious force to undermine the self through a relentless urge to be (own, display, be recognized as) something I am not yet. Whether by design or accident, consumerism locks us into a vicious spiral of avarice for the new; a desire for desire which cannot be sated since each new acquisition, once owned, is instantly eclipsed by a new object of desire. I argue that this poses a significant threat to a student's capability to formulate an individual sense of *self-in-the-world*, and an impediment, therefore, to the related capability to engage with the perspectives of others.

Consumerism can be cast as a psychological defence response to the confusing and isolating milieu of a globalizing world – a new opium for the masses. While, as suggested, consumerism might be most apparent within the wealthy capitalist economies, Ritzer (1993) detects its miasma as having spread much more globally, through processes broadly captured in the notion of McDonaldization. This is a commodification of identities on a global scale through the reach of dominating, homogenized, non-local symbols of what I need in order to be (let us say) 'cool'. In a later volume, Ritzer argues the commodification 'of nothing' (principally non-things and non-services, which having been created in some other place are devoid of any local/indigenous social worth) to be intrinsic to the processes of globalization, and proposes that this necessarily leads to the emptying of meaning from our lives, ' to the degree that consumption is increasingly dominated by nothing, people's lives are similarly involved with nothing and to an increasing degree' (Ritzer, George 2004: x).

Important to this book, is the thought that these chimeras of a commodified selfhood not only fail to offer any lasting solace; rather, they intensify 'our anxiety at finding ourselves with strangers in a world that holds no intrinsic meaning or purpose' (Rutherford 2007: 35). Education for the global student should seek to provide experiences and perspectives which reduce the anxiety of being with strangers.

Considering our discussions on the commodification of higher education, it is relevant to consider how Bauman portrays consumerism impacting also on the substantive values of education and the accumulation of knowledge:

> Today's consumerism is not about *accumulation* of things, but their one-off *enjoyment*. So why should the 'knowledge package' obtained during the stay in school or college be exempted from that universal rule? In the whirlwind of change, knowledge fit for instant use and meant for one-off use, knowledge ready-for-instant-use-and-instant-disposal, knowledge of the kind promised by software programmes coming in and out of shop shelves in an ever accelerating succession, looks much more attractive.
>
> (Bauman 2005: 41, original italics)

A colleague recently characterized this as a shift from 'just in case' knowledge to 'just in time' knowledge. And there may be validity in exploring further how higher education might better develop capabilities to access and utilize knowledge on a need-to-know-now basis, rather than focusing quite so much on knowledge accumulation. Crucially, though, between *access* and *utilize*, we need to provide an educational experience in which our students develop a capacity for sceptical engagement and critical evaluation of what they access, to know something's worth before they forge ahead. Furthermore, as Ron Barnett points out, what he terms the 'supercomplex' world 'presents not challenges of knowing but of *being*' (Barnett, R. 2000: 157); how much more important, then, is our students' willingness, reflective capacities and confidence to interrogate not only whether his accumulated knowledge, but also whether his accumulated identities have validity? And how much more complex is this task if, indeed, globalization is forcing them to replace 'relatively stable identities rooted in place' with 'hybrid identities characterised by mobility and flux' (Easthope 2009: 65)?

Appadurai's 'scapes' and Bauman's 'liquidities' offer vivid glimpses of the ways in which globalization is bringing new, varied, and rapidly moving forms and figures into our students' lives in unprecedented ways. In such a world, where our unconscious ease of flow among Heidegger's ever-familiar 'ready-to-hand' (1962/1998) hits against the new, the unknown, the beyond-experience, our students may hide in Nussbaum's chauvinism or romanticism, retreat into some form of fundamentalism, or protect themselves in stances concerning their 'rights' to consume. Whatever their defences, the cumulative impact of being surrounded by challenging newness is perhaps most likely to make many of them subject to the disjunctures of a kind of debilitating *culture* shock (whose classic symptoms include 'disintegration', withdrawal and a sense of impotence [Oberg 1960; Pedersen 1995]). It is largely the questions concerning how we and our students can reconcile ourselves to these radical (and 'radically incomplete') changes, and so make our way amidst their uncertainties and novelties, without recourse to personal deceptions, individualized colonialism, the comforting brotherhoods and sisterhoods of fundamentalism, or living inside extended personality traumas which are the concern of this book. An important part of the answer will lie in how we enable our students to be simply alert (mindful) to the impacts these novelties may be having upon them. For example, Jarvis notes with respect to mass media: 'The incidentality of learning means that individuals will acquire the information transmitted by the mass media without always being aware of what is happening to them' (Jarvis 2008: 98).

This neglected area of *incidental learning*, which we will return to in Chapter 4, adds a further perspective on the influence of our mediascapes, and it is important to remember that this holds true also for information 'transmitted' by, for example, social networking sites, the plastic heroes and heroines lauded by pedlars of consumerism, tax-avoiding corporations, the actions of the 'markets' and of the state, the university culture they temporarily inhabit, and, specifically, the norms of interaction with socio-cultural others which are evidenced in all those spaces. That the mass media, social networking sites, high profile individuals and corporations, and (even) our universities are part of the culture of consumerism means the messages surrounding our students, impacting their incidental learning, serve constantly to bolster and legitimize avarice and avatar. This does not seem conducive to an authentic life, and is anyway challenged abruptly by the counterpoises of conflicting global realities. These often visceral images of persisting global poverties, conflicts and inhumanities, disruptions of severe weather triggered by climate change, the destruction of eco-systems and the extinction of species, the discrediting treatment of migrants in our neighbourhoods, and so forth, penetrate our students' consciousness through the same and other technoscapes, mediascapes and ethnoscapes. If this is the world as significantly experienced by our students, then building opportunities, indeed requirements, for them to challenge and critique its assumptions and reconcile its contradictions seem requirements of a higher education.

As presented here, then, we see the void left for our students by the shrinking salience of the grand narratives being occupied by the transient narratives of consumerism, including the consumer-tourist and the consumer-media-voyeur, and at the same time by the expanding images and voices 'talking back' from around the globe. Inherent within those grand narratives are (or were) our personal 'projects' – which we form 'to advance or to protect what we care most about' (Archer 2007: 7). Archer asserts that it is impossible for us to live in society without our projects. Many of our projects may not be very 'grand' at all – simply the business of going about our daily business ('catching buses') – but even for these 'a change of circumstances' can jolt them from the 'successful social practices which have become taken for granted as embodied knowledge' (Archer 2007: 9). Globalization, in changing many circumstances, piles uncertainties upon our students, throws them out of their unexamined, established, and comfortable projects, and we need to enable them to build resilience if this is not to fragment their identities and their capacities to act. Postmodernism asserts the impossibility of building projects, but without them, as Archer points out, we cannot live in society.

We can of course reflect that in particular places and at particular times throughout history and in many places in the present, other lifeworld constructions have also been ruptured, and projects rendered nonsensical. Perhaps as invading colonialism or other fundamentalisms ripped through both sinew and state, perhaps as new gods relegated the once undeniable to the now laughably superstitious or terrifyingly heretical, perhaps as awful pestilence purged the population exacting atonement for unfathomable sinning, perhaps as the geocentric universe shifted its axes to the heavens. For those present, the traumas of these times were/are certainly not qualitatively less than the menaces of globalization; and humankind has survived. But in the process many have not survived, whole cultures have not survived; whole civilizations have been lost to the hegemonies of expanding empires or of self-seeking priesthoods and caliphates. And, unlike previous upheavals, globalization is not something confined within a particular place or felt only by a particular class or sect or ethnicity; its reach is, indeed, global. As noted earlier, the impacts of the multifaceted processes of globalization are certainly differentially experienced, but the uncertainties spawned in its advance affect everybody regardless of our location, our capabilities, or our worldview.

In this section, I have sought to illustrate a number of ways in which the postmodern, globalizing world is argued to challenge individuals' capacities to establish and maintain self-identity through a combination of turbulences, rendering the once-solid into the now-ethereal. In this vision, globalization is not about what we 'wish or hope *to do*. It is about *what is happening to us all*' (Bauman 1998: 60, original italics). Collectively, our scapes form the 'building blocks' of what Appadurai frames as *imagined worlds*, 'the multiple worlds that are constituted by the historically situated imaginations of persons and groups spread around the globe' (Appadurai 1997: 33). I employ the term *lifeworld* to refer to the uniquely individual representations of the world (our imagined worlds) which we each inhabit, or which inhabit each of us, and we will look at this in more detail in Chapter 3. Our individual lifeworlds are shaped through our individual *lived-experience* (Merleau-Ponty 1962). Global capital, its doctrine of consumerism, its unremitting push for market growth, and its capacity to dispossess and disenfranchise *may* be the hegemonic colonizing armada of our times, the significant features which give shape to our students' lived-experience, and hence to their lifeworlds. In its wake, dissolving certainties, daily encounters with difference, the invasive forces of mediascapes and technoscapes, the advancing commodification of our selves and those we tour, all represent some of the theorized social spaces within which we and our students flow or falter. And all of this, of course, is happening at speed and on many fronts; its accumulated impact raises 'the question of any homology with mental states being sustained or sustainable' (Archer 2007: 40). Bauman (1996: 18) encapsulates the postmodern problem of identity to be 'primarily how to avoid fixation and keep the options open', but this way, perhaps, madness lies. What I hold true and what I value over the times and contexts of my life may shift (otherwise what is transformative learning), but through that I retain a sense of *who* I am, and for *that* elements of fixity are needed. Precisely in these challenging times, 'it is those who have a strong sense of their own identity who offer the best potential for resistance' (Tennant 2009: 154) to the 'domination' of the postmodern self. Through the process of internationalizing the student experience, and in particular through building alternative perspectives and intercultural dialogue into that experience, we may help our students find security as individuals in the midst of diverse others. This is not 'only' a matter of security in the present, but of providing a basis upon which to build their future as global selves, for '[t]o adopt an identity, to make it mine, is to see it as structuring my way through life' (Appiah 2005: Loc 669). Woodward concludes his exploration of identity with an acknowledgment that our identities, while indeed shifting, need also to establish narratives which capture a sense of continuity:

> Identity travels, but it is about belonging. Roots are important, but an insistence on fixity and essential sources makes change difficult and stultifies development. Keeping in mind the journeys we have made and would like to make, and holding onto the moments that matter, make routes a more useful concept. We need to remember, in order to know where we have come from, so that we can create new stories of the self, while not losing sight of belonging.
>
> (Woodward 2002: 168)

Furthermore, what emerges strongly in the model of the lifeworld and of learning which I develop in the next two chapters as well as in the notions of social identity formation explored in the next section of this chapter, is that if we are to formulate any sense of the self it can only be done through/within encounters with others. Our project for the global student is one which fully recognizes that others are necessary to the constructions of the narratives of my-self, and so it is a project which then also asks, among these current and future turbulences, '[h] ow shall we find the common shared meanings that connect us to others? If they no longer exist, how shall we make them?' (Rutherford 2007: 9). Once again, I suggest, the ways in which we shape the spaces and experiences of university life to enable encounters across cultural boundaries are highly significant in enabling students to explore shared meanings, and so grow their own identities and locate their *selves-in-the-world*. In the next section we explore psychological perspectives on the social construction of our identity.

Reflective questions for Section 1

- To what extent, if any, do you identify with 'the puncturing of hitherto relatively closed systems of societal norms and rituals' in your own experience of living in a globalizing world?
- To what extent does your nationality give shape to/feature in your own identity? How about others you know? Do you have any sense that there may be generational differences to this within your own culture or communities, including between yourself and your students?
- Have the grand narratives lost their salience? Are any new ones emerging?
- To what degree have your own ethnoscapes changed in, say, the last twenty years? How are the ethnoscapes of your students different from yours at their age?
- If you reflect upon your own approach to/experience of international tourism, do you find any reason to question whether or not you claim rights over others, their cultures, or their homes? Are you a 'romantic' consumer of the exotic? Alternatively, have you experienced your own culture being the object of others' consumption?
- Can you identify anyone or any group who seem to you to live largely in the space between the shop and the garbage bin? Do you find any validity in the idea that this is a way to escape fixity and protect ourselves from seriously engaging with identity construction/maintenance?
- To what degree/in what ways do you see values in higher education being eroded by pulls towards superficial/instant/disposable constructs of knowledge?

Section 2: Social identity and ethnocentrism

By accident, I am who I am.

(Appiah 2005: Loc 4788)

The accidents of our birth and biography shape our values, beliefs, our sense of what is good and normal, our ontological relationship with reality, and the epistemology which underpins how we believe we can touch that reality – our lifeworld, as presented in Chapter 3. There are often quoted theories which seek to divide the macro cultures of the globe into types based upon sets of underlying values, (Hofstede 1984, 1991; Schwartz 1994). Of these, probably the most commonly cited is Hofstede's *individualism–collectivism* continuum (one continuum of six in his typology), upon which the 'Western' nations sit predominantly at the individualist end, with the collectivist end being dominated by South American and South-East Asian nations. Those with collectivist predilections are seen to favour group identity, preservation, action and reward over their more self-seeking, personal-merit and goal-driven individualist cousins. Schwartz divides the world differently, but his seven cultural values overlap Hofstede's at some points, and it is not of immediate interest here to critique one against the other since they are both potentially more dangerous than useful in the context of this book. These types of analysis *may* helpfully point to how national and supra-national cultures differ or find common ground in fundamental value dimensions, though recent analyses revealing levels of difference within national groups has caused Schwartz (2013) to seek to reassign macro-level cultural value differences to a kind of detached theorized system of social meaning, external somehow to the individuals who comprise the society. Nonetheless, they may provide interesting ways of thinking about what kinds of value domains can help us interpret aspects of behaviour or ways of thinking. Their danger lies in temptations to apply their generalized meta-cultural assignations to individuals who, by accident, may have been born into a particular cultural space (or, indeed, may simply *look* as if they were born into such a space). As noted in the opening of this section, it is the accidents of our birth *and our biography, our lived-experience*, which bring us to the individuals we are today. And, it is the *singular* complexities and serendipities surrounding each of us as individuals advancing through our future biographies which will bring us each to the individual we are tomorrow. It is important that we emphasize this at the beginning of this section because the discussion below on the social formation of identity, and in Chapter 3 on societal and cultural formations, must be read within this understanding. The social spaces each of us occupies vary in their heterogeneity; in the degree of heterogeneity between, within, and surrounding the social groups of any two individuals, and in the manners and intensities in which such heterogeneity is manifested. The opening section of this chapter sought to emphasize that a particular social consequence of globalization is the rate at which, for many of the global population, contacts with heterogeneous, *unready-to-hand* norms, rituals, and values are increasing. Whether those contacts are experienced as toured or as tourist can be considered an accident of birth (to the degree that for many their health, their continent, the repressiveness of the regime they live under, etc., has severe impact on the likelihood of having many of the capabilities needed to be a tourist); how *each* contact plays out can be considered an accident of biography, or rather of the biographies of each individual in the encounter. A highly significant accident of biography is, of course, the formal education we experience. Relatively privileged socio-geographical spaces and the reinforcing social encounters within those spaces have given shape to the biographies of the large majority of undergraduate students, in Western contexts at least (despite the enormous energy thrown at widening participation efforts), and their university experience in turn bolsters their individual *capabilities* (Sen 1999) and their *cultural capital* (Bourdieu 1986/2006). Bourdieu identified cultural capital as 'no doubt the best hidden form of hereditary transmission of capital', and said that it was the notion of cultural capital which made it possible for him to

> explain the unequal scholastic achievement of children originating from the different social classes by relating academic success, i.e., the specific profits which children from the different classes and class fractions can obtain in the academic market, to the distribution of cultural capital between the classes and class fractions.
>
> (Bourdieu 1986/2006: 108 and 106)

The differentials in capabilities and in all forms of capital are, of course, hugely magnified when viewed across diverse *global* contexts. Nonetheless, it is a belief in the power of education to help shape *who we are* and *what we can* which accounts for both its popularity, and its suppression or denial to some people under some regimes. It is the same belief which underpins this book; if higher education cannot have a significant impact on *who we are*, notwithstanding our biographies to date, then there is no sense whatsoever in the notion of transformative or significant education; education could only ever be the minimalist transfer of existing knowledge along the lines of Freire's (1970, 1972) banking paradigm. Much of what is said about social identity theory below, therefore, is to be read as applying also to the social processes of education, including university education – and under the proviso that good formal education is not about social reproduction; it is there, precisely, to make us better than we could be if left to our own devices.

Referring to Charles Taylor's (1991) proposition that we are 'dialogically' constituted, Appiah notes that: 'Beginning in infancy, it is in dialogue with other people's understanding of who I am that I develop a conception of my own identity' (Appiah 2005: Loc 589). As noted at the end of the preceding section, others are co-authors in the construction of the narratives of the self (Rutherford 2007). Rutherford goes on to advocate for 'identities of reciprocity' whose 'narratives can accommodate the presence of more than one voice', and 'in which esteem is mutually given' (Rutherford, op. cit.: 155). This aspiration, which may offer a valid response to the social dilemmas of a globalizing world, runs rather counter to the overarching principles of social identity theory explored below. An understanding of social identity theories helps appreciate why it is necessary, and complex, to shape university spaces and experiences in ways which will facilitate successful intercultural encounters.

Classic social identity theory (Tajfel 1978, 1981; Tajfel and Turner 1986) sees our social identity as a fundamental dimension to our self-concept, it evolves within, and therefore requires, group membership, and it carries significant emotional value. The evolution of our social identity rests upon a fundamental division within our constructions of self *vis-à-vis* others. There are those we identify *with*, our 'in-groups', and others we identify *against*, our 'out-groups'. Our social identity is forged through their respective realizations through three types of cognitive process – social categorization, identification, and comparison:

- *Social categorization* – whereby *groups or types* are identified. As discussed in Chapter 4 with regard to *schemes* and *schema*, seminal works on memory and on learning (for example, Bartlett 1932; Piaget 1972) deem categorization to be fundamental to the processes of knowing, storing, retrieving and interrelating our knowledge of the world. Social categorization of others as 'friend' or 'foe', and as 'blacks', 'police', or 'vice-chancellors' within those overarching categories can be read as one aspect of this schema work.
- *Social identification* – whereby we seek to take on the identity of the *in-group* we wish to adopt/be adopted by. Our need for a sense of 'belonging' is superseded in Maslow's (1954) classic hierarchy of human motivation only by the satisfaction of physiological needs (like air, water and food), and safety needs. And
- *Social comparison* – whereby we seek to strengthen the image of the *in-group*, and so our own sense of self-worth, through asserting the comparative negativity of aspects of *out-group* characteristics.

The world according to social identity theory is divided into 'them' and 'us'. The narratives we construct flow from both of these groups: 'I am/we are like this; I am not/we are not like that. I/*We* like this; I/*we* do not like that.' What I like is as much constructed by its contrast to that which I do not like as it is by itself. How members of my in-group *and* members of my out-group respond to me shapes my self-identity – that is my self as envisioned by myself, my self in the lifeworld. Furthermore, they shape how I relate to the social world, since according to social identity theory my in-group will seek to find (or create) negative representations of and take discriminatory actions against my out-group in order to enhance our own (my own) self-image. So, social identity theory creates space for the construction and reproduction of stereotypes (of both out-group and in-group members), for the loyalties of football fans, for the incitement of xenophobia, and for the de-humanization of others to make possible all manner of activities from individual acts of racism to national acts of genocide. Some of these may be triggered when we experience social identity *threat*. Social identity threat potentially surfaces most strongly in situations where, for example, we find ourselves isolated from our in-groups or where our in-group represents a minority, or in contexts which are to some degree 'alien' to our in-groups (spaces we do not commonly inhabit, places where accepted behaviour patterns or rituals do not conform to our expectations, institutions whose regulations or ideologies run counter to those with which we are familiar, for example). When our students encounter such situations, as they disrupt the ready-to-hand of self and other, they are in a space of emotional threat. In sum:

In encountering people who are culturally different from us, their dissimilar ways of thinking and behaving challenge our fundamental ways of experiencing. In encountering people who are culturally dissimilar, or when staying in an unfamiliar culture, our identities undergo turmoil and transformation. Emotional vulnerability is part of an inevitable identity change process.

(Ting-Toomey 1999: vii)

The psychology of social identity theory applies across any form of difference, whether 'real' difference such as gender or race, or rather more imagined/socially constructed difference, such as this or that football team (of course, gender and race characteristics are highly imagined and socially constructed, but also contain a biological validity of some kind). Clearly, the machinations of social identity construction and threat have strong salience in intercultural interactions, where others might easily be ascribed out-group identities. This field has particular relevance to this book, and is given further attention in the next section, on intercultural competence. However, it is important for us as educators responsible for students who embody all manner of diversities, to relate those intercultural discussions across these many individuals. As noted in Chapter 1, internationalization sets its gaze largely upon the global and the international, but is working in the same arena as those advocating for equality and diversity agendas. A particular aspect of social identity theory of relevance to our students who identify/are identified as outside the dominant groups is that: 'Research has suggested that both cognitive and affective components are more strongly aroused in minority groups and that members of these groups may experience a stronger need for in-group identification than members of a privileged majority' (Ward *et al.* 2001: 105). As discussed further in Chapter 5, establishing inclusive educational environments is a significant dimension to practice to ensure equitable opportunities across our diverse student body, including but not limited to the cultural diversities between home and domestic students.

In so far as all our students are concerned, however, the processes of global change suggest that they may all, whether in the majority or in a minority on campus, need to be prepared to face the prospect of being situated, for some time at least, as a member of a minority group. And, even if not, they need the capacity of empathy with those who are so situated if they are to go on to conduct their lives among them with the sense of *self-in-the-world* set out for the global self.

With an increasingly diverse pool of potential role models to hand among the mediascapes and ethnoscapes of globalization, there is a potential for expanding the frontiers of how I conceptualize the unique me. However, if it is the case as proposed in the previous chapter that the certainties of *us-and-them* social identity formation are losing their coherence, and adding to a sense of social identity threat, then can our students resist grabbing at the jetsam of consumerism or the life rafts of xenophobia as they struggle to stay afloat in the liquid turmoil? This book is premised upon a belief that they must, and that they can – but also that their university education has a significant role to play in developing their will and capabilities to do so. However, we have not yet done with the in-group. A particular conceptualization of in-group categorization, identification and differentiation is that of an *ethnocentrism–ethnorelativism* continuum (Bennett 1986, 1993), and because of the exposure this construct has had in particular in relation to university student exchanges, study abroad and international volunteering activities we will explore it in a little detail.

Milton Bennett's *Development Model of Intercultural Sensitivity* (DMIS) (Bennett 1993, 2008, 2009) has been utilized as the basis for scores of (invariably positive) studies into the effectiveness of university study abroad activities ('study abroad' is used here as in much of the literature as shorthand to refer to any form of international experience which is arranged by or on behalf of universities for their students). It is perhaps surprising (or perhaps not) that there has been much less effort made to research whether or not our inbound international students derive similar benefits from their 'study abroad' experience. The DMIS tool is one of 'tens, if not hundreds' (Jones 2010: 83) of similar instruments available commercially, and extensively favoured in the USA. The validity of these measures, or indeed the outcomes of the research projects which utilize them, is not our concern here. Rather, I wish to draw upon Bennett's framing of the ethnocentrism–ethnorelativism continuum as illustrative of *the kind of* personal transformation which may be associated with our students' journeys to a more global sense of *self-in-the-world*.

Bennett charts the journey from 'extreme' ethnocentrism to 'extreme' ethnorelativism through a series of stages and sub-stages, simplified in Figure 2.1 with descriptions extracted from both extremes and at mid-points on the continuum, and with reference to affective, cognitive and behavioural responses at each stage. Progression through these stages towards ethnorelativism is not suggested to be unproblematic or linear. Bennett describes a more complex ebbing and flowing as individuals adopt different perspectives in different contexts, so we can expect to find our students (and ourselves) moving to-and-fro when confronted with new knowledge, engaging in new encounters, reflecting upon past/recent experiences, and so forth.

Using the ethnocentric–ethnorelative continuum as a heuristic for responses across any type of in-group/out-group, we can consider some related propositions. Looking at different cultural conceptions of justice and social justice, Leung and Stephan (2001) begin by drawing upon earlier work by Opotow (1990) concerning 'moral exclusions'. Opotow posits that we establish boundaries outside of which our moral codes need not apply, or may apply differently: 'For example, within the family, the allocation of resources is often based on need, whereas in the workplace, reward allocation is often based on merit' (Leung and Stephan 2001: 377).

How far our moral codes might extend with regard to cultural others is likely to have strong correlations with where we sit on the ethnocentric continuum with regard to the group in question. Among the many manifestations of the differential applications of our own moral/justice norms are the ways in which many

DMIS stage		Affective quality	Cognitive structure	Behavioural emphasis
Extreme ethnocentrism	⬆	Benign on the surface ('live and let live'), but potentially genocidal when pressed into cross-cultural contact	No categories ('what difference?') or only broad categories for different cultures	Aggressive ignorance ('I don't need to know'), stress on the familiar
Borderline ethnocentrism		Insistently nice	Worldview is protected by attempting to subsume difference into familiar superordinate categories ('deep down we're all the same')	Active support for universal religious, moral, or political principles
Borderline ethnorelativism		Curiosity	Differentiation and elaboration of cultural categories; development of a meta-level view of cultural difference, including one's own culture	Acquisition of knowledge about cultures, including one's own
Extreme ethnorelativism	⬇	Confusion, authenticity	Worldview categories are seen as 'constructs' maintained by self-reflexive consciousness (cultures and individuals are 'making themselves up')	Formation and maintenance of constructed affiliation groups; cultural mediation

Figure 2.1 Simplified representation of Milton Bennett's stages of ethnocentrism and ethnorelativism

see immigrants as not being entitled to the same legal or economic rights as the home population, or are ready to allow asylum seekers to be returned to countries where they face torture while feeling proud themselves to live in a society where torture is illegal. More parochially, our domestic students might complain at the unfairness of being asked to work in groups with students whose first language is not English, while seeing no unfairness in their own expectations with regard to how communication is enacted within those same groups – an issue we shall explore in some detail in Chapter 5.

Related to social identity formation and ethnocentrism is the way in which Bruner encapsulates something of the dialogic processes between culture and the individual:

> But [culture] shapes the minds of individuals as well. Its individual expression inheres in meaning making, assigning meanings to things in different settings on particular occasions. Meaning making involves situating encounters in the world in their appropriate cultural contexts in order to know 'what they are about.' Although meanings are 'in the mind,' they have their origins and their significance in the culture in which they are created.
>
> (Bruner 2009: 161)

In their daily acts of meaning-making, the capacity of our students to situate what they see within appropriate cultural contexts is compromised by their own socialization into specific cultures, and the emotional resistance they have towards changing the worldview in which their identities are so strongly invested. However, as explored in the first section of this chapter, they live in a world in which they are exposed to difference, to changes in the relative powers of different groups to which they belong (most notably the nation-state), and to the diminishing credibility of their cultural grand narratives. Increasingly few of our students live/will live their lives in a static or mono-cultural milieu; journeying through their individual lives allows no simple passivity in absorbing an identity from a single set of coherent models as they shift towards 'the notion of 'multiple subjectivities', 'multiple lifeworlds', or 'multiple layers' to everyone's identity' (Tennant 2009: 151). A discussion we will return to in Chapter 3.

How do the dialogic processes of self- and cultural- meaning-making cohere for our students immersed in this context? If we accept the proposition that this is one of the challenges which an internationalized higher education must rise to, we need to look for something which might help us model conditions and develop capabilities for militating against the ethnocentrisms of in-group/out-group social identity formation and perpetuation among our students.

Finally, in relation to ethnocentrism, Triandis notes that 'many cultures define the word "human" with reference to their own cultural group, so that people of other cultures are not perceived as fully human' (Triandis 1990: 35). To the extent that this semantic distinction continues to have any salience in the imagination of the peoples of those cultures, we can see a potentially powerful resistor to the notion of the global self as one who holds a sense of *self-in-the-world*, which positions all humanity as equally human. As a particular example of the characterization of the cultural other as something less human, we can take Edward Said's representation of Orientalism (Said 1978/1987). I do not intend here to critique Said's propositions ascribing our will to *understand* the other to an overarching will to *dominate* the other (this is doubtless true of many relationships – but I struggle to believe it true of all). But Said's idea that 'the Orient' is a European invention is germane to earlier discussions on how we imagine the other, and to the possibility that our social constructions (be they European, secular, feminist, or whatever) of the other, as invented constructions necessarily render the other as less than human, or at least as less human than 'we' are. Said paints a persuasive picture (and painted pictures of oriental lasciviousness are a potent part of his argument); the oriental other of the collective Western imagination is a caricature, and a caricature is less than human. If I have no other contact (real or vicarious) with the oriental other, I am probably susceptible to the caricature; except that (and I posit this tentatively) in the fact of being human myself, and of having richer pictures and experiences of different humans – perhaps I am not as susceptible an individual as Said would have it. In any case, as I have said at length, today we have many more real encounters with alterity and many conflicting media images of the lives of others upon which to base our ascriptions and add nuances to our caricatures. Indeed, in so far as it challenges our certainties, this is part of the 'problem' of globalization outlined in the opening section of this chapter. More positively, it presents a countering set of images to any pervading socio-cultural or 'in-group' caricatures. Taking even a thin version of Said's general premise, though, we can see how our students, wherever they are from, are susceptible to carrying with them caricatures of specific or general others. Such caricatures may surface as stereotypes and in how individuals are identified as/by the cultures they are interpreted to represent. How some current university practices may serve to reinforce rather than to challenge such uncritiqued responses to the other is reviewed in Chapter 5.

In similar vein, Ting-Toomey points out that our on-going identity *negotiation* involves not only the identities of group membership, but also those arising though the unique *individual*:

> Beyond group membership identities, individuals develop distinctive personal identities due to unique life histories, experiences, and personality traits. We develop our personal identities – our conceptions of a 'unique self' – via our observations of role models around us and our drives and reinventions.
>
> (Ting-Toomey 1999: 34–35)

This adds significantly to the social identity picture as presented so far, since it allows for the individual self, like the other, to be more than that which is ascribed by group identifications. We each belong to multiple groups, we have each experienced being more or less 'successful' in particular groups, and we have each evolved (and continue to evolve) unique attitudes towards and capabilities to act among the others we encounter. Here again, perhaps, is the chink through which their higher education experience can influence our students' stances towards global humanity. Throughout the literature on study abroad and the like, developing beyond limited and limiting ethnocentric worldviews is argued to facilitate student adjustment to their new culture as well as to be developed by it. This sits within a broader field of enquiry which looks to what intercultural competence the individual brings to and takes from their encounters with alterity, and this is explored in the next section.

Reflective questions for Section 2

- Do you agree with my assertion that there are dangers in how typologies of macro-cultural characteristics/values such as those of Hofstede and Swartz might be employed? How about their usefulness?
- Do you accept that the accidents of our births and biographies are instrumental in shaping who we are? If so, what/how much responsibility does the individual have for her own shape?
- With respect to your own students, do you think I am correct to assert that: 'Relatively privileged socio-geographical spaces and the reinforcing social encounters within those spaces have given shape to the biographies of the large majority of our undergraduate students'?
- Would you agree that 'if education cannot have a significant impact on who we are, notwithstanding our biographies to date' there is little that could be called 'higher' about higher education?
- Is education there 'precisely, to make us 'better' than we could be if left to our own devices'?
- Do the processes of *categorization, identification and comparison* within in-groups offer a satisfactory account for how you see your own construction of your self?
- If you spend a little time reflecting upon your beliefs and attitudes towards one specific culture or social group of which you have limited experience, where would you position yourself on the (simplified) ethnocentric–ethnorelative continuum presented in this section?
- Do the boundaries of your moral code extend fully beyond your own culture/social group? Are there exceptions?

Section 3: Intercultural competence and communication

In theories of intercultural adjustment and 'acculturation', there is a basic premise 'that individuals exposed to heterogeneous cultural influences ... can either become or resist becoming intercultural' (Ward *et al.* 2001: 31). Ward *et al.* identify four types of response to being immersed in another cultural milieu:

- a rejection of first culture and adopting the new culture;
- a retreat into first culture;
- vacillation between the two cultures; or
- a synthesis of cultures into a bicultural (or multicultural) personality.

Two broad sets of factors are theorized to determine which of these paths an individual takes. First are the types and degrees of difference between the two cultures, and second are characteristics 'within' the individual (which are, we have proposed, formed within the complex of experiences which make up her biography, significant among which will be her culture and its scripts). Since we are not in the business of seeking to change cultures (except, perhaps, the culture of higher education), but rather of enabling individuals, the focus in this section is upon the second of these sets of factors.

Several interculturalists propose that an individual's underlying attitude towards the new culture is particularly salient in their acculturation journey. Berry (1990b, 1994, 2005) specifically maps four possible responses against two attitudinal questions, 'Is it considered to be of value':

1   To maintain existing cultural identity characteristics?
2   To maintain relationships with other groups?

'Yes' to both leads towards 'Integration', 'No' to both towards 'Marginalization', with other responses being 'Assimilation' ('No' to (1) and 'Yes' to (2)) and 'Separation'. This model is especially interesting if extrapolated to the multicultural milieu of our globalizing ethnoscapes, where establishing/maintaining relationships with alterity become something of an imperative for making our way in the world, while at the same time we may be inclined to cling more strongly to our existing cultural identities precisely because of the multifarious threats they (we) face. On the face of it, these suggest 'yes' 'yes' responses to Berry's questions and so offer significant hope for our quest for the global self. However, important though these fundamental attitudinal stances may be, there are other individual characteristics to consider.

The process of crossing cultures has been associated with acculturative stress, a variant of culture shock, extended over time and possibly accentuated by the circumstances which lead to the individual's long-term immersion in the new culture (for example, as involuntary political refugee or as voluntary tax exile). Our students, of course, are also different in the circumstances which bring them to their university lives, and in the degrees to which those lives represent immersion within a new cultural milieu. However, as already noted, and as will be discussed further in Chapter 5, the proximity of contact with socio-cultural others on our campuses may be a new experience for many domestic students as well as for their international peers. The various psychological phenomena which attach to acculturative stress loop back into the process through their impact on behaviours. Several individual biographical characteristics are posited to heighten or diminish the force of acculturative stress, including age and gender, educational background, previous experience of alterity and of acculturation, social and economic status, general health, and the availability of coping strategies and attitudes which are linked to each of these. However, it is significant that in the more recent iterations of acculturation theory those immersed in an intercultural context are seen to be, 'proactively responding to and resolving problems stemming from change, rather than being passive victims of trauma' (Zhou *et al.* 2008: 65). In this case, how we organize our students' experience of their university life may have some impact upon their coping strategies, attitudes, and proactivity, not least if we are able to enhance their experiences of intercultural contact.

One set of proposals for enabling sojourners to respond in their new milieu involve providing 'culture learning' – opportunities to acquire/learn appropriate behaviours through acquiring knowledge about a new culture's practices, values, and norms, and through experience of direct contact with host culture 'natives'. After all, for those 'who have been exposed to only one culture, there is no other Weltanschauung' (Triandis 1990: 34). This becomes a rather different task if we are seeking to equip students for unpredictable and multicultural encounters, but replacing a focus on how an individual culture approaches matters (culture-specific learning) with a focus on cultural difference *per se* (culture-general learning) is a possible approach. Culture-general learning 'the cornerstone of intercultural competence' includes 'an understanding of why and how cultures differ, including such concepts as cultural variability dimensions, variations in value orientations, mind-sets, stereotypes, and communication styles, among others' (Yershova *et al.* 2000: 47), and is something which we will look at in more detail as we consider practice in Chapter 5.

Another set of enablers is approached through 'stress and coping' approaches which look at supporting 'psychological well-being – the affective component' (Zhou *et al.* 2008: 65), perhaps through interventions such as stress management. A particular form of stress management (AUM – anxiety and uncertainty management) has been extensively advanced by Gudykunst and colleagues (Gudykunst 1994, 1995; Gudykunst and Kim 2003; Gudykunst and Mody 2002). In this model, an individual's ability to tolerate ambiguity, to empathize with strangers, to adopt the behaviour of strangers, and the rigidity of his attitudes towards strangers influence how he will react when in the company of strangers. Reducing anxiety and reducing uncertainty are independent, but necessary processes if the individual is to adapt. In other research, Hee Yoo *et al.* note that since emotional intelligence theory posits that emotion *regulation* of this ilk is predicated upon emotion *recognition,* this too must impact upon the process of intercultural adaptation: 'If emotion recognition is a necessary precursor to emotion regulation, and if emotion regulation predicts intercultural adjustment, then emotion recognition should also predict adjustment' (Hee Yoo *et al.* 2006: 347).

However, their findings in a study of international students demonstrated the complexities at play in interpersonal/intercultural encounters rather than pointing to any neat correlations. In terms of recognizing *anger* in others, they suggested this could be helpful in enabling more effective communication, and so 'affecting the quality of their social relationships and thus leading to better adjustment' (Hee Yoo *et al.* 2006: 359). By way of contrast, recognizing *contempt, fear* and *sadness,* were found to be 'consistently associated with worse adjustment', which they attributed to such recognition – leaving students 'more susceptible to the effects of stress'(Hee Yoo *et al.*, op. cit.). However, since emotional intelligence theory (Goleman 1995) itself would (crudely) propose that greater recognition of emotional states in self and others correlates to greater general well-being, there seems reason to suppose that this would apply also when in situations of intercultural contact. We might think of strategies to enable and require our students to reflect upon their own feelings and be mindful of the feelings of others within intercultural encounters as a strategy for building emotion recognition and regulation.

Several researchers have sought to identify how 'macro' cross-cultural differences, such as Hofstede's collectivism and individualism, and high-low uncertainty-avoidance clines might impact upon in-group/out-group ascriptions (as identified in social identity theory) and thereby upon the relative ease which such characteristics might lend to an individual's intercultural interactions and, possibly, acculturation to a new cultural milieu. As noted earlier in this chapter, these macro-cultural typologies are highly problematic at the level of the individual. However, it is worth exploring briefly some of the thinking in this area. The broad premise is that the greater the distance between two cultures on any one of these clines, the greater will be the difficulties of accepting/adapting to a new culture. The uncertainty-avoidance cline for example, posits that those societies which are uncomfortable with uncertainty will be strongly rule-governed, since rules reduce uncertainty and so provide emotional stability. The opposite will apply in societies who feel relatively at ease with uncertainty; such societies are also much more likely to be accepting of individuals and ideas which deviate from established norms. An individual crossing from one society which is highly rule-governed to another which is also highly rule-governed, even if the rules are radically different, will find the adaptation easier than if she were to travel to a society with rather looser approaches to rules (even if that society, therefore, was more tolerant to the individual continuing to live by her own set of rules). And so forth. The picture is complicated, however, because while a high uncertainty-avoidance and a low uncertainty-avoidance culture will differ in their fondness for rules, they might align more closely along other clines, and may have shared associations between particular behaviours and the values associated with them. As noted – but worth reiterating – these macro-culture typologies may have very little if anything to do with an *individual* engaging in an intercultural encounter. The broad point, however, is that the familiarity of what is encountered by an individual sojourner is likely to correlate with how easily she is able to recognize links between behaviours and their causes (isomorphic attributions); this in turn is a significant predictor of successful acculturation. Poor isomorphic attribution is manifested through the process of misattribution, which is illustrated in relation to intercultural communication below. A broad disposition to open-mindedness, a willingness to tolerate ambiguity, and a capacity for reflection are individual traits which might lead to a greater likelihood of isomorphic attributions within an individual's responses to encounters with difference. As such, building a curriculum/student experience which sets out to develop such characteristics would seem appropriate for enabling the global student.

A final important area to explore with regard to intercultural competence relates to how we communicate in intercultural spaces. Difference, to be recognized and reacted to, needs to be communicated. Communication, at its most simplistic level, requires a message sender, a message, and a message recipient, as in Figure 2.2. In reality, of course, messages usual flow in multiples and in many directions, with feedback loops from recipient to sender, and so forth.

Even in our simplified model, however, we easily identify that for the message to serve the intention of the sender, it must not only be received but, in receiving,

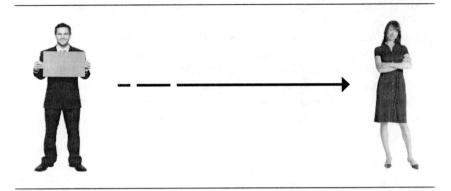

Figure 2.2 Simplified diagram of communication with message sender, message, and message recipient

the receiver must interpret its meaning 'correctly'. We can also see in the Figure 2.2 how the woman's posture and facial expression carry back messages to the sender. We do not need to look at communication flows across diverse cultures to find examples of communication breaking down because a message is differently inter-preted, but these situations provide some rich illustrations of the difficulties. We communicate through a very wide range of 'channels'. Indeed, everything we do, if it is not done in solitude, communicates something. Although choices are limited by individual circumstances, we all communicate through the symbols we select – the accessories of our lives from couture to coiffure, car to cutlery, or whether our furniture is traditional oak or designer veneer, and so forth. The extent to which we are 'free' to make these choices or are trapped within the expectations of our in-group affiliations is a moot point. However, whatever the case, those with whom I share cultural reference points and biographical contact points are more likely to interpret my symbolic signals as they were intended than someone who does not. A large hole in the ear lobe signals conformity in one culture and rebellion in another. Just as such messages are carried and communicated by the individual, they are also carried and communicated through the curriculum and the learning environments and experiences we create. These messages may be particularly strongly communi-cated through the 'hidden curriculum', as explored in Chapter 5. Of course, our most sophisticated symbolic tool for communication is language. In large measure (though far from entirely) we are alert to the idea that what we write and what we say may be open to misinterpretation. At the very least, when we speak to another we are aware that we are engaged in an act of communication. We tend to be less aware of the non-verbal communication which envelopes the spoken word. And yet researchers in this area claim this largely subconscious transmission may carry 'up to 93% of the social meaning of a message' (Singelis 1994: 268). In this dark-matter-world of non-verbal communication we encounter, for example, issues of proximity (stand too close and I threaten or intimidate, too distant and I am cold and indifferent), of haptics (where, when, and for how long can I touch whom without signalling sexual aggression or lack of affection), of oculesics (what's the length of gaze to convey honesty without compromising modesty, and to what extent is that a matter of our genders or of our relative social status).

We do not have space here to look in any detail at other aspects of communication which complicate and obfuscate cross-cultural interactions. However, I will briefly visit just two which further illustrate the complexity of this process. E.T. Hall (1959, 1966) identified that some cultures ('high-context') utilize the context (including the people who are actors within the context) to communicate a message much more than others, who transmit most of the message within the explicit linguistic code ('low-context'). Arguably, interpreting the messages of a high-context culture communication act then becomes more problematical for a cultural outsider since they need a wider understanding of the non-linguistic symbols which are doing more of the communicative work. Also arguably, in meetings involving both cultures, the high-context communicator may appear to her counterpoint to be taciturn, while the low-context communicator may appear verbose or patronizing. An associated point may be the relative importance ascribed to what *is said* and what *is not said*. Some researchers, for example, identify a preference for saying what's on your mind, with Western cultures contrasting with holding back and leaving what is *not said* to do the same communicative work in Eastern cultures (Knowles, E. D. and Ames 1999). The final area of difference to note by way of illustration of the complexities of communication is the concept of 'face' explored by Ervin Goffman (1967). Goffman proposes that in any interaction we are concerned with our own and the other's 'face' – our 'good-standing' in each other's eyes. Unless we are seeking to put down or humiliate our interlocutor, the communication act revolves around each of us seeking to at least maintain our own and the other's face: 'Face is something that can be lost, maintained or enhanced, and any threat to face must be continually monitored during an interaction. It is believed to be in everyone's best interest that face be maintained' (Bowe and Martin 2007: 28).

The mechanisms for maintaining face are highly complex, and each of the subconscious acts of non-verbal communication, along with aspects of the formal linguistic code (as a simple example, whether or not we employ titles like Mister or Doctor, or use first names) come into play. Apart from how face-maintenance is *enacted*, some argue that different cultures take rather different stances to face itself. For example, some suggest that 'Chinese prefer to seek compromise in the face of contradiction, whereas Americans pursue more exclusionary forms of truth and resolution' (Peng *et al.* 2001: 258). One explanation given for the commonly reported experience of Chinese students asking questions individually at the end of a lecture rather than asking when given opportunities to do so in the lecture, is that asking in public might imply the lecturer had not explained something well the first time – and cause her a serious loss of face. I can't comment on the truth of the explanation (or, indeed, on the generalizability of the situation), but the story illustrates the idea of face-maintenance very well. This is probably a good point to restate, though, that any individual is more than – and so different from – what might be taken from these macro-cultural characteristics.

Through the processes of childhood socialization we become (more or less) adept at performing the communication rituals of familiar culture(s). But cultural practices vary in all these regards, and more, in highly subtle but meaning-rich ways. Acceptable eye contact length is differentiated by micro-seconds, comfortable proximity by millimetres, for example – and of course both vary considerably *within* a culture dependant on variables such as the formality of the situation, the relationships between those present, the nature of the specific social activity, and so forth. In all of this, perhaps the most significant point to make here, though, is that these messages are predominantly sent and received subconsciously. We are left *feeling* mistrustful or intimidated by what for us constitutes inappropriate eye contact, or are embarrassed and angered by our loss of face, and we project those feelings onto the other – *he is* untrustworthy or intimidating – and rarely do we seek to reflect on how we have come to those judgements. In sum:

> Not only do we have certain expectations about the communication process; we have also learned emotional reactions associated with those expectations ... Our emotions, in turn, are intimately tied to value judgements, which we often make without a second thought ... emotions and values serve as guidelines in helping us form opinions about others and ourselves.
>
> (Matsumoto and Yoo 2005: 261)

Indeed, so strong are the messages of non-verbal communication, that 'culturally congruent non-verbal behaviours are a more powerful predictor of interpersonal attraction than ethnicity' (Ward 2001a: 423).

Our symbolic acts of communication are, to be clear here, *arbitrary*. We might wish to question extreme positions of cultural relativity when it comes to some values and practices in other cultures, but I think we can safely be complete cultural relativists when it comes to the rituals of day-to-day non-verbal communication. Making eye contact to convey honesty has no *intrinsic* superiority over avoiding eye contact to convey modesty. When we are faced with someone whose *behaviour* in our culture would signify a particular *attitude or value*, though, we tend to (mis)attribute the behaviour and believe it to mean they also hold that value or attitude. In short, when we encounter others who do not conform to our own arbitrary systems, communication flows are disrupted, emotional responses are conjured, attitudes are misattributed, and the simple business of getting on together is conflicted. And so, an important aspect of the intercultural competence required by the global student is the capacity, first, to remain aware that what she does in this respect is neither better nor worse than what 'they' do; second, to be alert to the signals she might be sending and be prepared to seek to modify her behaviours; and third, to be alert to emotional responses she might be experiencing on the basis of signals received, and be prepared to suspend judgements which they might otherwise prompt. Her attentiveness to self, other and situation suggested here relates closely to the concept of 'mindfulness' (Langer 1989), an attitudinal positioning, originating in Buddhism and adapted in behavioural therapy, in which we take responsibility for being attuned to what is occurring. As illustrated in this section, in so far as intercultural competence is concerned, the communication process loops back to the ideas around emotional recognition and regulation referred to earlier in this section:

> A failure to adequately communicate one's emotional and motivational state and/or accurately perceive the internal state of others is likely to result in interpersonal and personal problems. This notion is supported by theories and empirical data relating to nonverbal social skills and more general social competence, or psychopathology.
>
> (Philippot *et al.* 2005: 17)

Intercultural spaces, created in our encounters with alterity, whether in the wider world or in the learning spaces of our universities, then present emotional, behavioural, and cognitive complexities. Extending our understandings and engaging in successful experiences offer opportunities to hone our awareness, reduce our anxieties, recognize and regulate our emotions, and participate more successfully in communicative acts. We look next at what features of the interaction space itself might contribute to making those experiences successful in the first place.

Reflective questions for Section 3

- Would you prefer to live your own life by 'establishing/maintaining relationships with alterity' or by adopting the potentially more secure route of holding on to existing cultural identities by staying within your established communities? Which is most strongly reflected in your friendship groups? How about among your students?
- Have you experienced 'culture shock'? Do you think the university environment, with its sets of norms, values and rules, to be a potential site of culture shock? If so – is it so only for international students?
- Although mainly a question for Chapter 5, at this point can you think of ways in which you do or could 'enhance [students'] experiences of intercultural contact'?
- How much attention is given in courses and learning resources you are familiar with to developing academic writing skills in comparison to the focus on developing intercultural communication skills and concepts? Does the balance seem appropriate given issues raised in this section?
- How governed are you by your own cultural constructs of things like punctuality, use of names, the use of words like 'please' and 'thank you'? Do you agree that these are arbitrary?
- Can you identify any instances when you have experienced a discomforting emotional response to an individual on the basis of what would be considered a normal behaviour in her culture?

Section 4: Contact and conflict theories

In this section, we are most interested in how our students experience their intercultural encounters positively and take that learning forward as a capability to support their *selves-in-the-world*. We are faced with a rather fundamental question. Is it the 'natural order' in human affairs that individuals and/or groups seek to progress their work together through conflict or through cooperation? Or, perhaps, through whichever seems most likely to achieve the ends they seek in the circumstance? In *Leviathan*, Hobbes (2004/1651) proposed that in a 'state of nature' conflict and domination of our neighbours would be the order of the day, but to protect ourselves from the dangers of living in such a world, we form collectives (say our modern nation-states), and contract with each other to form laws and strong governments to enforce them. Hobbes' political theory is predicated upon conflict as the underlying human norm, but upon group cooperation, held together by the strong rule of a Leviathan state, as a mechanism to bring security and the kind of existence in which families and societies could flourish. Olssen proposes that our concerns for 'security, sustenance, safety and citizenship' in our global era are of far greater proportions than previously, and as such constitute 'a global *Leviathan*' (Olssen 2004/2006: 274). Olssen advocates a model for 'deliberative democracy' in which outcomes, beliefs and values are *seen* to be 'moulded ... in the process of discussion' and which is dependent for its success upon an education which helps 'construct a socially normative culture that provides security and builds the *capabilities* for democracy' (Olssen 2004/2006: 278 and 279, original italics). His normative thrust might give some cause for concern (just to return briefly here to our earlier discussions on the legitimacy of developing values in higher education), since taking the idea that cooperation rather than conflict is a better way to proceed is a value judgement. McGregor introduces other potential value positions if we are to be inclusive in the construct of deliberative processes, noting that '[r]ecognition and reciprocity are fundamental' (McGregor 2004: 97), and arguing a need to 'move beyond the privileging of male-centred, Eurocentric discourse methodology' (specifically by legitimizing more emotive and connective discourse strategies in a 'care-full' deliberative model). It seems to me that this is in large part a question of equalizing the deliberative space/process, as well as of engaging the whole person. Looking elsewhere, when John Rawls (1971) sought to devise a theoretical process for deliberations on how best (most justly) to order society, he proposed that those responsible for devising the principles of justice should be positioned behind a *veil of ignorance*. This meant that they should reach their decisions on the basis that they had no idea where they personally would sit in the society they devised – so the principles of justice they came up with ought therefore to be equitable. I bring this in here only because behind Rawls' metaphor of the veil of ignorance is, fundamentally, the idea that when people are aware of their relative positioning in an unequal society, it is less likely they will find or favour outcomes which do not privilege those in their position. The veil of ignorance is a mechanism for giving everyone an equal stake in finding an equitable outcome. 'Cut the cake without knowing which slice is yours'. It is, therefore, a tacit acceptance that we normally work to our own ends unless something in the process (for example, a veil of ignorance) neutralizes those ends.

In the grand narratives of Marxist interpretations, with class groups battling for resources, conflict theories of interaction predominate. People and their groups seek resources to secure power over other groups, and this is the basis upon which social order is maintained. The potential for social conflict is seen today to extend beyond 'class' and to spaces in which there is any type of inequality – for example across genders, ethnicities, and so forth. This is in part attributable to the inequalities in each participant's respective capabilities, but also arises because those inequalities tend to foster conflicting priorities, values, and objectives/aspirations. Whether or not the dissolution of the grand narratives, the multiple group memberships, and the emergence of the 'individual' posited in postmodern interpretations of the human condition, or the multiple exposures to the lives and values of others through the mediascapes, ethnoscapes and so forth of globalization, diminish the salience of group identities to the extent that conflictual approaches are also problematized seems a moot point. As noted, though, our capabilities to lead lives we have reason to value (Sen 1999) are highly unequal globally, and any individual's capabilities are now also impacted across continents by the different priorities, values, and objectives/aspirations of the various actors 'out there'. An important dimension to our project for the global student is precisely to enable her to adopt a stance towards others which recognizes equal claims to capabilities. What, then, might be the conditions which should characterize learning spaces and experiences in which cooperation might flourish and outcomes might be more just/equitable? This will be discussed at length in Chapter 5, but for now I suggest that the most significant dimension to seek to foster within inter-group (or indeed interpersonal) encounters is exposed in the brief forays we have had above into ideas of society, democracy and justice – the need to establish conditions of equality.

Equality is one of four requirements set out in Allport's Intergroup Contact Theory (1954/1979). The broad tenant of this theory is that just experiencing inter-group contact (and so for our purposes intercultural contact) in itself does not guarantee a growth in inter-group tolerance or respect. Coined in the concerns of his treatise, Dewey noted that '[p]ersons do not become a society by living in social proximity' (Dewey 1916/2012: Loc 123). Rather, unless certain conditions apply in the framing of the contact, prejudicial attitudes across the groups may actually increase through contact. However, if contact does lead to people coming to know and understand the other, then their prejudices will diminish. The most fundamental aspect of a successful inter-group contact situation is that it must involve people acting – *doing something* together, not just being co-present. This might seem obvious, but if we reflect upon the percentage of time which members of various cultural groupings in many 'multicultural' cities – or different student groups on our campuses – spend doing something together, it might give us pause for thought. Once engaged in a common action, Allport identified some thirty or so variables which might influence the outcome of inter-group contact. 'Equality' and three others seem to be of particular relevance:

- equal status between the participants;
- an emphasis on cooperative activities;
- a common goal in the activities;
- support from relevant authorities.

Dewey (1916/2012: Loc 116) recognized that we live in community 'by virtue of the things [we] have in common', but more importantly he noted that 'communication is the way in which [we] come to possess things in common' – giving support to the value of students exploring and forming their communities through working together in ways which emphasize cooperation and communication. Something which then demands that each participant in the experience 'has to assimilate, imaginatively, something of another's experience in order to tell him intelligently of one's own experience' (Dewey 1916/2012: Loc 146).

There is wide recognition, in many international declarations and treaties at least, that humanity is faced with several 'common goals' which are unsusceptible to resolution by any nation or group of nations. Bauman notes that this is no temporary situation, and contrasts the objective reality with the felt responsibility:

> Our mutual dependency is planetwide and so we are already, and will remain indefinitely, objectively responsible for one another. There are, however, few if any signs that we who share the planet are willing to take up in earnest the subjective responsibility for that objective responsibility of ours.
>
> (Bauman 2008: Loc 285–286)

It is arguable that this situation might be improved upon if more of us have more successful experiences of common goal activities involving more diverse individuals and leading to successful ends during our everyday lives. University learning spaces and experiences may offer the opportunity for such common goal activities. Bauman goes on to account for the lack of subjective responsibility by the differentials in our love for each other, suggesting that loving our neighbours as we love ourselves necessitates 'respecting each others' uniqueness – valuing each other for our differences' (Bauman, op. cit.: Loc 373). This suggests a particular role for the authorities in Allport's theory – giving their explicit support to the valuing of difference within the focused and common tasks which are being enacted in equalized spaces. Implicit in the framing of this discussion is the view, revisited in Chapter 4 when we investigate theories of learning, that what might be termed 'incidental' learning, learning *within* experience, is central to the human experience. Describing Dewey's ontological notion of experience, Elkjaer notes that '[m]ost of human lives consist of non-cognitive experiences as subjects continuously act, enjoy and suffer, and this is experience' (Elkjaer 2009: 89). Elkjaer is looking specifically at inquiry-based learning, but placing experience at the heart of human 'being' and of our learning is implicated in a variety of current approaches to learning, and the conditions of Allport's hypothesis are therefore pertinent to much learning activity in higher education today.

However we see the relative *weightings* within our biographies of our socio-cultural heritage, of the flowing ethnoscapes of a globalizing world, and of any 'hard wired' tendencies to in-group identification/ethnorelativism and human recognitions of each other in the creation of the individual self, we come to recognize that the self is, indeed, individual. I am unique, as is each of my students. From this perspective, all encounters are intercultural, and all education is necessarily also an intercultural act. Dunne (2009) argues this very point, and significantly points out how the power dynamics of the educational environment can reduce or increase the degree to which the educational act is truly an intercultural one. Where academics encourage intercultural participation among their students, we must also create conditions of equality, create purposeful activity towards common goals, and give validity to that participation if intercultural competence is to be positively impacted. We must add, though, that it is not only individual academics who hold power. Power resides also in the dominant student group, in the institution itself (for example through its academic regulations), and in those holding administrative and service functions. In Contact Theory, conditions of inequality are not conducive to prejudice-reduction. Inclusivity was identified in Chapter 1 as one of the two dimensions of an internationalized curriculum, and we noted that inclusive practice was important to fostering inclusivity in our students. So, when we come to examine our practice in Chapter 5, looking at the power dynamics we create or foster will be of particular interest. Power is in part dependent upon how I envision myself and the others with whom I interact, and this combined within all the other envisionings I hold, collectively constitute my lifeworld. In Chapter 3 I propose a model of the lifeworld which then acts as a heuristic for exploring some of its most salient dimensions.

Reflective questions for Section 4

- Conflict, cooperation, or a strategic choice based on which will deliver best personal outcome? Are these the only choices available to us in negotiating our way through our (authentic) lives?
- Do you agree that bringing diverse students into the same campus space is not a sufficient condition for reducing any prejudices they may hold or for enhancing their capabilities to act well in intercultural interactions?
- Can you think of group situations in which you have participated from a position of relatively limited power/authority? What have been the emotional impacts – at the time, and subsequently? How has the situation impacted on your capacity to act?
- Can you think of group situations in which you have participated from a position of relatively extensive power/authority? What have been the emotional impacts – at the time, and subsequently? How has the situation impacted on others' capacity to act?
- How would (or has) a life lived for a prolonged period in contexts where one or other of the above situations of relative power has predominated impact(ed) upon your self-image as *one who acts well* in that type of group situation?

Chapter 3

Questions of the lifeworld

We've been bewitched by countless lies,
By azure images of ice,
By false promises of open sky and sea,
And rescued by a God we don't believe.
Like coppers rattling from a beggar's plate
Guiding lights have fallen on our days
And burned and died.

(Yevgeny Yevtushenko, *Ballad about False Beacons*)

Packed in my mind lie all the clothes
Which outward nature wears,
And in its fashion's hourly change
It all things else repairs.
In vain I look for change abroad,
And can no difference find,
Till some new ray of peace uncalled
Illumes my inmost mind.

(Henry David Thoreau, *The Inward Morning*)

Introduction

So far, we have looked in broad terms at perspectives on the globalizing world, and its implications for students who must make their way within its challenges. In particular, we have focused upon the relationships between self and other, and what conditions might better enable those relationships to be enacted successfully amidst the multi-variant enthnoscapes of our times in general and on our campuses in particular. In this chapter we look at the individual and her representations of the world-to-herself, and also at culture and its relationship to the development of the self. Some of the discussions in this chapter might seem somewhat academic in the sense of being removed from the real world matters of internationalization. But how we frame our selves and the world around us is not an esoteric matter; an understanding or at least a point of view on this is necessary if we are to think at all about our students' learning processes.

As a single example of how the world may be differently framed, I take the pine tree. While pine trees (of various kinds) exist physically similarly in different cultures, what a pine *signifies* in one culture does not necessarily carry to another. In Japan, for example, the pine's strongest signification is as a symbol of longevity (when my first child was born in Tokyo, the local authority had a pine sapling awaiting my collection when I registered his birth). In Korea its association with longevity extends beyond life as it conveys souls into the next world. In many other cultures, a pine's primary signification will be as a quick-growing source of timber for cheap furniture or paper pulp – the white pine in Quebec may be a symbol of frontier development among the descendants of white settlers associated with logging, while simultaneously signifying the loss of homelands and own cultural heritage to the indigenous Algonquin. In Greece the pine, as the source for the distinctive ingredient in Retsina wine, holds both culinary and social significance. The Cedar pine holds the central position on the Lebanese flag, and has significance by virtue of its religious neutrality. In many other cultures, the pine will hold no particular signification. The pine is by no means exceptional in its range of cultural significations, and how specific objects and actions hold different significations to individual students becomes highly salient when those individuals come together in learning spaces – where meaning-making is embroiled in meanings-already-made. Importantly, these meanings do not only relate to objects (like pine trees), but to actions, values, self and others.

This chapter offers an interpretation of our being-in-the-world (Heidegger 1962/1998), and our knowing of the world. In doing so, it begs a fundamental ontological question, which needs to be acknowledged, but cannot be explored in any depth at all. The question concerns whether human existence is entirely in and of the world, or is mind (or 'self') distinct/separated from the world? Is there an 'I' from which 'I' envision the world which is not fully implicated as a constituent of the world? This is often posed as a question of *Cartesian dualism* (for a brief introduction to the mind–body distinction, see Skirry 2006), though it has dogged philosophy since well before Descartes and ever since he put his 'I think therefore I am' stamp on it. I raise it, because I will be drawing upon a number of sources in the discussions which follow, not all of which would necessarily answer this question in the same way.

Perhaps it is a heresy both to those who would say 'yes' and those who would say 'no' to a self–world duality, but my own *lived-experience* (the primary source of truth for the phenomenologist) suggests something of a 'yes and no'. Craib proposes a formulation which might fit to this response:

> It is, I think, arguable that at different levels of experience both are right; our consciousness breaks any causal chain that links our subjectivity to the outside world. Yet at the same time our subjectivity is caught up in the outside world in all sorts of ways, through our body and through the language and belief systems into which we are socialized, and the social structures in which we are situated.
>
> (Craib 1998: 35)

In the framing of the discussions which follow, I will often imply the existence of distinct 'inner' and 'outer' worlds in various ways. These formulations are used as heuristics, and not intended as literal representations of the complexity of human being-in-the-world. My personal overall current interpretation is that we are, indeed, entirely of the world, our sense of self like our sense of all else flows in and through the world. However, my *lived-experience* includes experience of a self standing back, taking stock, thinking *from*, albeit temporarily. This self I also experience as having been and once again continuing to be within/ of the world; in its flow and shaping its flow. This interpretation is fundamental to how I frame the lifeworld, and thence to how learning is understood, as we will explore in Chapter 4, and to the questions of practice in Chapter 5. I have already introduced the general notion of the lifeworld, and the largely unexamined flow which makes up our daily experiencing of the world, and these will be elaborated on in Sections 1 and 2. Specific features of lifeworld and experience which relate to intercultural being will be explored in Sections 3 to 6. The theoretical discussions in this chapter are intended to frame in particular how the individual student, represented to himself through his lifeworld, can only experience his learning among others from within the worldview, self-identity, and personal characteristics accumulated through his biography. We gain nothing by simply expecting a student to understand our own perspectives and those of others simply because those perspectives are aired in his presence. Our task as educators, I suggest, is to offer through the learning spaces and experiences we create, new dimensions to biography which can shape the on-going business of lifeworld construction. Internationalization, as presented in this book, is about the development of lifeworld dimensions better fitted to the globalizing world – encompassing self-identification and agency – *self-* and *act-in-the-world*.

Section 1: A model of the lifeworld

> People tend to weave their images of the world out of the yarn of their experience.
>
> (Bauman 2008: Loc 595)

> We must not, therefore, wonder whether we really perceive a world, we must instead say: the world is what we perceive.
>
> (Merleau-Ponty 1962: xvi)

Although we are looking in this section at the *individual* and her unique representations of the world, a good illustration of how the meaning of reality, the truth-to-me, can be found in changes to broader socio-cultural meanings (truths-to-us) which occur over time. We have mentioned already major shifts in the collective imagination of the world brought about by new observations in science such as the Copernican revolution to a helio-centric solar system. But considering a shift in our *sensibilities* not wrought by a change in scientific interpretations perhaps offers a more grounded illustration of the somewhat arbitrary nature of our lifeworld (re)fomulations, (and our commitment to maintaining arbitrary lifeworld constructions is a crucial consideration for supporting the development of the global student). Today, millions are drawn to hike, ski, climb, or simply sit outside their camper vans and enjoy the views among mountain ranges across the world. Calendars and screensavers resplendent with panoramic mountain scenes bring 'beauty' to our living rooms and offices. Not only would this have been considered very unsophisticated in our relatively recent past, but prior to their exploration by a few adventurers in the late nineteenth century, all mountains, like the European Alps

> were as distant from the normal world as was the moon. Anything could happen in this icy semi-circle of teeth that bit off Italy from the rest of Europe. To many they represented hell ... When people approached them, it was only to scuttle over their passes as speedily as they could, alert for impending danger. Many travellers were carried blindfold lest they be overwhelmed by the awfulness of the scenery.
>
> (Fleming 2001: 6)

The mountains have changed little since then, but their *representation* in the imaginations of millions has. Of course, their accessibility has tamed them and removed some of their tangible threat. But this ease of access has resulted at least as much from the change in our sensibilities as it has enabled that change to occur. In Britain, William Wordsworth and his fellow Romantic poets helped change sensibilities to the Lake District in particular, and to nature in general; in the USA, John Muir and Henry David Thoreau may have performed a similar feat.

I give this example to illustrate something of what is implicated in framing the lifeworld. It illustrates how we hold a *version* of reality to be true – and true not only in a *cognitive* sense; wearing blindfolds was a *behavioural* response to protect against being *emotionally* overwhelmed. You will easily be able to identify other shifts in widely held sensibilities over time – and differences in widely held sensibilities across cultures (though again, we should not fall into assumptions about individuals from those cultures).

In most cases, most of the biographies which shape our lifeworld – and especially our young lifeworld prior to university – are experienced in a particular socio-cultural milieu. We will investigate aspects of *how* a biography experienced in a particular cultural milieu may give shape to the forms and figures in our lifeworld in subsequent sections of this chapter, but there is one macro-cultural formulation which should be mentioned here. We have emphasized the idea of the rapidity of change as central to the lived-experience of globalization. We might find among the swiftly advancing fronts also a change in the very *type* of culture in which different generations formulate their sense of self and world. The culture in which I experienced growing up *seems to me* to be best described in cultural theory as 'postfigurative' – where 'change is slow and socialization occurs primarily by elders transferring their knowledge to their children' (Matsumoto and Juang 2004: 156).

Now in my late middle age, I seem to be experiencing something more akin to a 'prefigurative' culture which 'is changing so rapidly that young people may be the ones to teach adults cultural knowledge' (Matsumoto and Juang, op. cit.). It is difficult to be sure whether it is the world or me which has changed, of course, so it is possible that those now young still *experience* their life as largely one of being acculturated by their elders. But I suspect not. An example, for me, would be the ubiquity of the technological-social world in which almost constant connectivity with friends-at-a-distance takes precedence over contact with others physically present. Texting back-and-forth at the dinner table or in the lecture theatre is a cultural act, and one which I am very slow to *accept* into my lifeworld, even though I know I must. If a prefigurative culture is how their milieu is experienced by our students, it offers a radically different context for the formulation of their lifeworlds; one which will likely have much more profound effect on their sensibilities than even the Romantic poets were able to set in motion.

However, we need to return from these collective, social, representations of reality to capture the entirely *individual* nature of the lifeworld. A short look at my personal relationship with those Alpine peaks might help. I have visited several mountain ranges, including the Alps, as a middle-grade climber and never really fit enough mountaineer. I have done so with different friends, with my then-teenage children, with my partner, and alone. My experiences have ranged from very fearful moments, weary and stressful hours, periods of cold and boring inactivity, and points approaching ecstasy. Other climbers and mountaineers will recognize all of these and will have their own experiences to relate to each. But nobody else has *my* combination of experiences – and mountains in general, the Alps, the gendarmes of Petit Mont Blanc, or the steps out of the Torino hut above Courmayeur do not *mean* the same to anybody else – not even to those who have been there with me. Each visit, each act of remembering, each re-telling of a tale is imbued with what I have experienced, thought, felt at each previous encounter, in each previous act of remembering, and in all my previously told tales. And with all the other threads of the tapestry which have made up my biography. I can describe some of this; you can find what will pass for similarities within your own lifeworld. But you, even if you have traversed that same ridge, even if you traversed that same ridge at my side, did so as my friend, my daughter, my son, not as me. A part of my companion's experience of that day is of walking beside me; that is never part of my experience. Each lived-experience is unique to me, and together they comprise my unique lifeworld. This should be a cause for wonderful celebration, and an indication of what we could really mean when we speak of human diversity. It emphasizes the *individual* nature of a student's current understanding and the need to recognize the individual nature of her learning of new understandings. It points us towards a notion that, to some degree, all encounters with others are intercultural encounters. The discussion on practice in Chapter 5 is largely about how we enable our students to recognize and explore the *individual* within the diversity around them as a central part of the process of creating their global selves.

In the quotation which opens this section, then, it seems to me that Bauman rather understates the case when he says that we 'tend' to weave our images from our experience; it is *only* from our experience that we come to imagine the world. Crucial to this assertion, though, is that our experience includes *everything* we have *done*, everything we have *thought*, and everything we have *felt* – our encounters with others, the books we have read, the education we have had, the altitude sickness we did *not* have, the reflections we have undertaken, *and* the ways in which all these things have come together in consciousness (or have not) at a particular moment. This resonates with the lifeworld in Edmund Husserl's foundational work on phenomenology (Husserl 1936/1970), as summarized by Ashworth: 'A particular experience lies within the whole lived world ... In general, the meaning of an experience can only be understood within an understanding of its relevancies to other parts of the person's subjective world' (Ashworth 2003: 99). In my interpretation, this means it can only ever be fully understood by the experiencing subject. This is not to deny the potential for qualitative research in general, and phenomenology in particular, to open windows on the experiencing of others, but open windows still give access only to an outsider's perspective on a limited portion of the home in which I dwell. Indeed, as I will explore below, even I do not fully know myself, but I do know my lifeworld. Our students, too, know only their individual lifeworld and their self-representation within that private realm. Building a representation of the self which includes that as someone who can be *comfortable* among alterity is an important ingredient in the development of the global self.

My self-identity is part of my subjective world – a question of how I appear to myself, here and now – I too am a figure in my lifeworld. This may strike us as a strange way to think of ourselves, a kind of Gordian knot or Mobius strip which leads us round an impossible loop. But how else can we describe it? There is, of course, also the person whom I am to others – but this is not my self-identity, however much it may shape and inform it. We might reasonably hope that there is some contiguity between the me-to-you and the me-to-me (but I suspect that at some times most of us also hope you do not always see me as I see myself, and at other times wish you would see me rather more as I see myself than you appear to do). How I present myself to myself is also not the whole story of who I am, but it is the whole story of who I know myself to be. A critical aspect of our task is to facilitate for each individual student a more globally situated and interculturally competent representation of her self to herself. Giddens, in his work on reflexivity notes the importance of our feeling of 'biographical continuity' in our self-representation; stability in a person's identity is to be found

> in the capacity *to keep a particular narrative going.* The individual's biography, if she is to maintain regular interaction with others in the day-to-day world, cannot be wholly fictive. It must continually integrate events which occur in the external world, and sort them into the ongoing 'story' about the self.
>
> (Giddens 1991: 54, original italics)

This must not lead us to conclude that how we see ourselves cannot change over time (again, our lived-experience (Merleau-Ponty 1962) tells us that it does), but for all the change, we somehow still identify continuity in *who* we are – if not, necessarily, in *what* we are.

How our students imagine themselves, how they are represented to themselves in the lifeworld, is central to the construct and to the construction of the global self. Their *self-in-the-world* is how they each *identify their selves* in relation to the (global) other. If/how/how successfully they engage with the process of constructing their global selves (and any other process of change) will depend in no small measure upon how they identify their capabilities and their inclinations. If we are seeking, as I suggest we must, to enable our students to develop their sense of *self-in-the-world*, then establishing opportunities in classroom and campus spaces for a student to *experience* himself in successful interactions with diverse others, and to build such lived-experience into his biography would seem essential to the project. This implies that there needs to be opportunity, perhaps even a requirement, to reflect upon the interactional *process* as well as the product of seminar discussions, group projects, and the like, with a specific focus at times on 'what did I do?' and 'how did I feel?'

Before moving on to present a model of world–lifeworld which will underpin all further discussions in this book, there are a couple of reference points which might help emphasize the totality of lifeworld as I am representing it. Ingold suggests that

> the world imagined as a globe, far from coming into being in and through a life process, it figures as an entity that is, as it were, presented to or confronted by life. The global environment is not a lifeworld, it is a world apart from life.
>
> (Ingold 1993: 32, cited in Urry, 2000: 45)

While the point that we do not *directly* experience the globe as a globe is obviously true, the globe does have representation in my lifeworld, or it does not exist to me as globe at all. Ingold's broader concern that the ways in which a global representation of the environment may diminish its salience and lead to local disempowerment is not in dispute here; but his formulation that 'globe' is somehow apart from lifeworld cannot fit with our lifeworld model. As with everything else, if I have a representation of 'globe' in my lifeworld, that *is* 'globe' to me. If I do not, it does not exist.

In Chapter 2, I cited Tennant's reference to 'multiple lifeworlds'. He posits this, in a broader discussion on Foucault's 'technologies of the self', as a response to 'decentring of the self away from the notions of a coherent "authentic" self', which defines the postmodern condition (Tennant 2009: 151). I recognize (perhaps more so than Tennant) that we are multi-layered and that different facets of ourselves emerge under different circumstances. However, if the postmodern interpretation demands we accept the idea of multiple lifeworlds, this does not fit with the lifeworld I am presenting here. To reiterate, the lifeworld is the totality of my representation of the world to myself. That there are conflicts and incoherences within anyone's lifeworld is likely true, and the cause of much individual concern, possibly discomfort, as we seek their resolution. This has important implications for how we interpret the learning process, as we will explore in Chapter 4.

Peter Jarvis, whose work informs much of Chapter 4, presents the possibility that, given the mediascapes and enthnoscapes explored earlier in the context of globalization, we might 'now recognize that all of us live in multi-cultural lifeworlds .... Consequently, we learn a diversity of interpretations of reality from the outset' (Jarvis 2006: 56). This provides an opportunity for me to re-emphasize that lifeworlds are formed through biography – but biography is not just being there, it is being-someone being there. In a generalized view we might say that an international student has significant dimensions of difference within the classroom space when compared to a domestic student. These differing dimensions of her respective being-in-the-(classroom) world *necessarily* mean she experiences whatever activity and knowledge flows through those spaces differently. I will explore in more detail in Chapter 5 why such a generalized view needs to be critiqued, but it is a valid consideration when it comes to how learning experiences are, in fact, differently experienced. Jarvis' appealing possibility of a gain in the capabilities of 'all of us' to formulate multicultural lifeworlds which enable us to live at ease with diversity, does not echo the rather more disjunctive postmodernist tales of identity disintegration in response to the uncertainties of lives amongst alterity and the loss of our grand narratives. For many (and I would argue, actually, for all of us), rubbing shoulders in the bus queue and enjoying an ethnic festival or two is most likely insufficient to override the unease of identity-uncertainty. The same caution surrounds how effective we can expect isolated campus diversity events and un-constructed/un-deconstructed classroom pair and group work activities to do anything similar.

In this book, then, my lifeworld *is* the world *in all its aspects as it appears to me here and now*. Those aspects of the world with which I am in most regular interaction are likely to feature more strongly in shaping my lifeworld and to be more strongly represented, more colourfully hued, within my lifeworld – let me call this my 'socio-cultural-world'. Other aspects of the world, less frequently or less directly encountered, may have been less influential and be less clearly represented – let me call this my 'extended-world'. As discussed above, my lifeworld also holds my construction of my self – let me call this my 'self-world'. In my modelling, as represented in Figure 3.1, lifeworld and the 'real' world(s) beyond are co-existent, dialogically co-constructed. I flow as part of the world, but my lifeworld contains (and constrains) my reality. Furthermore, it is the only reality I know, and it is a reality which only I know. This does not mean that we have no means to connect, no ways to explore each other; lifeworlds are permeable, or there could be no learning. This modelling of our being-in-the-world does mean, though, that we cannot ever expect to wholly know another or ourselves. What becomes important, then, is how to enable our

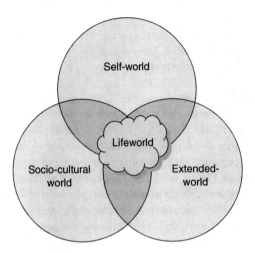

Figure 3.1 Representation of the lifeworld with the self-world, the socio-cultural-world, and the extended-world

student to *better* know himself and other; how his lifeworld might take shape such that he both recognizes the limitations of his lifeworld (a sceptical bent) and identifies himself as one who can and who wishes to become more through the opportunities offered (or confronting him) by the (globalizing, interconnected) world.

Reflective questions for Section I

- How shall I talk of the sea to the frog, if it has never left his pond?
- What sort of picture does your own lived experience present to you of how you exist in relation to the 'outer' world?
- To what extent, at this point in your own life, have you experienced your biography 'in a particular socio-cultural milieu'? How about your students?
- Do you see any validity in the claim that 'our' cultures are shifting from a 'postfigurative' to a 'prefigurative' mode?
- Can you think of *any* representation of the world which you *entirely* share with someone else? If yes – please deconstruct it further. If still yes – please let me know about it.
- Do you accept that you can never fully know yourself or another?
- If 'rubbing shoulders in the bus queue and enjoying an ethnic festival or two is most likely insufficient to override the unease of identity-uncertainty', does this validate the intervention of higher education in the process of lifeworld construction? Can you accept the construct of lifeworld 'as all' as it is modelled in this section? If not – how would you represent it differently?

Section 2: The habitus and the ready-to-hand

There is no way out of this game of culture.

(Bourdieu 1984: 12)

Experience is no stream even though the stream of feelings and ideas that flows upon its surface is the part which philosophers love to traverse. Experience includes the enduring banks of natural constitution and acquired habit as well as the stream.

(Dewey 1934: 7)

How much of the life we are living passes us by? How much are we *of* the stream, where do our acquired habits come from, and are we indeed unable to exit the game of culture? As noted previously, Martin Heidegger (1962/1998) presented our being-in-the-world as predominantly an unexamined flow – precisely caught in the stream. In his view, life passing us by dominates our experience of existence, and

we human beings start pondering the essence of something only when that 'something' goes bust on us: when we can't find it in the place in which it 'always was,' or if it begins to behave in a way that for all we know and are used to expecting can be described only as odd, surprising, baffling, and puzzling.

(Bauman 2008: Loc 1915–1918)

When we first encounter the world, of course, nothing is as it 'always was', and any parent will recognize the transformational nature of their child's relationship with the world – the phenomenal alacrity with which they come to recognize and then to manipulate all manner of aspects of their environment, from feeding themselves to speaking their first language. These early encounters are, for most of us, enacted within a particular socio-cultural milieu, and therefore the norms and practices of that specific context come to be most readily to hand, and hence least examined – until they 'go bust' on us.

In his construct of the 'habitus', Pierre Bourdieu (1984) posited the individual's *embodiment* of the socio-cultural attitudes which permeate a society into her values and pre-dispositions. Habitus formulates her 'logic of practice'; unexamined by the individual, it is/becomes the place which she perceives and understands the world *from*, and so also the place *within* which she engages with the world and others within it. In other words, habitus is an unexamined lifeworld shaped through and within the socio-culture norms of the familiar. Tied to the habitus (inhabiting the habitus) are a range of forms of 'capital', including cultural capital already mentioned, and discussed further in the next section. Bourdieu describes such 'embodied capital' as 'external wealth converted into an integral part of the person' (Bourdieu 1986/2006: 107). We might think of such embodied capital as being akin to strengths or capacities to act which are imbued by an individual's existence at particular place(s) within particular culture(s). Thus, habitus is not formulated simply through a homogeneous experiencing of a culture, but through who/where/what I am *within* that culture; how that culture recognizes, empowers, establishes this 'who/where/what' which I am. Echoing discussions in the previous section, when we recognize that our learning spaces and the activities we create within them are also cultures, how students are recognized, empowered or disempowered through *that* culture will also impact their habitus. Importantly to our later review of learning, Bourdieu does not propose a completely static model, in which there can be no personal development; habitus can change, but at each point in time, in each encounter with the world, in each lecture, seminar, field trip, and assessment task, the individual brings her now-existing logic of practice and her culturally imbued capital to her perceptions, interpretations, actions, and ways of valuing. As, of course, does each 'other' in the encounter. Thus, the students themselves are co-creators of each-other's habitus, and of the culture which may empower or disempower their peers. When we speak of creating inclusive of equitable learning experiences, therefore, we cannot do so without considering how those spaces challenge or endorse existing differentials in cultural capital and students' in-habited sense of who/where they are within those spaces.

We see similar interpretations of how individual 'meaning-making' is, rather, a process of communal/social meaning generation and transmission in theories of social constructionism (Gergen 1994, 1999). The texts or discourses which are available to me for interpreting and exploring the world are limited by the social contexts with which I am familiar/in which I dwell. In this view, 'truth' replaces 'Truth' as 'a way of talking or writing that achieves its validity within a local form of life' (Gergen 1999: 38). Furthermore, discourses, including those of specific disciplines, and their social enactors, including students and discipline 'experts', assume/are imbued with differential status/power (cultural capital), and become the mechanisms for perpetuating social order and structure; so:

> Consider, for example, the disciplines of medicine, psychiatry, sociology, anthropology, education, and the like. These disciplinary regimes, as Foucault called them, generate languages of description and explanation – classifications of selves as healthy or unhealthy, normal or abnormal ... along with explanations as to why they are so. These regimes also employ various research procedures, whereby we are scrutinized and classified in their terms. In effect ... we are giving ourselves over to the disciplinary regimes, to be labelled and explained in their terms. And when we carry these terminologies into our daily lives, speaking to others of our cholesterol level, our depression ... we are engaging in power relations – essentially extending the control of the disciplinary regimes. As our disciplines of study begin to influence public policy and practices, we become further ordered in their terms. Ultimately, we participate in our own subjugation.
>
> (Gergen 1999: 39)

The same discourses, of course, similarly limit how we interpret and explore ourselves. And how our students experience their own being-in-the-world. When our campuses are alive with diversity, and our students are to enact their lives amidst alterity, we as educators must feel a little despair when Gergen goes on to assert that

> the explorations of other cultures draw us into questions of similarity and difference. We are fascinated by what we share, and the ways in which we are alien. However, all such distinctions are drawn from our own vernaculars, the conventions of construction with which we attempt to make sense of the other. And such distinctions are necessarily saturated with the values they sustain. Thus every telling of similarity and difference – every essay of the other – is not so much a reflection of the real as it is a reflection of our own modes of being. To read the other is to make manifest our own existence – how it is we construct the world and with what end.
>
> (Gergen, op. cit.: 107)

The way out of the game of culture does indeed seem at best highly constrained, and Heidegger's, Bourdieu's and Gergen's models of our being-in-the-world find echoes in psychological accounts of development within a particular cultural milieu:

> Culture is a macrolevel social construct that identifies the characteristics and attributes we share with others. But culture also influences the very core nature of our beings as individuals. Because culture shapes and colors our experiences, behaviours, attitudes and feelings, it helps mould our fundamental sense of self – our self-concept, self-construals and self-identities.
>
> (Matsumoto and Juang 2004: 319)

The somewhat limiting representations of our being-in-the-world presented in this section are, of course, not left unchallenged. And, if we fall back to our own experiencing of how our identities are shaped and enacted in the world, I suspect most of us will find strong resonances with Craib's (1998: 7) assertion that '[h]owever many times I rewrite and erase my identities, it is I who does it, not you or my grandmother or anybody else'.

If we consider the underlying premise for this moulding of our self, the formulation of the habitus, the absorption of the ready-to-hand, the circularity of available social discourses, etc., it seems likely that the process and the capabilities to formulate some way out, are constrained to greater or lesser degrees depending on (i) the stability/fixity of the cultural context in which we grow up and (ii) the degree to which it is the only space in which we live out our lives. As explored in the preceding chapters, both of these are shifting in the context of global connectivities, and so we must acknowledge that some of the banks which shape the flow of the stream may also be less stable:

> The new array of shifting, temporary, and precarious positions is too fluid to be consolidated into correlated dispositions, which are inherited and shared

by those similarly positioned .... The implication is that the relevance of Bourdieu's 'semi-unconscious' or 'quasi-automatic' 'habitus' peters out towards the end of the twentieth century.

(Archer 2007: 38)

There has been a general change in the global conditions of life-worlds: put simply, where once improvisation was snatched out of the glacial undertow of habitus, habitus now has to be painstakingly reinforced in the face of life-worlds that are frequently in flux.

(Appadurai 1997: 56)

In this book so far, I have presented this, as Appadurai suggests, as a fundamental *challenge* of the global age. It may, however, also be a milieu in which the constraints of the game of culture are weakened and tapestry threads are less tightly woven, allowing space for greater personal agency concerning who/how we become. In the next section we look towards what we might carry with us to enable some of that to happen.

Reflective questions for Section 2

- To what extent do you recognize your own life as being one of largely unexamined flow within the norms constructed for you by your culture, which only gets serious attention when something 'goes bust' on you?
- Would you say that you carry a relatively 'rich' amount of cultural capital in your social existence? What forms of cultural capital do you see yourself blessed with or deprived of?
- Does the shift towards 'employability' in higher education indicate that it is less salient in imbuing students with other forms of cultural capital than once it was?
- Thinking about socialization processes through membership of or exclusion from discourse communities, do you recognize Gergen's assertion that 'Ultimately, we participate in our own subjugation'? Do academic discourses make higher education an active agent in the subjugation of, for example, cultural others?
- On balance, would you see the process of globalization, in loosening the cultural threads in their individual tapestries, more likely to liberate our students to 'be themselves', or to leave them uncertain of how to make their way in the world?

Section 3: Capital, capability and agency

In the previous section I referred briefly to Bourdieu's notion of cultural capital. We might use Gergen's example of the social structuring enacted through medical discourse to explore cultural capital a little further. The power imbued in/through Gergen's discourse is, let's say, 'owned' by those within the medical sphere. Their cultural standing within *this* sphere brings access to other powerful discourse communities; opens up gateways to learning; attracts wealth and the wealthy; encourages engagement with highly regarded forms of cultural activity; promotes self-confidence and a sense of self-worth; and so forth. However, the influence of all of this is not restricted to the current generation of health professionals. It contributes also to framing the habitus for their progeny, gives them access to high-status forms of education, passes down the trappings of the cultured or the powerful (as 'symbolic' capital) – and these individuals go on to carry this cultural capital forward and so perpetuate the social order. Many would point to the English aristocracy as a longitudinal example of the perpetuation of power through cultural capital, regardless of either individual merit or the prevailing political discourse around notions of a democratic state and its principles of citizen-equality. To reiterate, such social constructions are seen to be replicated in/perpetuated through lifeworld constructions in which (simplistically put) both those with and those without power, wealth, and so forth, tacitly 'know their place'. If we apply the construct of cultural capital on an international or global scale it might account in part for the perpetuation of inequitable power distribution across continents, races and ethnicities. Such inequalities, in turn, accentuate existing concerns about equity and inclusivity within our (culturally) diverse classrooms and campuses. University spaces themselves, and disciplinary spaces within universities, carry their own cultures and, as we shall explore in Chapter 5, convey these to students through the hidden curriculum as well as through more overt regulations and expectations. Some of our students hold a cultural capital which facilitates their presence in these cultures, others do not. Arguably, those who do not but still manage to successfully negotiate their university lives have had a richer education at the end – but in general their levels of measured success continue to show academic disadvantage (as indicated in degree attainment percentages, for example).

However strongly or weakly our individual societies and cultures shape lifeworld formation, including individual construals of self-identity, the process involved is not a simple transfer from 'outside' to 'inside'. There is a dialogic process in motion; I bring myself (albeit a socially/culturally constructed and incompletely known self) to the table. This dialogic process we can represent figuratively as taking place along *lifeworld horizons*, metaphorical semi-permeable membranes which enable us to contain our sense of self and world while yet existing in the world, as represented in Figure 3.2. In Chapter 4, I will present this dialogic process as 'learning', and its outcome as a reshaping of the lifeworld – coming to 'know' (cognitively, affectively, behaviourally) something differently, and so 'to stand in a new relationship to the world' (Barnett, R. 2007: 31).

The process of dialoguing with one's self is argued by many to be fundamental to how we deal with novelty – intrusion or disruption to the ready-to-hand. John Dewey and others refer to the process as reflection, others speak of 'reflexion'. Both terms are somewhat differently nuanced across writers, but for now, I will draw upon both terms to indicate the kind of 'internal conversation' with which we are all familiar, and which forms part of our response to something new along

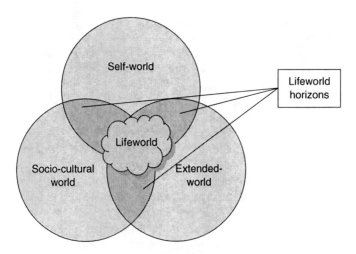

Figure 3.2 Representation of the lifeworld and its horizons with the self-world, the socio-cultural-world, and the extended-world

our lifeworld horizons, and through which we may come to shift something of our relationship with the world. Archer argues that the speed and novelty of global change is forcing a more critical engagement with this process: '[f]or the first time ever, there are pressures on everyone to become increasingly reflexive, to deliberate about themselves in relation to their circumstances' (Archer 2007: 53). To the extent that this is true, it has implications for our approach to the design and the delivery of our curricula, and is something we will return to in Chapter 5. For this section, though, I present reflexivity and cultural capital as (different) forms of *capability*, and propose that it is our capabilities, as set out below, which give shape to our agency – how we can *act-in-the-world*.

Amartya Sen's (1992, 1993, 1999, 2008) work on capability has been influential in framing how we might interpret the relative 'well-being' of people and peoples across local or global contexts, initiating a move from relative economic wealth/poverty as the sole, or even the dominant measure. Sen's work contributed significantly to the creation of the United Nation's Human Development Index (details at: United Nations 1990, 2010). It also offers a very helpful model for thinking about how any of us is able to make our way in the world. Sen's capability represents 'the alternative combinations of things a person is able to do or be – the various "functionings" he or she can "achieve"'; '[t]he freedom to lead different types of life is reflected in the person's capability set' (Sen 1993: 30 and 33). Central to the idea of freedom to lead different types of life, is people's right to determine what 'kinds of lives they value – and have reason to value' (Sen, op. cit.: 18). In Sen's terms, then, we can consider reflexivity as one 'functioning', which when combined with other functionings comprise an individual's capability set. I refer to these as individual capabilities rather than 'functionings'. Martha Nussbaum (2000) set out ten fundamental capabilities – illustrated by examples in parenthesis in the following example. If I have the, let's just call it, 'mental' capacity for reflexivity ('Practical Reason'), but no right to freedom of expression ('Senses, Imagination, and Thought'), or the state of health ('Bodily Health'), or the security brought by the absence of fear of rape ('Bodily Integrity'), etc., then my overall capability, my freedom to lead a life I have cause to value, is compromised, as it would also be compromised if I had all of these, but not the capability of reflexivity. The strength of my cultural capital might, reasonably, be expected to impact more, or less, on any of these. Higher education *may* hope in the long term to bring about economic, social and political changes which will expand what we might call people's objective capabilities (refer again to the dichotomies presented in the Introduction to this book). In the shorter term, however, there is perhaps a more attainable role for higher education in helping students formulate their subjective capabilities; escape routes from the differential capitals and capabilities of their diverse biographies. For our students, how they see themselves, their self-confidence, their self-efficacy, their self in relation to other, or the capabilities of 'imagination' and 'voice' (Walker 2010: 229), etc., are at least as much a part of their capability set as, for example, act-in-the-world capabilities such as a capacity for reflective thinking, disciplinary knowledge, or managing their time effectively. Our concern, in these terms, then becomes the creation of learning experiences which enable each of our students to develop her capabilities to enact her life based upon the things she has reason to value (Walker and Unterhalter 2007). The contentious part, I suppose, is the presupposition in this book that everybody should hold other human beings as something they have reason to value. If we accept this as a legitimate, and indeed a fundamental, aim of higher education, then what formulation of our students' learning spaces and experiences might best enable the development of the capabilities which will support them to enact this?

A different encapsulation of 'capability' was advanced for higher education in the UK, led by John Stephenson (1992, 1998). Although the 'capability movement' did not approach the concept with the same complexity or criticality which Sen and Nussbaum advanced in their fields, there are similarities with regard to what we have termed the subjective capabilities of the individual. According to Stephenson, capability development, as a legitimate objective of higher education learning is

> not just about skills and knowledge. Taking effective and appropriate action within unfamiliar and changing circumstances involves ethics, judgements, the self-confidence to take risks and a commitment to learn from the experience ... Capability embraces competence but is also forward-looking, concerned with the realisation of potential. ... A changing world needs people who can look ahead and act accordingly.
>
> (Stephenson 1998: 3)

With specific regard to the focus of this book, it is also relevant to note the development from these more generic notions of capability of the construct of 'cross-cultural capability' as the basis for curriculum internationalization (Jones and Killick 2007). This will be given some further attention in Chapter 5, but in brief the cross-cultural capability approach seeks to embed cross-cultural understandings, competencies, communication skills, and ethics *within* the disciplinary focus of a student's programme of study, in order to enable students to *enact their personal and professional lives* in complexly diverse local and global contexts.

Capability, in each of these constructs, is strongly related to individual agency – the ability to take responsibility for our actions because we have a measure of control over them. Cross-cultural capability argues for agency which is underpinned by a personal ethic, and that such an ethic must be built from global perspectives on personal and disciplinary/professional practice. As discussed in Chapter 2, the picture of fragmentation, flow, lack of fixity, and consumer identities in the postmodern envisioning of our times threatens individual agency, perhaps precisely at a time when our students most need it. As discussed in the previous section, various propositions around the influence of society or culture on the development and enactment of the self also throw individual agency into question, and may act to limit our students' capabilities to adopt a global perspective. Archer proposes our internal dialogues, introduced earlier in this section, to be 'crucial to how we make our way through the world today', since 'they account for our being "active agents", people who make things happen, not "passive agents" to whom things happen' (Archer 2007: 65). Freirian education (Freire 1970, 1972) can be couched in the terms of this chapter as setting out to deliberately interrupt the transmission of cultural capital or the perpetuation of enveloping cultural discourses and to enable capability development precisely in order to liberate individuals to be critically reflexive beings. In models of *reflexive modernity* (Beck 1994; Giddens 1994) the types of dissolving certainties we have briefly discussed are seen to open up spaces in which society (or perhaps humanity) begins to reflect upon itself, and its systems, and individuals are more free to find and assert counter-positions to the prevailing forces. Freed from the yokes of tradition and nationhood and tight social structure and a *narrative I fit within*, with an almost enforced self-awareness, we may individually and collectively take reflexive stances to shape our ways of being. If reflexivity is so important in offering the potential of an individual and a collective agency 'fit for' our postmodern, globalizing world, then it would seem to be something we need to focus upon in our higher education learning processes and objectives. Jarvis (2008: 72) proposes the 'obvious outcome' of reflexive modernity to be the learning society, since individuals 'have to be free to think and learn for themselves – to construct their biography', a state of being which is not without its problems for both the individual and her 'society'. For the global student, then, the capacity for reflexion becomes a capability for dealing with on-going change and challenge, and for her teachers establishing learning experiences which develop a reflexive capability is a critical pedagogical act.

Before looking in detail at perspectives on learning in Chapter 4, I will seek to ground some of the discussions in this chapter in specific examples of lifeworld formulations which are particularly relevant to our students' relations with the global other.

Reflective questions for Section 3

- What forms of cultural capital do you see different students blessed with or deprived of? Do any differentials that you identify raise 'concerns about equality and inclusivity within our (culturally) diverse classrooms and campuses'?
- I asserted that we are familiar with the process of 'internal conversations'. Are we? Can (should) higher education impact upon the quality of such conversations (for example by seeking to enhance the degree of critical reflexivity involved)?
- Sen's iteration of capability proposes a measure of the quality of human existence to be our freedom to lead the kind of life we have reason to value. Do you accept this formulation? If not, can you articulate what you would regard as a more legitimate alternative?
- If you accept Sen's general premise, do you also accept that it follows that: 'Our concern ... then becomes the creation of learning experiences which enable students to develop their capabilities to enact their lives based upon the things they have reason to value'? If not, how would you formulate the (ideal) central concern of higher education today?

Section 4: Cultural icebergs

Competent adults in their home culture come to feel like helpless children in another.

(Ward *et al.* 2001: 52)

I have brought 'culture' into several of discussions so far, but given little consideration to what we mean by the term. A commonly used metaphor for culture is the iceberg – with a relatively small proportion riding visibly above the level of consciousness, and the bulk (and the bulk which is most likely to collide and cause damage) lying below. Those sitting upon a particular iceberg are likely to have an even more restricted conscious view of its features than does the outsider: 'From the perspective of an outsider looking in, culture is seen as affecting the way people think, feel, and behave ... But from the insider's perspective, culture is basic and natural' (Kim 2001: 58). The ready-to-hand is the more unexamined precisely because of its familiarity. However, as discussed earlier with regard to Edward Said's Orientalism (1978/1987, 1985), we must also acknowledge that what the outsider sees, may be rather distorted by the prisms erected within his own culture, the 'mythologies that obscure and deny the reality of the others' (Robins 1996: 80). The same prisms, of course, also fragment our views of our own cultural territory.

What might constitute the visible and the hidden dimensions of a culture? Some of the answer to this question was considered in relation to intercultural communication in Chapter 2. Behaviours such as eye contact may, effectively, be hidden – as may the emotional responses they generate as well as the misattributed values they might be interpreted to betray. The same is true of the more visible culturally significant symbols we might individually *display* such as our 'revealing' clothes or the status-signifying extended ear lobe hole. The English aristocracy may *display* their pomp through ermine robes in Parliament and tweed on their country estates, but the habitus which is the embodiment of their cultural capital works largely, and powerfully, in unseen (unfathomable?) ways. In our encounters with other cultures, above the waterline are the exoticism sought out by the tourist: the grand symbolic gestures of architectural wonders; the 'typical' foods and their forms of presentation ('Oh, what a wonderful tagine') and consumption ('Oh, aren't chopsticks such fun?'); the idiosyncratic means of transport such as the rickshaw, the New York cab, or the London bus; traditional cultural events like a public fertility rite, a Noh drama, or a baseball game; and so forth. Those things which the tourist-as-consumer lays rights to. In the more immediate contexts of this book, above the waterline might be the rituals of our graduation (or commencement) ceremonies, the explicit processes through which access is granted to library resources and classrooms, the academic regulations laying down the penalties for plagiarism and collusion. Less visible, in the hidden curriculum, are the social rituals which govern where to sit within a classroom space, how to enact the student–master relationship, or where cooperation ends and collusion, actually, begins. Just to reiterate, these remain also and possibly even more so, below the conscious awareness of the student who is a cultural native. She, though, has the tacit understanding of how they are to be negotiated and enacted (what we will refer to in the next section as her procedural schema or scripts). With respect to our quest for equitable and inclusive learning spaces, this has profound and possibly insurmountable implications.

I have discussed culture so far in this section as though it were a static and homogenous entity, but it is neither. Cultures, while seemingly somewhat fixed, glued together by common practices and traditions, achieving cohesion through long-held systems of values and the processes of socialization discussed above, are rather more slippery. We saw in the opening section of this chapter how there has been a collective shift in how nature and mountains are valued and experienced, and how some cultural practices of the youth of the technological age have shifted from those of my own generation. We have also referred to the detraditionalization (Giddens 2002) of our cultures as part of the postmodern condition. Rather than static, then, 'culture is a never-ending and inherently unstable process of negotiation and change, a process of becoming rather than a state of being' (Donald 2007: 295). Cultural change is not a new phenomenon, and while sometimes the pace of cultural change may *seem* inordinately slow, consider the radical transformation in the positionings of women in Western societies since the suffragette movement of barely more than a century ago, or that of homosexuals within the span of my own lifetime, and so forth. However, the *seeming* fixity is important. Arguably, cultural change is not commonly something which happens so fast or so widely that it *intrudes* upon the ready-to-hand daily existence of most people. Arguably, also, there are moments in time when it does; the upheavals of conquering empires and faiths were cited in Chapter 2, for example. Arguably, also, the pace and spread of cultural change in our present times is more pervasively abrupt than at any/most times previously. Not unlike the acceleration we are witnessing in the melting of the icecaps and the icebergs they calve. Featherstone (1995: 5) has also argued that with the 'intensification of cultural goods and images within consumer culture', the task of just *reading* culture has become more difficult, making the '[t]aken-for granted tacit knowledge about what to do, how to respond to particular groups of people and what judgement of taste to make … more problematic'. To the extent that an increased speed and spread of change and the obfuscation of intruding consumerism are true of our age, our students need not only the capabilities to adapt to/adopt other cultures, but also to adapt to changes and unreadable messages within their own.

Apart from recognizing the changing nature of culture over time, the idea of cultural homogeneity is also to be questioned. The landscape of any cultural iceberg is full of crevasses, differentiated seracs and variously angled snowfields. We recognize sub-cultures *within* national cultures. These may be based upon ethnicities, age, sporting affiliations, music or fashion choices, and all the rest. In some countries, we are accustomed to speaking of (though perhaps much less frequently of actually engaging in) a multicultural society. Sometimes dissolving homogeneity is raised to consciousness and becomes perceived as a threat; so in recent times we are witnessing the resurgence of pulls to dilute the recognition of cultural pluralism (with somewhat vague notions of national citizenship and the introduction of tests to demonstrate immigrant citizenship allegiances, for example) in some contexts, and more fundamentalist demands for the stricter observance of established quasi-religious rituals in others. At the same time, as discussed already, the globalizing world 'has made the myth of a cultural homogeneous state even more unrealistic' (Kymlicka 1995: 9) as it confronts us with deterritorialization, detradionalization, and daily encounters with multi-variant ethnoscapes. In such a world, Welsch argues the metaphor of cultural islands (and presumably icebergs, too) to be 'factually incorrect and normatively deceptive' (Welsch 1999: 197). Since, in the internal relations of today's culture 'there exists as much foreignness as in its external relations with other cultures', and in their external networking cultures are 'extremely interconnected and entangled with each other' (Welsch, op. cit.: 198 and 197), Welsch proposes we have entered a state of 'transculturality'. For us, and our students, transculturality is 'a matter of readjusting our inner compass: away from the concentration on the polarity of the own and the foreign to an attentiveness for what might be common and connective whenever we encounter things foreign' (Welsch, op. cit.: 201). It seems to me that there remains something, though, of the cultural iceberg implicit in this, since 'things foreign', while we may find them close by, are still being defined as 'foreign'. The *physical geography* of cultures is certainly shifting, and topographical islands it is true are home to, and host to, and partner to increasingly diverse others. But it is too early yet, I think, to see the shifting of inner compasses on a mass scale. Indeed, as noted, there are signs of some shifting to the opposite pole of increasing intolerance of difference and change. It is, then, the job of education, especially education with aspirations for developing the global student, to create spaces where transculturality can be experienced. In terms of cultural icebergs, this means enabling students to see the complexity and arbitrariness of the taken-for-granted in their own cultural norms as much as enabling them to appreciate better the hidden values and beliefs upon which the visible behaviours of others rest. As referenced in Chapter 2, the need is not to know any one culture in depth, but to take a 'culture-general' approach. In Appiah's version of cosmopolitanism, he proposes that, '[w]e can live together without agreeing on what the values are that make it good to live together; we can agree about what to do in most cases without agreeing about why it is right' (Appiah 2006: 71). This seems to me to be broadly true, but in order to do so, we first need to understand the ways in which we are occupied by our cultures as much as, or possibly more than, we occupy them.

Given the influence of culture on the individual, and the strength of our affiliations to what are essentially arbitrary sets of norms, rituals, artefacts, and attitudes which make up our individual cultural iceberg, we should look again at what psychological considerations might be driving us to accept such levels of assimilation. In Chapter 2, we identified the sense of self and of belonging which develops through/within the in-groups and out-groups of social identity theory (Tajfel 1978). As an extension of this, we can see that culture also provides emotional, cognitive and behavioural security through the frameworks it provides for decision-taking and living in communities:

> Culture enhances survival. Cultures provide rules for living, tell people how to interact, and how to work and play with each other. Culture provides a hierarchy for decision-making and sets the standards for group cooperation and division of labour. With culture there is some order to life; without culture there is chaos.
>
> (Matsumoto and Yoo 2005: 258)

This leads us back into the construct of 'culture shock' as the psychological impact of finding ourselves in a context in which the complex and hidden rules with which we are familiar no longer appear to hold good. These considerations of social and cross-cultural psychology, however, do not fully explain *how* it is that we come to find ourselves at home in one culture and at sea in another. In the next section we pursue a different psychological focus as we briefly explore aspects of cognitive psychology which might offer some insights here, and which will also be useful when we come to look at learning in Chapter 4.

Reflective questions for Section 4

- Has your own experience as an adult placed you in contexts where you have come to feel somewhat like a helpless child?
- What examples can you identify of cultural norms, behaviours, values, etc., which are largely enacted below the level of consciousness by natives of a culture?
- Am I right to cite a baseball game and a public fertility rite alongside each other as examples of cultural events?
- How quickly do you feel culture changes? What kind of thing (if anything) endures over time?
- Is there any sense in my assertion that 'our students will need not only the capabilities to adapt to/adopt other cultures, but also to adapt to changes and unreadable messages within their own'?
- Does the 'fact' that a single nation might now encompass many cultures mean that those cultures are any less metaphorically 'islands' (or icebergs) than has hitherto been the case?
- Are we 'occupied by our cultures as much as, or possibly more than, we occupy them'? For example?

Section 5: Schemata, scripts and types

Categorisation is one of the most ubiquitous and important human mental activities and provides efficiency in memory and enables communication. Moreover, categories aid survival by allowing us to make educated guesses about unseen properties of categorized objects.

(Peng *et al.* 2001: 243)

In Jean Piaget's (1954) seminal studies in children's cognitive development, schemata are posited to be the constituents of the mental framework which develops through interaction between the child and her environment (be that interaction with objects, actions or people). Concepts are categorized and grouped into a schema, which is subject to extension and revision through new encounters with the world (a process we will explore in more detail in Chapter 4). Schema creation is posited to be the fundamental mechanism for the cognitive structuring of our representation of the world. Schemata may be more or less 'accurate' at any given time, but for the individual concerned, they *are* how the world is at the time (so, we see a direct parallel with our representation of 'lifeworld'). Schemata are also central to Bartlett's (1932) work on memory, and as such come into play not only in how we come to structure the world in the first place, but also in how we go about the business of reconstructing our representation of the world in each act of recall (including subconscious recall, which is particularly important to the discussions which follow). So we, and our students, as adults have developed highly complex, interrelated, and mutually re-enforcing sets of mental representations of the world which act as the basis for our recall of 'how things are' in this or that particular situation. Where our schemata seem to mesh with the world as it is being experienced in a particular situation, we generally go along easily and possibly with little if any real conscious engagement, little exceptional emotional dissonance, and 'automatic' behavioural responses: Heidegger's largely unexamined flow among the ready-to-hand. When the meshing is more of a grinding, less comfortable reactions may follow. Simplistically, the *physical* configuration of our brain has become arranged in ways which work better in some contexts than others. It would not, then, be surprising to find some level of psychological resistance towards a non-conforming world, and a will to defend the schemata we and our world have worked hard to construct. In this view, learning environments and experiences which themselves conform to a student's schemata for 'learning environments and experiences' may be seen to facilitate learning by reducing psychological resistance or easing their flow within the learning act. Alternatively, learning environments and experiences which enable students to experience new ways of being/doing may offer deeper learning opportunities through reconstructing existing schemata. Balancing these so that levels of unfamiliarity and challenge are not so great as to cause disengagement or so low as to offer no learning opportunity is the role of the educator.

To ground this in our concern for developing the global student, I will briefly explore types of schemata and some of their characteristics, in so far as they impact upon how we may make our way in different cultural spaces. I'll take what is on the face of it a simple concept by way of illustration of schema types. For most 'impact' I'd ask you, the reader, not to read on beyond the next sentence until you have acted as requested. Please, close your eyes just for a few seconds and imagine yourself walking through a farm.

Did you play the game? If you did, which of the following farms has most in common with the place in which you took your imaginary walk? Farm (a) has chickens in the farmyard and cows and sheep at pasture in small green fields. Farm (b) has large areas of wheat or corn rolling towards the horizon, with large mechanical harvesters to bring the crops home. Farm (c) has neat rows of rice growing in wet terraced landscapes, perhaps being tilled by oxen. Apologies if you had a farm (d) which fits none of these. That would spoil the impact – but not the point. You can probably easily picture any of the farms sketched above, but when you closed your eyes your 'farm' schema brought to the fore the *objects* and their *organization* which are most salient to you. In addition to objects and their organization, our schemata also guide us in how we are to proceed in the world. If you have not experienced walking through (let us say) an English dairy farm, you may be justifiably unsure about your right of way, not know if/how a yellow paint spot directs your passage, be nervous and unsure how to shift the beasts which block your way, not know by what process you are to make payment for the 'free range eggs' displayed on the table at the gate, and so forth. All this uncertainty, it should be noted, even before there has been any direct interpersonal contact. The schema in which you are deficient here still concerns the farm, but it goes beyond the objects and their organization to matters of *how you are to engage* with them. Well-formed *procedural* schemata of this kind are often referred to as 'scripts', and serve to guide how we go about the routines of daily life – buying a newspaper, ordering food in a restaurant versus at a hotdog stand, apologizing for bumping into someone, interjecting in a lecture theatre, constructing a piece of academic writing, locating a book in a library, and the rest. Into this sphere we can also propose 'scripts of the self' – the ways in which I know myself to enact my role within the range of options available culturally.

Another small scenario illustrates the importance of this for some of our students. Am I someone who proceeds in the world by regularly interjecting in lecture theatres, or by never doing so? My schema for this has also developed through my experiencing the world. Let us say, then, that in my experiencing of the world to date, my lecture script is one of a time/space of student non-interjection and respectful silence. I enter a new world and my experience is one where others are indeed interjecting, and seemingly successfully and appropriately so. It might be argued that in this case, my script 'should' be open to modification – adaptation. This may be true, and may well happen – but if you revisit the scenario as described above, there is nothing which has changed in my experiencing of *my* interactions in the world. My script for how *others* behave in a lecture theatre has new evidence available which might indeed lead to change; but there is still no new evidence for how *I* behave in that context. Framing it differently, a change in a cognitive schema which says *that* something is true in the world need not lead to a change in a behavioural or affective schema which says that it is true for how I behave or feel at ease in the world. This is highly significant when it comes to the frustrations we might hear concerning student behaviour, along the lines of 'I've told them to do it like this, but they just keep doing it like that'. It also suggests another area of development for all students who will go on to make their way in contexts for which they have no 'appropriate' scripts. The global student needs to be enabled to see herself, to hold a script of herself, as someone who can find her way within and among the unfamiliar, and so her learning experiences need to be ones within which such a script can be built.

Schemata are also posited to be activated in certain ways, of which formulating prototypes and their *predictive* use are of particular interest. Unless a particular farm had special salience for you when you closed your eyes earlier (you may live on a farm, have recently spent a holiday on a farm, have a strong fearful childhood memory of a farm, for example), then the farm schema you initially activated in the small exercise above could be referred to as your *prototypical* farm. Our overall schema for 'farm' may be very complex and comprehensive (including far more varieties and features than the few examples I gave); prototype theory suggests that we categorize some aspects of farm (in my case, say, chickens and sheep) as more representative of a typical farm. This prototype is then most readily available for recall, and so speeds cognition; where I mix with people whose prototype shares these features, it will also speed communication. It may also ease or inhibit our rubbing along together – perhaps more obviously so if we were activating our schemata for, say, 'immigrants' or 'the English aristocracy'. Speed of cognition and communication are not only facilitated (or inhibited) by the prototypes which are immediately activated, but by the array of related schema which then may become more readily available through that activation. By way of further example, suppose a lecturer, with a similar chicken-and-sheep prototype in mind, asks a group of students to name some of the key features of effective supply chain management for a farm. For me, as someone sharing the lecturer's prototype: chickens lay eggs, eggs need sexing, sizing, date stamping, protective packaging, regular collection, smooth transportation, and overall rapid battery-to-breakfast turnaround. Rice does not. I am 'primed' for a rapid and appropriate response. My Indonesian classmate may be less so.

Care needed to be taken with the last sentence. It was straying dangerously close to what for our purposes is the most problematic manifestation of the prototyping process, which is of course stereotyping. Since we have established schemata for ourselves and our 'in-groups' as well as for others, we similarly hold, respectively, *autostereotypes* and *heterostereotypes*. You might enjoy thinking about some of your own cultural group's autostereotypes – if you are an academic in a Western university one may be that 'we' have the 'best university education' in the world. Odd to me that this persists among colleagues in America, the UK, Australia and elsewhere. Clearly, at most, only one 'we' can be correct.

For what follows, I will concentrate on our stereotyping of others, and use the term 'stereotype' throughout. Following from the theories of cognitive categorization which we have introduced in this section, stereotyping is a particular example of a natural, and in the main helpful, process which facilitates our abilities to represent, recall and engage with the world, and to communicate with others. However, since we are now talking about categorizing people rather than objects, the process, no matter how 'natural', becomes more problematical, including concerns such as:

- stereotypes can cause us to be blind to any characteristics (positive or negative) of a group which do not conform with the stereotype we hold;
- stereotypes can lead us to characterize an individual on the basis of what we hold to be a true of a group, regardless of her actual affiliations to that group;
- stereotypes often come 'loaded' with normative positions concerning what is 'good' or 'bad' regarding any attributed characteristics;
- stereotype schemas are not amenable to being easily dis/reassembled

  o dis-confirming evidence tends to be unseen, unremembered, or explained away as anomalous;
  o conversely, any behaviour which can be interpreted as congruent with a held stereotype tends to assume prominence and act to reconfirm the stereotype;

- we tend not to be aware that we are operating from within a stereotype schema when involved in a social interaction;

- our stereotype is likely to include some elements which lead us to predict how the other will act in a given situation, and will therefore also (mis)guide our own actions and reactions.

Unsurprisingly, then, stereotyping is a threat to successful intercultural interactions and likely to impact negatively on openness, engagement, and our capabilities to learn from others or adopt 'objective' stances towards the behaviours, beliefs, or aspirations of others. Stereotyping runs counter to a project for developing the global student or enacting the global self. Precisely because it is 'natural', it requires educational interventions if our students are to gain some degree of mindfulness concerning its impact on their encounters in the world.

As noted above, stereotypes often embody normative beliefs – what we might more simply refer to as attitudes. The final section of this chapter takes a broader look at attitudes.

Reflective questions for Section 5

- What have you categorized today?
- Has anything you have read in this book so far challenged your existing schemata? If so – how have you reacted – have you experienced any 'level of psychological resistance towards a non-conforming world'? If, by any chance, you have found nothing in the book to challenge your existing schemata, have you felt instead any sense of psychological comforting? (And, otherwise, why on earth are you still reading?)
- Thinking over the last 24 hours, can you identify some of the scripts you have played out?
- If your discipline area sets out to prepare students for the 'world of work' – what kind of scripts do you seek to familiarize them with? If you consider higher education has a role to play in helping students make their way in the world beyond the world of work – what different kinds of scripts will they find themselves playing out in their future lives? Do we know?
- Whisper to yourself at least five stereotypes you activate from time to time.
- Stereotyping 'requires educational interventions'. Is this really part of the remit of higher education?

Section 6: Attitudes and heuristics

[Attitudes are] the most distinctive and indispensable concept in contemporary social psychology.

(Allport 1935, cited on Wikipedia, May 2013)

We looked briefly at Allport's Contact Theory (1954/1979) in Chapter 2. Allport set out specific conditions for intercultural contact to lead to prejudice reduction. Prejudice, in a sense, could be considered another word for 'attitude towards', since to hold an attitude is to have a disposition towards something. Our prejudices, like our attitudes, may be favourable or unfavourable dispositions. Prejudice, though, denotes an attitude which is there before the act, which shapes our response to the individual prior to (and thence within) our encounters. Since we generally hold that prejudices are unsatisfactory ways with which to approach the world, and something which any higher education would seek to enable students to minimize in their approaches to the world, might it be that we hold other types of attitude which require consideration from an educational perspective?

We hold attitudes towards many things, (including the attitude to prejudice which opened the previous sentence); indeed it is likely that we hold attitudes towards anything which is salient to us at any given time. Our attitudes (defined broadly) may be cognitive, affective or behavioural, and they may be the most powerful determinant of how we respond to a given situation, object, encounter, dilemma, and the rest. They may, alternatively, be rather weakly held, or may (perhaps because of other attitudes we hold) be suppressed and kept out of how we respond (or at least so we like to believe). Some attitudes are so intertwined with our self-identity as to be defining characteristics of that identity ('I am not a racist'). It also seems that to varying degrees our attitudes can be rather temporary, inconsistent over time, and activated differentially by variables in the context or situation (how often do white racist attitudes dissolve when someone's health is at stake and in the hands of a black nurse or doctor? And how often do they return when their situation is returned to 'normal'?) Any of these forms of attitude may, I suggest, not be operating at the level of conscious awareness at any given time, but may still be impacting upon how I am 'dealing with' whatever is at hand.

We may reuse existing attitudes *even if they no longer fit*, or replace them based upon 'internal' rather than any 'external' factors:

> Under time pressure, fatigue and other cognitive or motivational constraints, people may rely on old attitudes even though they are not suitable. On the other hand, people may well have stored an attitude but in the situation other information may be more accessible, for example one's mood. As a consequence it is more likely that a new attitude will be constructed rather than that the old one will be retrieved.
>
> (Bohner and Wänke 2002: 113)

Our attitude towards an individual and/or what she might be saying or doing can also be influenced by what are essentially extraneous factors – such as matters of non-verbal interaction like proximity discussed in Chapter 2. Although arguing for a 'multi-stage' processing model which gives more salience to the role played by processing the *content* of a persuasive argument, Reimer *et al.* cite various pieces of research which provide 'ample empirical evidence' that

> communicator cues can (a) influence how systematically messages are processed ... (b) determine the interpretation of ambiguous arguments ... and

(c) instigate expectancies to which arguments are then contrasted ... These various effects are examples of indirect effects of communicator cues: the cues affect attitudes by directing processing goals and the interpretation of the arguments.

(Reimer *et al.* 2005: 1837)

How much of (how little of) our work in higher education helps our students become alert to the attitudes they bring towards a subject under study, or the responses of a peer in a lecture theatre (for example)? There is much attention, of course, given to notions such as critical thinking, but are these framed in such a way that a critical evaluation of self is a required part of the process? Given, also, that attitudes have been discussed above as extending beyond the cognitive realm, to what extent does a focus on critical *thinking* address the issue anyway?

Despite their apparent fickleness, attitudes are held to gain strength over time, to be more robust when they 'sit comfortably' with other schemata, and are more likely to be activated coherently if they are activated frequently (I might 'forget' to be racist if I infrequently encounter situations where an attitude to race is relevant). The *selective exposure hypothesis* (as noted with regard to stereotypes in the previous section) suggests that we seem to ignore non-confirming, *hostile*, evidence and seek out or give additional weight to confirming, *congenial*, evidence. Therefore, encounters with the world might tend towards *polarizing* existing attitudes rather than displacing them. In respect to in-group membership, this might be expressed as 'group polarization', and some researchers posit that we align ourselves with what we *believe* in-group attitudes to be even before we have come to experience them. To the extent that this is true, creating learning spaces and learning experiences which do not *explicitly require* students to expose to themselves if/how they are being pre-disposed to attitudinal stances might be considered as being complicit in the group polarization process which I am suggesting we should be working to dismantle.

As noted in Chapter 2 with particular regard to Berry's two questions concerning attitude to own and host culture (Berry 2005), research on intercultural interaction and acculturation sees sojourner attitudes as key ingredients in the success or failure of the process. Some researchers in this area propose that attitudinal responses to other cultures are influenced by the degree of separation between the norms, values, practices, etc., of the two cultures; unsurprising if 'individuals who are more culturally distant are likely to have fewer culturally appropriate skills for negotiating everyday situations ... [and] ... the transition between more distant cultures may entail greater life changes and engender more stress' (Searle and Ward 1990: 452). Most of the research in this area is based on macro-cultural constructs, such as collectivism: individualism introduced in Chapter 1, or degrees of preferred social hierarchy, acceptance of uncertainty, and the like. Work in this area by Triandis (1994) proposed that cultural difference might be related to three 'cultural syndromes', which he later summarized:

> A cultural syndrome is a shared pattern of beliefs, attitudes, self-identifications, norms, roles, and values organized around a theme. The first syndrome is complexity-simplicity and contrasts information societies with hunters and food gatherers. The second is tightness-looseness. Tight societies have many norms about social behaviour, and people are punished severely when norms are disregarded. Loose societies have relatively few norms, and members of the society tolerate deviations from the norms. Individualism and collectivism is the third cultural syndrome.
>
> (Triandis 2001: 43)

Although, as already noted, we might treat such macro-cultural constructs with some scepticism, particularly with regard to their salience for any individual, the basic premise is that the success of intercultural interactions is related to the real *and the perceived* cultural distance between those involved. Where higher levels of dissimilarity are perceived, this causes 'individuals both to desire less contact and to experience fewer rewards from the contact that they do have with dissimilar others' (Shupe 2007: 752). In other words, the attitude towards a more culturally distant other impacts within the interaction to limit its rewards, and is thereby reconfirmed within the experience of the interaction, so limiting the likelihood of experience enhancing an attitude of 'desire to have further contact'. This relates directly to the often observed phenomena that simply creating spaces in which others are present, say through the recruitment of international students, does not bring about greater tolerance, curiosity or respect across cultural groups. Not even, necessarily, when we engineer cross-cultural group work. The conditions *within* the group work need also to be engineered to maximize the reward which derives from successful interaction.

One specific aspect, or type of attitude, seems particularly relevant to how we might respond to individuals 'of difference'. We noted in the previous section that a feature of schema activation is proposed to be the activation of a prototype. We might think of 'heuristics' as prototypical attitudes (I suspect some social and cognitive psychologists might take issue with this – but let's use it as a heuristic in itself). The use of heuristics to guide how we *act-in-the-world* is contrasted with more systematic approaches to our getting along. Either, or both, processes might be activated in particular situations, but (as with prototypes) when time is short, attention is not mindfully *of* the encounter, and so forth – the heuristic predominates.

Bohner and Wänke (2002: 119 and 120) note that heuristics may be re-enforced or even reconstructed through internal states of mind, as when we have experienced ease in some act of mental processing – which entails 'implicit heuristic inferences like "if generating this argument feels easy, it must be valid"', and also applying our decision-making rules on the basis of 'external cues':

> Typical examples of such persuasion cues are a message source's expertise and likeability, or the social consensus that is perceived for a certain attitudinal position. Thus, people may use the heuristics 'experts' statements are valid', 'I agree with people I like' or 'the majority is usually right'.

Put simplistically, heuristics are the 'rules of thumb' we employ to guide our decision making, working on a kind of algorithm built around 'if-x, then-y'. Pre-existing heuristics require less 'work' in negotiating a situation. Heuristics of 'authority' provide common examples, along the lines of:

People in authority are to be believed.

He is in authority.

I believe him.

Start with a different initial premise, and the attitudinal response to the individual might be radically altered:

People in authority are to be feared.

He is in authority.

I fear him.

Inject some particular symbols of authority deriving from culture-specific experience, and the attitudinal response to the individual might be 'incorrectly' triggered when outside the familiar milieu:

People in authority are to be feared.

People in authority wear uniforms.

He is not wearing a uniform.

He is not in authority.

I do not fear him.

Part of what we mean by 'critical thinking' in higher education, it would seem to me, is about developing the capability to question our own heuristics (and those of others). But, it would be naïve to suppose that we can 'train' ourselves or our students out of natural habits of mind such as employing heuristics when it comes to making our way in the world on a daily basis. Perhaps, instead, we can 'refine' some of the heuristics.

Our heuristics are part of the lifeworld, and we can think of them as applying to the dimensions of self-, socio-cultural-, and extended- worlds proposed in the lifeworld model. In terms of self-identity, I'd suggest a common heuristics might work something like:

I'm not someone who feels comfortable with difference.

She is different.

I won't feel comfortable with her.

How much more comfortable might we all be, and how much more easily might the world go round, if we were able to provide learning experiences for our students which enabled them to replace the original premise of heuristics like these? Replacing or re-forming our heuristics, like all other matters of change to the lifeworld, is a learning process. In the next chapter, we look at aspects of the learning process as the basis for discussion around practice in Chapter 5.

Reflective questions for Section 6

- The opening citation of this section drew upon Wikipedia. What was your *attitude* to that?
- 'I'm not a racist' is a powerful attitudinal marker of my own self-identity. Can you articulate some of yours?
- Suppose you were to switch your role and become a student (or if you are a student, you were to become an academic), what attitudes would you identify as being appropriate to membership of your new group?
- If you come from a monogamous society, to what extent do you feel your attitudes towards a second marriage after legal separation, a legal bigamous relationship, and a polygamous relationship (say Brigham Young, with between 25 and 55 wives) differ? If they do, is this an example of the impact of degrees of cultural difference?
- Is part of higher education's objectives regarding critical thinking about developing the capability to question our own heuristics?
- Do we have any legitimate right to set out to provide 'learning experiences for our students which enable them to replace the existing premises of their heuristics'?
- Go back to your response to the third bullet in this section – to what degree was your answer based upon known facts about the group, and to what extent was it based upon a kind of group stereotyping?

Chapter 4

Questions of learning

I know who I WAS when I got up this morning, but I think I must have been changed several times since then.

(Lewis Carroll, *Alice in Wonderland*)

To know yet to think that one does not know is best;
Not to know yet to think that one knows will lead to difficulty.

(Lao Tzu, *Tao Te Ching*)

Introduction

... it surely matters ideologically what kind of 'model' of the human mind one embraces ... Indeed, the model of mind to which one adheres even shapes the 'folk pedagogy' of schoolroom practice.

(Bruner 2009: 147)

You may have hoped that we had left behind the 'Cartesian' question of mind–world dualism raised in the introduction to the previous chapter. Not quite, since the issue continues to haunt how we interpret the process(es) of learning which this chapter is concerned with. Engeström (2009: 54) notes that in the views of learning developed by Lev Vygotsky (1978), and adopted enthusiastically by many educationalists over Piaget's (1929; 1977) more dualistic modelling, '[t]he individual could no longer be understood without his or her cultural means; and the society could no longer be understood without the agency of individuals who use and produce artefacts'. However, arguably, the developments within constructivist models of learning have not been consistent in banishing the Cartesian ghost, and may have effectively reintroduced a dualism which is 'incongruent to the monist philosophy guiding Vygotsky's writings' (Liu and Matthews 2005: 389). Bruner (1966, 2009) promotes instructional approaches built on strong assertions concerning the ways in which 'culture shapes the mind', because '[a]lthough meanings are "in the mind", they have their origins and their significance in the culture in which they are created' (Bruner 2009: 161). Jarvis appears confident to assert that: 'The person is body and mind, and both are constituted in extremely complex ways ... They are not separate but inextricably intertwined, so that there is no Cartesian dualism' (Jarvis 2005: 9). However, he also says this of the learning process: 'Our experience occurs at the intersection of the inner self and the outer world and so learning always occurs at this point of intersection' (Jarvis 2006: 7). Unless the 'intertwining' body exists separately from the intersecting 'outer world', this seems to me still to beg some degree of dualism. I, then, resort again to operating with a kind of 'yes and no' answer in the following examination of learning. This allows for a kind of 'thin' dualism which, while not theoretically 'tight', is again reflective of my own lived-experience – and perhaps yours, too?

We have developed a picture of aspects of student *being* – in particular in terms of relationships towards others and the formulation of the lifeworld. We have also looked at ways in which the 'outer' world, in particular our own societies and cultures, play particular roles in shaping the lifeworld. This chapter builds upon those pictures by asking about the *process of learning* – how might it be described in itself, what might trigger it, and so forth. These are important if we are to consider in Chapter 5 how we might build our students' learning experiences in ways which contribute to the development of the global self.

There are several permutations on a small number of different basic theoretical perspectives on learning as a process. Within those theories and their permutations, there are elements which 'must always be present', even if differently privileged. Jarvis characterizes these as 'the person, as learner; the social situation within which the learning occurs; the experience that the learner has of that situation; the process of transforming it and storing it within the learner's mind/ biography' (Jarvis 2006: 198). This chapter looks at each of these in various ways, but it does not attempt an overview of all learning theories and their permutations (for excellent attempts at more comprehensive pictures see the several volumes by Jarvis cited in this chapter, and also Illeris 2002). Instead, I focus mostly towards a broadly 'constructivist' learning paradigm, which is currently the most influential in shaping what happens (or at least shaping what is supposed to be the most effective kind of thing to happen) in Western higher education. The key theorists I bring into this chapter, then, broadly align with the basic tenet of constructivist interpretations of learning (though some pre-date the introduction of the term) that 'knowledge is not mechanically acquired, but actively constructed within the constraints and offerings of the learning environment' (Liu and Matthews 2005: 387). From a focus in this chapter on theories of learning, we move to a focus on our approaches to teaching (or facilitating learning) as part of Chapter 5.

Section 1: (Re)forming the lifeworld

Our net conclusion is that life is development, and that developing, growing, is life.

(Dewey 1916/2012: Loc 963)

Life is about being: human life is about learning.

(Jarvis 2006: 133)

In Chapters 2 and 3 I offered models of the lifeworld and its permeable horizons with the self-, socio-cultural- and extended- worlds 'beyond'. I proposed that we take the lifeworld of each of our students to be the complete and unique representation of the world-to-her, developed/developing through her unique biography; and in that journey, influenced particularly by what we can term the socio-cultural experiences of her life. In that formulation, we can see that any 'learning' which takes place in our student constitutes a change in her lifeworld. Something previously represented as x is now x-changed.

Employing the terminology presented in Chapter 3, the lifeworld comprises a series of schemata (or 'schemes' as preferred by some authors quoted in this chapter) in which 'the self is born' (Jarvis 2006: 14). Internationalization, as proposed here, seeks to present opportunities for the birth of a more global self through the experience of university. So, what further do we believe about the qualities, types, or degrees of change which our students' schemata might undergo? In Piaget's model, 'to learn something means to mentally structure something, namely, to incorporate it in a mental scheme' (Illeris 2004: 83). Piaget proposed two types of mental incorporation when we encounter something new in the world:

1   we might *change a schema* in the light of the new information (*accommodation*); or
2   we might somehow misrepresent the new information such that it can still *fit within our existing schema* (*assimilation*).

As it happens, a good illustration of these arose today in a conversation with a colleague. In preparation for their expected second child, he and his partner had just moved their first child from his cot (crib) to a bed. The boy had gone to bed the previous night clearly excited by his new-found grown-up-ness. The parents' anticipation was that when he woke up, having 'accommodated' the new reality he would get out of bed. Instead (somewhat to their chagrin) he cried out at the usual early hour for someone to 'let me out' – just as he had always done in his cot. Although the bed obviously had no protective/ constraining sides to bar his exit, and he had made his own way *into* bed the previous night, his schema for morning liberation requiring someone to 'let me out' had not changed. Each parent's schema, on the other hand, having somewhat prematurely changed to a world which afforded them a more leisurely morning routine, had quickly to 're-think' itself.

I suggest we treat *assimilation* and *accommodation* as principally a heuristic for possible modes of response, and that we might better regard them as working in tandem or as a continuum rather than as distinct and separate. A sort of tandem model is drawn when Tennant argues the growth of 'knowledge' to be 'based on the interplay between assimilation and accommodation, between the person acting on and "constructing" the world and the world acting on the person' (Tennant 2005: 64). This allows for a helpful recognition that learning is a continuously on-going iterative process, in which no learning act is undertaken in isolation or can ever really be said to be complete. It succinctly captures much of the constructivist paradigm. Viewing the processes as a continuum helps capture the idea of *partial* accommodation, with perhaps accommodative change to a small 'bit' of one schema or other which has yet to (if it ever does) entail accommodative changes to related schemata. Returning to an earlier example, through new experience, I come to recognize *this black nurse* as helpful, knowledgeable, comforting, competent, of equal standing, a person-whose-colour-is-irrelevant. I have experienced some accommodation with regard to my schema for individuals. However, this is not a guarantee that my larger schema for *all black people* will also change as a result. (This is not a normative justification for racism, but an attempt to illustrate a process which might account for the continuation of racism, notwithstanding evidence which should refute its biases). Important to how we might enable students to develop a more global sense of *self-in-the-world* is the view that even small schema changes might sometimes have highly significant impacts upon larger schema changes depending upon the point at which they occur in our experiencing. Simplistically, my first experience of a *black-nurse-as-person* might make less difference than my twentieth; or might have radically different impact if I encounter her from an initial position of embodied racism or from a position of broad indifference. The completeness or complexity of the accommodation is also likely to depend upon a range of other factors – the intensity/intimacy of the encounter, the emotional charge in the situation (do I find significant solace), and so forth. This takes us back to (and a little beyond) Allport's Contact Hypothesis discussed in previous chapters. In brief, then, we can represent the learning process as a continuum stretching from no internal change through to small-scale, isolated, and perhaps incomplete change to a single schema through to large-scale change across multiple, interconnected schemata. Non-accommodative learning, interpreting the world so it continues to fit existing lifeworld representations, is almost a process of learning to deceive ourselves. We will go on to consider that some change is so profound or 'systemic' as to constitute a kind of change to our 'meta-schema' when we look at Jack Mezirow's *transformative* learning and Carl Rogers' *significant* learning, each of which has something to contribute to a model of learning for global students. We can represent this continuum as in Figure 4.1.

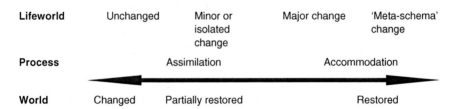

Figure 4.1 Learning as an iterative continuum between assimilative and accommodative processes

From initial research showing 'perspective transformation' among women who were returning to education through community college re-entry programmes in the USA, Jack Mezirow (Mezirow 1978, 1991; Mezirow and Associates 2000) developed an influential theory of *transformative learning*. 'Perspective transformation' is

> the process of becoming critically aware of how and why our presuppositions have come to constrain the way we perceive, understand and feel about our world; of reformulating these assumptions to permit a more inclusive, discriminating, permeable and integrative perspective; and of making decisions or otherwise acting on these new understandings.
>
> (Mezirow 1991: 14)

Mezirow distinguished the pervasive change involved in the transformation of 'meaning perspectives', as above, from more specific (but important and contributory) 'meaning schemes':

- Meaning perspectives: 'broad sets of predispositions resulting from psychocultural assumptions which determine the horizons of our expectations'.
- Meaning schemes: 'the constellation of concept, belief, judgment, and feeling which shape a particular interpretation ... Meaning schemes are specific manifestations of our meaning perspectives'.

> (Mezirow 1994: 223)

Clearly, perspective transformation lies at the meta-schema change position on our learning continuum, and is indeed characterized by Mezirow as 'epistemic' change. It also clearly has strong echoes of Freire's conscientization model. Mezirow was, indeed, struck in his original research by the way in which the return to education was a process of emancipation for the women concerned, whose standing in their own lifeworlds, their self-identities, took significant new form. While Freire's model requires the learning cycle to go through the further stage of remediating the learners' unequal position in the world, Mezirow recognizes that limitations in other regards (we would say, in their objective or subjective capabilities) might not make this possible, but this does not negate the transformative nature of their *learning*.

Since, '[l]ife abroad places students in situations where transformations are called for if they are to maximize their life conditions' (Murphy-Lejeune 2002: 226), it is perhaps unsurprising that Mezirow's model has been cited in several studies on the impacts of study abroad (Bamber 2008; Hunter 2008; Kiely 2004; Whalley 1996), including the impacts of international experience on academics (Hamza 2010). The kinds of personal change which are implicated in developing the global self make 'perspective transformation' a helpful construct for this book. Here, and with regard to the influence of our culture/society on our learning, it is relevant to note that Mezirow specifically identifies cultural paradigms as a locus for transformative change:

> Our identity is formed in webs of affiliation within a shared life world. Human reality is intersubjective; our life histories and language are bound up with those of others. It is within the contexts of these relationships, governed by existing and changing cultural paradigms, that we become the person we are. *Transformative learning involves liberating ourselves from reified forms of thought that are no longer dependable.*
>
> (Mezirow 2000: 27, my emphasis)

A special characteristic of meaning perspectives is their influence on how aspects of the world more generally come to be experienced. They form the lenses through which further world-interpretations are judged; they 'determine the horizons of our expectations' (Mezirow 1994: 223). They are central constituents of the habitus from/within which we engage with all that is encountered. To shift the habitus depends upon alternative worldviews becoming available to us across our lifeworld horizons. We might, therefore, propose that 'a university that hopes to prepare students adequately for supercomplexity and uncertainty would offer an undergraduate programme that affords rich opportunities for students to be exposed to conflicting frames of reference' (Kreber 2009: 16). The particular frames of reference which would facilitate the global self are potentially to be found amongst diverse students on our campuses and within the range of sources and activities they engage with through the formal curriculum.

Mezirow (1994: 224) described four types of learning (none based solely on assimilation), which I include in Figure 4.2 as an elaboration on our previous assimilation–accommodation continuum.

While each of these represents change in the lifeworld, perspective transformation represents a change to 'self' which permeates how we define our *self-in-the-world*, and may be our escape route from the game of culture. This

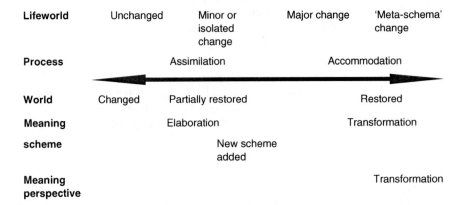

Lifeworld	Unchanged	Minor or isolated change	Major change	'Meta-schema' change
Process		Assimilation	Accommodation	

World	Changed	Partially restored	Restored
Meaning		Elaboration	Transformation
scheme		New scheme added	

Meaning perspective			Transformation

Figure 4.2 Learning as an iterative continuum between assimilative and accommodative processes with Mezirow's four types of learning, including 'meaning perspective' transformation

kind of change finds echoes in Meyer and Land's (Meyer and Land 2005; Meyer *et al.* 2010) proposition that some forms of 'troublesome' knowledge require considerable effort to work through/work into and are often associated with what they refer to as a 'threshold concept' which is

> akin to a portal, opening up a new and previously inaccessible way of thinking about something. It represents a transformed way of understanding, or interpreting, or viewing something without which the learner cannot progress. As a consequence of comprehending a threshold concept there may thus be a transformed internal view of subject matter, subject landscape, or even world view.
>
> (Meyer and Land 2003: 1)

Linking the idea of threshold crossing with the 'trigger' of culture shock as a particular type of dissonance, Cormeraie explicates how both are implicated in the process of crossing cultures, and cautions the consequences of unsuccessful transition:

> For an individual's perceptions to move, to make the imaginary leap from the familiar to the uncharted, a 'break-through' has to happen, a temporary disintegration of one's irrefutable and hitherto congruent Weltanschauung, through the experience of shock, stimulating the affective dimension. ... [W]e also know that, if left unprocessed, the consequences of this shock, of the misunderstanding resulting from seeing the validity of one's beliefs dismissed, misunderstood and thwarted, can mean conflict and closure; in other words, a negative behavioural response.
>
> (Cormeraie 1998: 49–50)

The idea of crossing thresholds, gaining new meaning perspectives or a more authentic state of being at least *implies* a rather tight moment in time when substantial change takes place. This is not to say that the process leading to the moment may not have been long and characterized by backwards and forwards movements, but there seems also to be a tipping point which leads the learner from one state of knowing/being into the other. Illeris (2002: 163–229) cites work by Nissen (1970) on 'learning jumps' – necessitated when 'life conditions change, for the individual and society' (Nissen, op. cit.: 51) – requiring both to 'adjust themselves radically in order to keep up, and ... be able to transcend the adaptation that was appropriate to the earlier conditions' (Illeris, op. cit.: 163). Learning, then, might proceed in small or large degrees and by slow accretion or more sudden tippings across significant thresholds. Potentially, every little helps.

Meyer and Land propose that learning thresholds, once crossed, are 'probably irreversible' as the perspective change is unlikely to be forgotten or will require 'considerable effort' to unlearn (Meyer and Land 2003: 4). While this appears distinctly possible for change of such magnitude, Illeris proposes that any learning, if it is to qualify as such, involves change which is 'relatively lasting' (Illeris 2002: 17). However, this seems not to be necessary to me; indeed this requirement seems at odds with a model of learning as an on-going and iterative process. Why the need for anything learned to be stable? The parents of the child in the example given earlier had 'learned' that their child was now in a bed and being in a bed meant he no longer needed to call them from theirs in order to get up. This learning (a change in their lifeworld) was quite impermanent and had to be quickly un-done. It is true that their initial learning was based on less data, but we learn everything based on only part of the data which might be relevant to its Truth. Our truths are always incompletely founded; if we never learned anything until we had all the possible data, we would never learn anything. So, a student's learning, and making his way in life more generally, proceeds always on the basis of what his until-now encounters with the world have made available to him, *and* upon how he responds to ('incorporates') that data. A further change in what the world presents *or* a change in how he responds offers new learning opportunities. If this were not so, little of significance could happen at university; if it is so, then universities do hold the potential to enable students to develop into more global selves. This resonates with Mikhail Bakhtin's (1984) principle of *unfinalizability*, whereby, since learning is a life-long process and includes learning 'to be' who we are, none of us is ever complete or completely knowable. Briefly relating this back to our explorations in Chapter 2 – among the characteristics of a postmodernist world, Bauman notes consumerism to be 'a life of rapid learning – and swift forgetting' (Bauman 2008: Loc 1544) – in so far as the urge to consumerism is an urge to identity formulation, such rapid changes make our selves more un-finalized and more difficult to 'read'. Learning, then, can never be said to be complete, it can be un-done and re-done, even if meta-schema change such as might be entailed in crossing learning thresholds is more resistant to revision.

Without labouring our attention to the cot incident – it offers helpful grounding for re-emphasizing two important points. The parents' initial new learning ('now the world is kinder to us in the morning') was *wrong*. This is an obvious point, but not one which is necessarily in our mind when we speak about learning. Learning is *change*, but that does not mean it is necessarily change for the better. We can, and do, learn things which take us to a less 'accurate' position *vis-à-vis* the world. The second point is to ask – what was the basis for the parents' initial learning? It might have been nudged by a degree of wishful thinking, but it was not plucked from thin air. There was, rather, a drawing upon their existing knowledge of the world: knowledge that beds don't prevent unilateral exit; that children (including themselves when younger) can and do get out of bed unassisted; that their own child had already found he could get into bed; that he liked his new resting place; and so forth. Learning, as I will labour at some length, is presented as a process deriving from our interactions in the world. However, it also derives from our representations of earlier interactions – our prior learning, embodied in the lifeworld. Thinking about what we already 'know', quickly reveals that not everything we know is to do with our thoughts, we also know ways to *do* things and ways to *feel about* things. And this takes us on to a more holistic view of the learning process – a view which it seems to me has much to offer any work on internationalization of the curriculum.

Reflective questions for Section 1

- Can you think of any examples of incidents, like the child and his new bed, which illustrate a distinction between assimilative and accommodative learning?
- Do you accept my characterization of learning as 'a continuously on-going iterative process, in which no learning act is undertaken in isolation'? Are there no exceptions?
- Have you experienced any kind of learning which you would recognize as changing your 'meaning perspectives' or meta-schema? Is there anything in the notion of *higher* education, or in the objectives of the courses you teach on, which implies this kind of change for your students?
- In what ways do 'the kinds of personal change which is implicated in developing the global self' make 'perspective transformation' a helpful construct for this book'?
- Do you accept Kreber's assertion that 'a university that hopes to prepare students adequately for supercomplexity and uncertainty' should 'offer an undergraduate programme that affords rich opportunities for students to be exposed to conflicting frames of reference'? If so, where do such opportunities arise in the courses you teach on?
- What are some of the threshold concepts in your own discipline?
- Are you happy to accept that 'learning' need not imply knowing something 'better', need not be at all long-lasting, and is only ever a stage in an unfinalizable process?

Section 2: Holistic learning

In her becoming, the student has to be right within herself, has to believe in herself, have faith in herself, and have a measure of confidence in herself before anything of worth can happen in her learning.

(Barnett, R. 2007: 48)

... it is not possible to separate reason from passion, so that the person is a thinking, feeling, acting individual.

(Jarvis 2006: 13–14)

Our schemata, intimately linked though they are, can be considered to differ in kind – for example, representing:

- what a farm is comprised of;
- what it is that I need to do in order to make my way in a farm; and
- what my attitudes are towards farming and farmers.

In turn, these are principally concerned with my understanding (cognitive) of farm, my acting (behavioural) within farm, and my feelings (affective) about farm. Of course, they overspill and overlap; for example attitudes alone 'may encompass affective, behavioural and cognitive responses' (Bohner and Wänke 2002: 5).

Once again, however, a heuristic of lifeworld with these three dimensions can help us to look at learning. These overlapping 'A' affective, 'B' behavioural, and 'C' cognitive lifeworld dimensions are represented in Figure 4.3. I also acknowledge that many would add a fourth, spiritual dimension to their experiencing of the world, and if that is your lived-reality, you will frame what follows around the 'four dimensions of being', or perhaps frame spiritual being as so pervasive as to, effectively, constitute the lifeworld. However you envision your being, I hope the heuristics I am using will continue to make sense.

It seems to follow from this that learning must also take place in any/all of these dimensions of our being. This is highly significant when we reflect upon the (im)balance of attention given to each of these in the formal curricula of university courses. Carl Rogers offered a holistic framework for development in his theory of *significant learning* (Rogers 1959, 1983), and Howard Gardner's work on multiple intelligences (Gardner, H. 1985) provided a framework for reshaping the cognitive bias in theories of learning.

From Rogers' humanistic perspective, learning (or at least what can be crudely described as 'good' learning) involves the whole person, and is a journeying

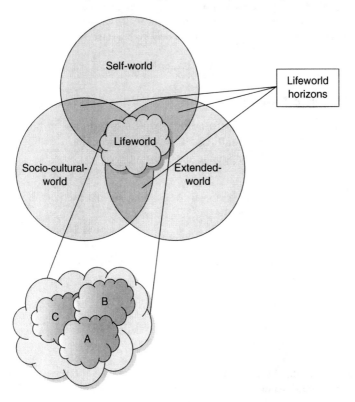

Figure 4.3 Representation of the three dimensions of the lifeworld and its horizons with self-, socio-cultural, and extended-worlds

towards a more authentic way of being (becoming a 'fully functioning person', or 'self-actualization'). He characterized significant learning as

> learning which makes a difference – in the individual's behaviour, in the course of action he chooses in the future, in his attitudes and in his personality. It is pervasive learning which is not just an accretion of knowledge, but which interpenetrates with every portion of his existence.
>
> (Rogers 1961: 280)

Although reminiscent of Mezirow's characterization of 'perspective transformation' discussed in the previous section, *significant learning* is more 'embodied', of the whole person rather than the cognitive favouring in Mezirow's work. Central in the process of becoming a fully functioning person is Rogers' holistic interpretation of 'self-concept', in which we see self–other representations which are particularly relevant to our *self-in-the-world* dimension of the global self:

> ... the organized consistent conceptual gestalt composed of perceptions of the characteristics of 'I' or 'me' and the perceptions of the relationships of the 'I' or 'me' to others and to various aspects of life, together with the values attached to these perceptions. It is a gestalt which is available to awareness though not necessarily in awareness. It is a fluid and changing gestalt, a process, but at any given moment it is a specific entity.
>
> (Rogers 1959: 200)

As hinted at in the idea of fluidity and change above, Rogers recognized that in a world which is characterized by change we need a disposition, a willingness, to change and adapt. In the process of self-actualization, becoming my 'ideal person' is a grasping to be more than I am. This yearning is active in pushing us into and through the 'painful' (Rogers 1969: 339) learning process. It now takes us on to look more specifically at considerations of the role played by emotion specifically.

You might recall that we cited 'emotion recognition' (Hee Yoo *et al.* 2006) and 'emotion regulation' (Matsumoto *et al.* 2001) as potential determinants of the success of acculturation in Chapter 3. In the terms of this chapter we can represent the process of acculturation as meta-schema change akin to perspective transformation, but within which all dimensions of learning are involved. Recognition and regulation are specific facets of *emotional intelligence* (Goleman 1995), which includes other aspects such as tenacity, motivation, and empathy. Collectively, emotional intelligence is posited to be the *principle driver* of our daily decision making, and highly influential in our underlying capacity/inclination for cognitive work. Emotional intelligence is in some part anticipated in Gardner's (1985) *multiple intelligence* theory, in which he proposed eight intelligences: linguistic, logical-mathematical, special, musical, bodily kinesthetic, naturalist, interpersonal, and intrapersonal. I would have presented these as 'areas of intelligence' rather than 'intelligences', but Garner himself was more inclined to separate them:

> ... the conviction that there exist at least some intelligences, that these are relatively independent of each other, and that they can be fashioned and combined in a multiplicity of adaptive ways by individuals and cultures, seems to me to be increasingly difficult to deny.
>
> (Gardner, H. 1985: 8)

Whether integrated 'types' or 'relatively separate' intelligences, the paired *interpersonal* and *intrapersonal* seem particularly salient areas for the development of the global self. If our students *feel* uncomfortable in their interactions with others, how then will they find the capability to engage in respectful dialogue or to seek out how the world looks from others' perspectives? Emotion is not only part of the affective dimension to being, then, it is also significantly involved across the learning process. Following her own explorations of this area, Moon (2004: 54) summarized emotion to relate to learning in the following ways:

- emotion influences the structure of knowledge;
- it influences the process of learning;
- it may arise in the process of learning;
- emotions that are not directly relevant to the learning facilitate or block learning;
- there is emotional insight where the emotional orientation of the person changes.

How we structure our students' learning environments and experiences, and perhaps most significant to our enterprise, how we structure their intercultural encounters, must in this view pay particular attention to the emotional charge they generate/diffuse if our intended learning is to take place.

George Gardner (1962: 248) specifically framed the kind of intelligence needed for successful intercultural living as five characteristics of the 'universal communicator': an unusually high degree of self 'integration or stability', an 'extrovert type' orientation, valuing 'all men', a sort of habitus embodying 'cultural universals', and 'a marked telepathic or intuition sensitivity'. Later authors have defined cultural intelligence as a 'capacity for successful adaptation to ... unfamiliar settings attributable to cultural context' (Early and Ang 2003: 9), and propose that individuals have this form of intelligence in different measure, and irrespective of other intelligences they might possess. Significantly, in this cultural intelligence model, someone's self-concept is highly implicated in their motivation towards and capacity for adaptation to new cultural contexts, behaviours, etc.

From the discussion so far in this section, I now suggest that learning, as well as being characterized as types of learning on a continuum, also involves learning *in and through* the affective, behavioural and cognitive (and spiritual) dimensions of our being, as represented in the amended model of Figure 4.4. In this, the affective, emotional dimension may well be particularly impactful across if/how we engage the others, and *any* change, but particularly meta-schema change, might advance through 'jumps' over learning thresholds, sometimes occasioned by seemingly small experiences.

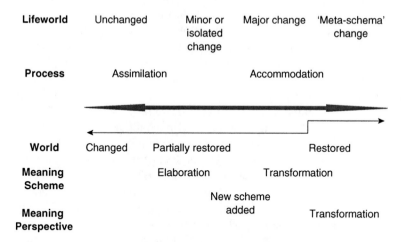

Figure 4.4 Learning as an iterative continuum, perhaps with 'jump' points, between assimilative and accommodative processes across the affective, behavioural, and cognitive dimensions of being

As noted with regard to other aspects of being and learning, the presentation of three (or four) dimensions of learning is a simplified model, and it is important to briefly re-introduce their essentially integrative nature. The transfer of learning across/through learning dimensions may herald what I will refer to as a *virtuous learning circle*. Illeris captures something of this:

> … strong cognitive accommodation can … be accompanied by strong accommodative restructuring in the emotional patterns. If a sudden event or the kind of cognitive processes that have earlier been referred to as reflection, meta-learning or transformative learning cause a radical reconstruction of the individual's comprehension of a certain set of conditions and contexts, there may also be a correspondingly radical shift in the emotional patterns, not as obsessions, but more what could be described as a toning: the nature of particular parts of the emotional patterns shift generally in strength and direction. For example, if on the basis of various experiences and influences, one reaches a point of eliminating one's prejudice concerning the opposite sex or other ethnic groups, it will probably also bring about general shifts in the emotions concerning these groups.
>
> (Illeris 2002: 74)

I suggest that a virtuous learning circle may run its round further, though, since the shift in our affective responses described above will lead to shifts in our behaviours when again among the opposite sex, and reduce our resistance to prior disconfirming, hostile information – hence, supporting further cognitive change. A specific example of the virtuous circle which is particularly relevant to our students as global selves is Bandura's (1997) notion of *self-efficacy*, a confidence in one's own capabilities to perform an action successfully – informed by/enabled through having witnessed one's self (I have done this, so I can do it again) and/or others (he has done this, so it can be done) doing so. Creating for our students opportunities to see, and reflect upon, themselves and others engaging successfully in experiences of intercultural (or, indeed, mixed-gender) being seems to hold significant promise for endeavours to enable the global self.

So, we flow (and sometimes jump) in the world in our thoughts, our actions, and our feelings. Through these we know the world, we interact with the world, and we learn from and as part of the world. Although cognitive learning has received more attention in learning theory work as well as university curricula work, the way I describe learning processes in the following sections should be read as applying apply across all dimensions. Whatever types or degrees or dimensions of change are involved, however, until some assimilation or accommodation of whatever is new occurs, we find ourselves and the world in an uncomfortable misalignment. Learning is driven by an urge to return to a state of equilibrium; what is more, the greater the 'cognitive dissonance' the stronger the drive to resolve it. This is seen across learning theories as the fundamental hammer which sparks the learning reaction. But what are the triggers which set the hammer itself in motion?

Reflective questions for Section 2

- Do you agree that there is a general imbalance in the attention given to different learning dimensions in university education? If so, do you see that as problematic or appropriate?
- Rogers' work is characterized by his view that learning involves the whole person in a process driving towards (more) authentic being. How would you interpret the idea of 'authentic being' or a 'fully functioning person'?
- Emotion, specifically our emotional intelligence, is suggested to be the *principal driver* regarding our daily decision making. This seems to be at odds with the emphasis put on *reasoning* in dominant Western perspectives. How much weight would you give to emotional intelligence in your own decision making?
- If self-concept is important in our willingness and our abilities to adapt to new contexts, how great a role do we in higher education have to play in constructing positive self-concepts – for example a strong sense of self-efficacy in our students?
- I introduced the notion of virtuous learning circles to represent how, for example, affective learning can facilitate changes in behaviour which can then influence how we might also cognitively process new information in a particular context. Can you identify examples of this in your own experience?
- Anticipating somewhat the next section – do you experience learning as a process being driven by a need to resolve 'cognitive dissonance'? Always?

Section 3: Learning triggers

> We reflect on the unexamined assumptions of our beliefs when the beliefs are not working well for us, or when the old ways of thinking are no longer functional. We are confronted with a disorienting dilemma which serves as a trigger for reflection.
>
> (Mezirow 1994: 223)

> The term 'cognitive dissonance' has been used to describe the – often uncomfortable situations – in which new material of learning is in conflict with the learner's cognitive structure.
>
> (Moon 2004: 19)

> The point about learning is that it begins when [the] taken-for-granted is interrupted and disjuncture occurs: we are no longer in harmonious relationship without world – we now no longer fit into our world – disjuncture has occurred and we experienced dissonance.
>
> (Barnett, R. 2007: 10)

With conditions like 'disorientation', 'disequilibrium', 'disjuncture' and 'dissonance' as drivers of learning, we might first remind ourselves here that there are alternative means for achieving 'cognitive consistency' than undergoing a painful 'personal' change process. The first, fitting what we experience to that which we already know has already been noted as 'assimilation'. A second, related, strategy was discussed with regard to stereotypes in Chapter 3 – ignoring what doesn't match, and seeking out what does:

> According to the principle of cognitive consistency, consciously considering information that challenges one's attitudes should cause an aversive state of arousal ... It follows that people should actively search for and pay close attention to information that matches their existing attitudes (congenial information), and should try to avoid or ignore information that is incompatible with their attitudes (hostile information). Numerous studies have addressed this selective exposure hypothesis.
>
> (Bohner and Wänke 2002: 196–197)

We might read the tendency for socializing with people who share our own preferences, knowledge base, political perspectives and the like as a strong indicator of the power of this 'defence' mechanism; perhaps it accounts in some measure for the tendency among many students to seek out like-minded, similarly dressed, and broadly ethnically similar friendship groups. But, despite the pain, we do learn, undergo change, at various 'levels' and in various 'dimensions' as described. And, most learning theorists seem to agree, 'comparatively little change occurs ... in situations of equilibrium' (Gmelch 1997: 487). These perspectives point towards *experience* as the most fundamental condition or trigger for learning to occur – since outside of experience there can be no encounter with anything different to occasion disequilibrium.

John Dewey was clear about the importance of experiential learning:

> An ounce of experience is better than a ton of theory simply because it is only in experience that any theory has vital and verifiable significance. An experience, a very humble experience, is capable of generating and carrying any amount of theory (or intellectual content), but a theory apart from an experience cannot be definitely grasped even as theory.
>
> (Dewey 1916/1966: 144)

Lucas, in a paper in which he seeks to align intercultural learning with experiential learning theory, differentiates experiential learning from other major learning theories: '[t]he process is fundamentally different from cognitive learning, which focuses on the acquisition of abstract symbols and empirical or behaviourist views of learning, which focus on the acquisition of appropriate behaviours in specific contexts' (Lucas 2003: 302). In much higher education today, the call for 'student-centred' learning extols a range of practices which hinge upon students being *experientially* engaged in their learning.

In most constructivist models of learning, the primary locus for learning through experience lies in intersubjective encounters – learning in social contexts where our lifeworld horizons encounter each other. This will be explored further in Section 4. For now, we see that experience in/of the world is a necessary constituent in the learning process, and education for the global self then suggests that our students should experience their learning-world as globally situated. However, experience *per se* is not in itself considered a sufficient constituent – at least not for maximal learning to occur. When Dewey, and others, speak of 'experience', they use the term 'to denote the relations between subject and worlds' (perhaps what we might commonly mean when we talk of 'having an experience') 'as well as between action and thinking' (Elkjaer 2009: 78). The second implicated trigger is that of *reflection*. A third is that of *application*, since in the experiential model 'the learner examines his or her own experience and, through a process of reflection and observation, arrives at abstract theories or generalizations, *which he or she then tests*' (Lucas 2003: 302, my emphasis).

This 'reflective cycle' has received a great deal of attention in higher education (although I would say rather differentially across the disciplines), perhaps due in large measure to the influence of David Kolb's (1984) work. What often gets lost in the idea of learning through experience (and, I suggest, also lost in the application of Kolb's work in higher education), is its holistic nature as explored in the previous section. Elkjaer presents this as a fundamental distinction between an epistemological and an ontological interpretation of experience; a distinction which lies at the heart of the question about our higher educational enterprise:

... experience is traditionally understood as an epistemological concept in which the purpose is production and acquisition of knowledge ... Dewey's concept of experience is ontological and based upon the transactional relation between subject and worlds. The epistemological orientation of experience means that it is possible to overlook situations in which knowledge is not the primary content or purpose, and not be able to see that experience is also emotional and aesthetic ... Most of human lives consist of non-cognitive experiences as subjects continuously act, enjoy and suffer, and this is experience.

(Elkjaer 2009: 79)

We will return to this shortly as we look at incidental learning, but prior to that there is one further aspect of reflection to introduce – the temporal. The reflective cycle model implies a process over time – experience, then reflect, then apply or 'experiment'. Donald Schön (1983) proposed also that we might experience (or seek to engage in) 'reflection-in-action' – casting a critical eye on the here-and-now *and* responding there-and-then to any problems with a 'solution'. Although some have cast doubts on such multi-tasking as a channel for learning, we might here look again to the idea of *virtuous learning circles* through the specific example of *mindfulness* (Langer 1989) which was introduced in Chapter 2. Mindfulness can be framed as a form of reflection-in-action, although the requirement to be open and non-judgemental might be interpreted to be at odds with a critically reflective stance. Specifically relevant to the experiencing of the global student, Ting-Toomey characterizes mindfulness as encouraging participants in an intercultural encounter to:

tune in consciously to their habituated mental scripts and preconceived expectations. *Mindfulness* means the readiness to shift one's frame of reference, the motivation to use new categories and to understand cultural or ethnic differences, and the preparedness to experiment with creative avenues of decision making and problem solving ... To be mindful communicators, individuals need to learn the value systems that influence others' self-conceptions. They need to be open to a new way of identity construction. They need to be prepared to perceive and understand a behaviour or a problem from others' cultural and personal standpoints.

(Ting-Toomey 1999: 46)

So, on reflection, mindfulness is entirely 'at evens' with being critically reflective, since a critically reflective stance also requires that we seek to stand outside our expectations and existing frames of reference if we are to identify what might be wrong and what new approach might make it better. It was suggested in Chapter 2 that being mindful in an intercultural encounter would help a participant to be aware of a fissure in communication, and so to seek to repair it in the here-and-now. If successful, we can see that the continuing experience of the encounter is likely to be more successful than it might otherwise have been. In terms of our virtuous circle of learning, the learner has experienced herself taking successful action and has experienced successful intercultural communication, bolstering self-efficacy and perhaps also feeding forward to motivate further encounters.

The reflective process of standing back (later or in the here-and-now), taking stock and taking action, then, is fundamental to what is understood as 'experiential learning' in general, and is proposed by most interculturalists as 'crucial' and part of the process of using an intercultural encounter to 'learn something about themselves as well as learning about others' (Sen Gupta 2003: 160). However, returning to the position that most of our lived-experience consists of 'non-cognitive experiences as subjects continuously act, enjoy and suffer, and this is experience' (Elkjaer 2009: 79), we have to ask if there is no learning to be derived from this most pervasive state of existence? Dewey was quite unequivocal on this:

> Activity that is not checked by observation of what follows from it may be temporarily enjoyed. But intellectually it leads nowhere. It does not provide knowledge about the situations in which action occurs nor does it lead to clarification and expansion of ideas.
>
> (Dewey 1938/1963: 25)

Modern exponents of experiential learning are no less adamant on the point:

> Reflection is the element that transforms simple experience to a learning experience. For knowledge to be discovered and internalized the learner must test assumptions and hypotheses about the outcomes of decisions and actions taken, then weigh the outcomes against past learning and future implications. This reflective process is integral to all phases of experiential learning, from identifying intention and choosing the experience, to considering preconceptions and observing how they change as the experience unfolds.
>
> (National Society for Experiential Education 2013: n.p.)

On this point, I have to part company with Dewey and others who would agree with him. This is not to undervalue the value of reflection, and I would probably agree that reflective learning is 'richer'. However, my own lived-experience is highly suggestive of learning taking place without conscious attention. Furthermore, such learning is highly implicated in the socialization to own culture which has been indicated at length in this book to be so strong in shaping our worldviews (those highly generative meaning perspectives). Freire and Dewey, and others, would not actually dispute this – and the precise point about learning 'for democracy' or for 'conscientization' is that these seek to set out mechanisms for (let's say) 'overriding' that undeliberative learning. But I believe it is not helpful to a model of learning to leave out incidental learning as a highly significant contributor, or to (if only by implication) relegate it to less sophisticated processes of pre-adulthood. In terms of the focus of this book, incidental learning is fundamental to the kind of learning which 'transfers' through the hidden curriculum and through on-going being within the campus community. As such, failing to acknowledge its importance risks neglecting how those spaces might be constituted to support the more deliberative activities encouraged through our formal curricula. Barnett, arguing for a need to develop students' 'will' to learn, brings together the points made about learning dimensions and the import of incidental learning when he asserts that our learning is 'mostly unintended, incidental and non-reflective' and it is 'far wider than just the cognitive dimension' (Barnett, R. 2007: 121). He characterizes learners who engage in non-reflective learning as 'gullible' and accepting 'what they are told'. This might be true, but *our* acceptance (for this is not the preserve of naïve or unengaged students but the dominant mode of being for most of us most of the time) in incidental learning is triggered by much more than what we are *told* – it is triggered also by what we see and feel, how the world is arranged around us, how others interact (or don't) with us, and all the rest of the world in which we flow. Little wonder that Jarvis characterizes the 'moments' in which we escape from the flow and 'become aware of the world' as 'episodic' (2006: 73).

Learning, then, is triggered by/in our experiencing of the world. Experiential learning theorists in the main incorporate into their definition of experience a process of reflection and reaction, and we can include in this a notion of reflection-in-action, mindfulness, contributing to the learning process through virtuous learning circles. However, modelling lived-experience as being largely one of an unexamined flow leads us to see that incidental learning (while potentially less rich) plays a significant role in triggering the shaping and reshaping of the lifeworld. A particular site of flow for most of us lies in our encounters with other people, and the social world is possible the most significant cauldron for human learning, as we go on to consider in the next section.

Reflective questions for Section 3

- Would you 'read the tendency for socializing with people who share our own preferences, knowledge base, political perspectives and the like as a strong indicator' that we seek out 'selective exposure' in order to avoid having to reconsider our attitudes?
- Is 'an ounce of experience ... better than a ton of theory'?
- Do you subscribe to the view that experience–reflection–action provides for optimal learning? How does 'reflection-in-action' figure in this?
- Is experience 'also emotional and aesthetic'? If so, can learning be only cognitive?
- To what extent are you *mindful* as you make your way in the world?
- Am I right to insist that incidental learning must feature in any account of the learning process? And is incidental learning necessarily an indication of 'gullibility'?
- Can you identify learning in your own life which has not been triggered by experience of some kind?

Section 4: Situated learning and communities of practice

> As an aspect of social practice, learning involves the whole person; it implies not only a relation to specific activities, but a relation to social communities – it implies becoming a full participant, a member, a kind of person …. Activities, tasks, functions, and understandings do not exist in isolation; they are part of a broader system of relations in which they have meaning. These systems of relations arise out of and are reproduced and developed within social communities, which are in part systems of relations among persons.
>
> (Lave and Wenger 1998: 53)

> When we do get our disjunctures resolved, the answers are social constructs, and so immediately our learning is influenced by the social contexts within which it occurs.
>
> (Jarvis 2009b: 27)

Situating learning in the social/cultural-historical context as in socio-cultural, constructivist views of the process is not only to say that learning can occur when we are with people. More significantly, our cognitive (and, let's also say, our emotional and behavioural) development *is dependent upon* the social context in which it is situated and, by some accounts at least, is also involved in the (re)construction of those contexts. Lev Vygotsky has had a significant impact on how learning is viewed since the translation of his works brought him into Western 'social' contexts. Vygotsky postulated a 'zone of proximal development' (ZPD) which is a border area between what a learner is currently capable of by herself and what her further development currently has the potential to make her capable of 'under adult guidance or in collaboration with more capable peers' (Vygotsky 1978: 86). On either side of the ZPD borderlands are development and learning, which Vygotsky saw as separate:

> … the most essential feature of our hypothesis is the notion that development processes do not coincide with learning processes. Rather, the developmental process lags behind the learning process; this sequence results in zones of proximal development.
>
> (Vygotsky, op. cit.: 90)

Taking an everyday interpretation of 'development, and 'learning', we could perhaps couch this in terms of our schemata heuristic along the lines that something becomes available as a procedural schema (capability for performing) only after it has been accommodated within a propositional schema (understanding a thing to be true). However, this interpretation does not fit well with the idea that we often make our way in the world utilizing procedural schemata for which we appear to lack propositional schemata – as when we subconsciously employ the 'hidden' communication rituals of our culture even though we would not ordinarily be able to articulate what those rituals were, or even that they existed as anything other than 'normal' behaviour. Less problematic is to consider the journey across our ZDP to represent a deeper level of accommodation. More important to our discussion here is Vygotsky's central and original premise that the socio-cultural (and therefore historical) context in which our learning (and our being) is situated *shapes* our cognition – facilitating and constraining us in its own terms; our consciousness is 'imposed on humans through participation in sociocultural practices' (Wertsch 1986: 187). For Vygotsky, developing *meaningful* perception is actually about escaping the limitations of a singular framework to that of a more generalized consciousness. Clearly, in these terms, where the knowing adult or more capable peer who is guiding us across our development zone is a product of the same historico-cultural context, he is complicit in the constraining act. It is not difficult here to see the implications for those who experience higher education largely as engagement with peers and adults whose habitus is similarly formulated to their own.

In this reading, Vygotsky's ZPD becomes a space in which we risk becoming either further embedded in our culture, or finding some liberation through intersubjective engagement with more (or differently) knowing others. I am not sure that Soviet-Vygotsky would fully approve of such a reading. His compatriot, Mikhail Bakhtin (1984) was, however, very clear that without difference between social inter-actors, there is no space for the dialogic process necessary for learning to take place. Certainly, Vygotsky's 'more knowing' other is a dimension of difference, but a limited dimension if she is caste in the dominant milieu. In contrast to propositions in culture-learning theories and ethnography that to understand the other we should seek to adopt an insider (emic) view on cultural practices (as represent in the quote from Ting-Toomey in the previous section), Bakhtin saw this as simply taking us into further replication, and rather advocated the strength in etic perspectives:

> In order to understand, it is immensely important for a person who understands to be *located outside* the object of his or her creative understanding – in time, in space, in culture ... in the realm of culture, outsidedness is the most powerful factor in understanding.
>
> (Bakhtin 1986: 6, cited in Jackson 2008: 18)

I am personally unsure of the validity of this, and would suggest that such etic perspectives come most easily (so less examined) to us and are generally so wrapped in the obscuring veils of our own cultural perspectives as to be unlikely to enable us to understand except from within the perspectives of our existing meta-schemes. Significant value does lie, though, in trying to see *our own* cultural being from the 'outsidedness' of others.

Other people, and perhaps most effectively 'different' other people, then provide a special trigger for our students' learning/development. They are the observed/experienced actors of (social) practices and their guides across as yet incompletely accommodated schemata, helping them bring as yet vaguely shaped forms and figures across lifeworld horizons.

As may have been discerned from the brief discussion on Vygotsky, his primary focus was, again, on 'knowing'/'being' in the cognitive dimension. A more holistic, and more 'dialogic', account of social learning is found in Lave and Wenger's work on learning situated in communities of practice, which '[i]n contrast with learning as internalization', is 'an integral and inseparable aspect of social practice' which 'concerns the whole person acting in the world' (Lave and Wenger 1998: 31 and 49). Not only does Lave and Wenger's holistic approach align more closely with the perspectives on learning built in this chapter, their construct of communities of practice is also important for our purposes because, in its focus on participant positionings, it opens up questions of power dynamics in the learning field. The question of power dynamics is especially important when we consider the power differentials which might be experienced by minority and majority students, and by those more and those less familiar with the academic milieu in which they enact their learning. The act of social practice 'implies not only a relation to specific activities, but a relation to social communities – it implies becoming a full participant, a member, a kind of person' (Lave and Wenger, op. cit.: 53). The mechanism for arriving at full 'membership' of the community of practice is a kind of inward spiralling from an initial position of 'peripheral participation'. In such a community, peers or 'near-peers' can play a powerful role as knowledge circulation among these (near) equals 'spreads exceedingly rapidly and effectively' (Lave and Wenger, op. cit.: 93). When we see 'becoming a full participant, a member, a kind of person' as such a central feature of the learning community, the importance of inclusive learning environments and curricula is again highlighted – not only as an ethical issue, but also as a matter of learning effectiveness. This represents an important dimension to the social construction of knowledge by bringing the learning community into play, perhaps (not necessarily) as a counterweight to the broader socializing (or teaching) community which might more ordinarily be seen to set the learning agenda. In terms of learning generally, both Lave and Wenger's and Vygotsky's works *require* engagement in a social act and a social context. Intersubjective encounter is a necessary condition, and in these and other constructivist accounts, the learner and her environment co-construct each other. In this space, co-participants, perhaps as more knowing others, perhaps as peers, perhaps as dwellers in a similar world, but perhaps more powerfully as different others, help shape all the learning. In general, all of this plays well in the considerations of practice in Chapter 5, although it is not entirely unproblematical and will be further discussed when we come to look at the highly influential theory of constructive alignment on the shaping of the formal curriculum (Biggs 1999; Biggs and Tang 2011).

> ### Reflective questions for Section 4
>
> - In part, Vygotsky's account of learning brings us back to the idea of habitus and the cultural impacts on lifeworld formulation. Does he trap us again in the game of culture?
> - Can you see circumstances in which crossing the ZPD might *not* require a more capable other? Where does reflection come in?
> - If your own biography has led to lifeworld formulation in similar socio-cultural contexts to those of your students (or some of your students) do you see yourself as 'complicit' in constraining their development?
> - How best to 'learn' cultures? Emic or etic perspectives?
> - What 'questions of power dynamics' would you think relevant to the learning field of your teaching spaces?
> - Reflecting on your own experience as a student, can you identify circumstances when any of your communities of practice provided learning which was at odds with that 'required' by the teaching community? How about now, in other communities of practice in which you engage?

Section 5: Learning stages

We have already looked at some aspects of what might be termed 'learning stages': The move from partial or minor schema change to meta-schema transformation, and crossing learning thresholds to open up new worlds for discovery. In this section we will look at two other aspects of learning stages. First, at stages which might relate to stages in the broader developments distinguishing child and adult, and second, at stages in our more immediate state of being which might influence our receptivity to learning.

Setting out, already in 1992, an agenda for 'Education for a Global Society' through study abroad, Kauffman *et al.* (1992) summarize a three-stage model for the development from adolescent to adult, as represented in Table 4.1. Each stage in the development of autonomy is accompanied by/represented through

Table 4.1 Three-stage pattern of development from adolescent to adult

Autonomy	Belonging	Values	Cognition/vocation	Worldview
Level I: other-dependent	conventional diffuse	inherited	dualistic	encapsulated ethnocentrism
Level II: inner-dependent	self-selected group	searching	relativistic	empathic ethnorelativism
Level III: inter-dependent	open	owned	commitment in relativism	integrated ethnorelativism

Source: Kauffman *et al.* 1992: 128.

holistic change involving our sense of belonging, our values base, and 'vocation' – 'what one's life is to be and how one wishes to serve humanity' (Kauffman *et al.*, op. cit.: 138), as well as purely cognitive change. Their specific focus is upon the development of a worldview through study abroad, and this they associate with a developmental move from 'encapsulated ethnocentrism' to one of 'integrated eth-norelativsim', which would form a reasonable goal in our journey for a global self. The majority of undergraduates, by virtue of their age, would be 'expected' to be moving out of Level I and through Level II during their university years.

Echoing strongly some of the ways in which we have described the moves which might enable us all to make our way in the globalizing world, the authors summarize an important dimension to change through these development stages:

> As young adults gain more autonomy, they must confront new questions about boundaries of relationships. At this stage their connections are diffuse …. [then he/she] realizes that other people are essential to his or her search for a new pattern of knowing and being in the world, and so moves on to the next level: identifying with a self-selected group.
>
> (Kauffman *et al.* 1992: 132)

Such changes are commonly reported across the study abroad research literature, but I would have to say that it is not my experience, nor that reported in most of the literature which has investigated home–international student integration, that this type of transformation occurs among those who stay on our campuses. Indeed, this lack of spontaneous integration is a very strong indicator that we as educators need to be doing more to enable our students to be more than they would otherwise be, and is something we will discuss further in Chapter 5. Nonetheless, the question of who/what our undergraduate students might be in terms of development stages related to learning is important, and not a subject of much discussion in higher education learning theory. If our students are in a hinterland between adolescence and adulthood, this would impact upon whether teaching theories most strongly associated with 'child' education (pedagogy) or those relating to adult education (andragogy) (Knowles, M. 1980) provide the best basis for our practice.

Summarizing this field of *life-span psychology*, Illeris (2002: 206) tells us that 'it becomes quite clear that people in different life ages generally have essentially different motivational structures and different perspectives on learning and education'. Importantly, in the 'youth' stage, our focus is 'very much orientated towards the formation of identity and can only be understood in this light', and only in adulthood do we accept responsibility for the management of our own lives – a psychological development process which, it seems 'has become longer and longer, to the extent that today it is most often accomplished well into a person's twenties or perhaps never' (Illeris, op. cit.: 214 and 219). This begs several questions, but for our own purposes there is the issue of the demarcation line between 'youth' and 'adult'. Whatever the veracity of claims for an ever-receding point of adulthood, this model strongly suggests that identity-work is a strong, perhaps a primary, driver for our undergraduate students. This is important in the context of a book which is advocating for a particular form of self-identification, but also more generally in the implications it has for ensuring that learning experiences at university allow for, or build upon those identity drivers.

Elsewhere, extensive research involving over 300 students between the ages of eighteen and thirty led Baxter Magolda (2001) to propose a four-stage 'journey towards self-authorship' – which the author characterizes as 'complex and arduous' (Baxter Magolda, op. cit.: 331) – as summarized in Table 4.2. This model presents being in terms of our epistemological understanding ('how do I know what I know?'), our understanding of self ('who am I'?), and our desired relationships with others. Investigating her students during and beyond their university lives revealed a picture which might broadly support Illeris' review of life-style psychology with regard to adulthood coming later in life, at least in the inter- and intra- personal dimensions:

> Across their twenties, at varying paces in varying contexts, participants shifted to contextual knowing, assuming that knowledge was relative to a context, could be judged on criteria, and better or worse choices made after an evaluation of relevant evidence. In both independent and contextual knowing participants were aware that they were now in charge of deciding what to believe and choosing their own paths. However, their way of being in the world up to now had been to rely on external authority and guidance. Despite their progress on conceptualizing more complex ways of knowing, they did not have the corollary progress on the intrapersonal and interpersonal dimensions to genuinely enact contextual knowing. In their attempts to function independently and contextually, they began to internalize external 'shoulds' to decide knowledge claims. This resulted in adopting formulas or doing what others determined would be successful. Participants also internalized external 'shoulds' to answer the 'who am I' question; defining their internal sense of self through what they perceived that others thought was appropriate. Thus in the interpersonal dimension, other voices overshadowed those of the participants. Because they were focused on thinking for themselves and functioning independently, they framed their stories about all three dimensions as though they were internal. Hearing them in detail revealed that these processes were formulas – prescribed plans or predetermined scripts – adopted from the external world.
>
> (Baxter Magolda 2001: 72)

Baxter Magolda identified her most important finding as being how her research 'revealed the central role internal self-definition plays in self-authorship', a fundamental point for our endeavours towards the development of the global self, since our self-definition is 'crucial' to how we go about relating to others (Baxter Magolda 2001: xvii).

Table 4.2 Baxter Magolda's 'four phases of the journey towards self-authorship'

	Following formulas	Crossroads	Becoming the author of one's life	Internal foundation
Epistemological dimension: how do I know?	Believe authority's plans; how 'you' know	Question plans; see need for own vision	Choose own beliefs; how 'I' know in context of external knowledge claims	Grounded in internal belief systems
Intrapersonal dimension: who am I?	Define self through external others	Realize dilemma of external definition; see need for internal identity	Choose own values, identity in context of external forces	Grounded internal coherent sense of self
Interpersonal dimension: what relationships do I want with others?	Act in relationships to acquire approval	Realize delemma (sic) of focusing on external approval; see need to bring self to relationship	Act in relationships to be true to self, mutually negotiating how needs are met	Grounded in mutuality

Source: Baxter Magolda 2001: 40.

We have, then, a suggestion that pre-adulthood individuals are strongly driven by needs for identity formation (in relation to self and other), and that this stage of their motivation for and priority for learning extends not only into their lives at university but also beyond. To what extent this might arise *because of* the focus which universities give to cognitive development, as previously mentioned, is not in any way clear. However, it does hold implications for our approaches to facilitating identity-learning, suggesting among other things that offering students some foundational experience at university may be very salient to the continued building of a global self in the world beyond their studies. We will return to Baxter Magolda's (Baxter Magolda 2009; Baxter Magolda and King 2004) 'learning partnerships' model for supporting students in their journeys to self-authorship in Chapter 5.

The other type of learning stage to briefly consider to close this chapter is probably relevant at all stages of development, from infant to adult, though perhaps with shifting degrees of emphasis. We have looked at the role of emotion in learning with respect to emotional intelligence, and noted the influence this is proposed to have on our overall approach/motivation to engage in learning at all. Maslow's (1954) theory of a hierarchy of human needs has been highly influential over several decades. Although the theory is open to criticism for presenting an overly simplified and in a sense de-personalized taxonomy, I suggest that we should consider that it can provide helpful insights when treated as just that – a generalized model. The proposition here is not strictly that an individual has to pass through stages, but that there is a hierarchy of human needs such that the more fundamental levels of need must be satisfied in order for higher levels to be addressed as effectively as possible. Only when the physiological needs basic to human survival (from breathing through nutrition to sleep) are satisfied will needs for our security, health and property become the dominant drivers. We then are motivated to satisfy needs around friendship and love, and onwards through self-esteem, confidence and self- other- respect before reaching Maslow's pinnacle of 'self-actualization'. At this peak, we find space for matters of morality and the resolution of prejudices, for example. At one level, this appears to be rather a case of common sense, and at another it opens up space to be dismissed because we can all think of exceptions. However, I would propose there is a level of general truth here, and one which is not such common sense as to always translate into our practice in higher education. Establishing learning conditions which promote a sense of security, equality, and self-esteem has been variously alluded to through this chapter and others, and forms a substantive area for consideration in Chapter 5.

Reflective questions for Section 5

- Do you see our development through childhood to adulthood as including the development of 'our sense of belonging, our values base, and vocation'?
- Do you think the 'lack of spontaneous integration' between home and international students is 'a very strong indicator that we as educators need to be doing more to enable our students to be more than they would otherwise be'?
- How do you see your own undergraduate students in terms of their point in life – more as children or more as adults? Do you (does the university more broadly) treat them as such?
- How much support does/should your own work with students give to facilitating the development of their self-identities?
- To what extent do you think psychological drivers such as those identified by Maslow are relevant to student motivation and learning? To what extent do they feature in your own approaches to constructing learning environments and experiences?

Chapter 5

Questions of practice

Prejudices, it is well known, are most difficult to eradicate from the heart whose soil has never been loosened or fertilised by education: they grow there, firm as weeds among stones.

(Charlotte Brontë, *Jane Eyre*)

And so these men of Indostan
Disputed loud and long,
Each in his own opinion
Exceeding stiff and strong,
Though each was partly in the right,
And all were in the wrong!

(John Saxe, *The Blind Men and the Elephant*)

Introduction

It is relationships, and how we engage the diverse other, both within a university community and beyond, that reveal ethical value.

(Robinson and Lee 2007: 15)

As the European Union's (EU) principal vehicle for understanding and addressing diversity, much is expected of intercultural dialogue.

(Kaur-Stubbs 2010: 38)

- knowledge is retained and reinforced through practical application;
- learning is a holistic process, crucially involving the self-awareness of the learner;
- learning is best achieved through collaboration with others.

(Major 2005: 18)

A well-known folk tale concerns the contrasting descriptions offered of an elephant when a number of men encounter only restricted parts of one. It offers a metaphor for the kind of educational experience which is constrained within a particular point of view, where alternative perspectives do not contribute to a broader understanding, and where communication could significantly enrich everybody's understanding. This particular folk tale is interesting in that it is found in seventeenth-century Japan and China, appears to be based on a story circulating in India several centuries earlier, appears in Jainism, Sufism, Hinduism and Buddhism – and was translated into the English poem quoted in the opening of this chapter in the nineteenth century (my source for all this is Wikipedia). Some truths do cross continents, cultures and generations.

Ron Barnett calls for a radical reformulation of university education around a 'constellation of fragility' as a response to his interpretation of the fragmenting certainties and rapid changes faced by our students in the postmodern, globalizing world. He proposes for this a 'threefold educational process':

> Firstly, it has to create epistemological and ontological disturbance in the minds and the *being* of students: it has to pose cognitively and experientially the radical uncertainty presented by supercomplexity. Students have to come to *feel* in every sense the utter insecurity of the post-modern world. Secondly, higher education has to enable students to live at ease with this perplexing and unsettling environment. Thirdly, it has to enable them to make their own positive contributions to this supercomplex world, while being sensitive to the unpredictability and uncontrollability of the consequences of what they say and do.
>
> (Barnett, R. 2000: 154)

Though I am drawn to Barnett's general thesis, I am not convinced that 'utter insecurity' is a good starting point. I suggest that, whether as a consequence of the complex scapes of the postmodern globalizing world outlined in Chapters 1 and 2, or as a consequence of their stages of being as referred to in Chapter 4 (or both) many students already feel very insecure, and insecurity is not a good place from which to learn. As outlined in Chapters 2 and 3, identity threat does not push us outwards but draws us to type and limits both the will and the capacity to see how the world might be to others. In particular, it is insecurity with and ignorance of the (global) other which leads some to retreat to defences such as racism and sexism. Yes, in a world where change is 'radically incomplete' there is a need for us all to be comfortable *not knowing*, but radical uncertainty is more likely to lead to fundamentalism than scepticism, dismissal rather than curiosity. I suggest our primary task is much more about creating cognitive, behavioural and affective security, important to which is a developed values base, in order that the second and third stages in Barnett's three-fold process might be achieved. In the preceding chapters I have sought to develop a representation of student identity and capability development as lifeworld change, in which learning is seen as three-dimensional reformulations of schemes and meta-schemes driven largely if not entirely within social interaction. We have seen various perspectives which indicate that such interactions are most comfortable to us when they occur among communities of similitude, but we have also seen that such contexts are not fertile grounds for new learning. Given the continuing shifts in the postmodern/global environments in which our students enact their lives, characterized by change, uncertainties, increasingly diverse 'ethnoscapes', ethereal consumer-identities, and the related threat of agency/capability loss, I argue for a university experience which focuses *primarily* on establishing global identity/self-realization. As Walker (2010: 229) points out, a capabilities approach to higher education looks beyond the capabilities brought by the student to 'the social arrangements, for example pedagogic conditions or normative processes of universities that enable or diminish student capability formation'. The practice questions of this chapter, then, concern how we might formulate university spaces (learning environments, activities, experiences, disciplinary perspectives, and the like) which have greater potential to open up curiosity (the affective quality associated with *borderline ethnorelativism* in Bennett's continuum summarized in Figure 2.1) than fear, suspicion, or romanticism towards others and their worlds; to allow our students (and ourselves) to recognize the limitations in their own perspectives without feeling under threat; to allow for more truths to be respectfully shared and critiqued; and to enable the development of reasoned values with global applicability. In such spaces, our learners cannot successfully make their way without enhancing their *act-in-the-world* capabilities. They will be challenging spaces, but I suggest if they are carefully constructed they are also the spaces in which a more global sense of *self-in-the-world* may flourish. The recurrent issue throughout this chapter, then, is how our learning spaces might lead to cross-cultural capability development – enabling our students to engage in communication and community *among* diverse others *for* a globalizing world. All of this entails the introduction of more global perspectives, the challenging of established truths, and requirements for ethical and values-based approaches to a discipline and its practices, and so relates back to discussions in the opening chapters on values in higher education, critical pedagogy, and education as conscientization (Freire 1970, 1972).

At university, students experience, and so learn from, the *formal* curriculum as set down in course/programme documentation and experienced through the planned learning activities and resources which support the aims, objectives, and outcomes of those courses. Students also engage with a very variable *informal* curriculum through a combination of activities and experiences which are made available for their participation, but are not a requirement of their programme – and in many cases are not provided by the programme itself. Additionally, and significantly, all students experience a *hidden* curriculum. Unplanned but ever-present, the hidden curriculum carries messages about values, preferred behaviours, favoured characteristics (in the iceberg metaphor of Chapter 3, the *culture-below-the-waterline*) of the discipline and of the institution – through their own practices, discourses, organization of spaces and time, regulations, charters, choices of logo or motto, and the like. For the student, these three curricula constitute a holistic experience, and their learning is shaped within all these dimensions of university life, (and the many more matryoshka of their wider environments, of course). Considerations of practice, therefore, need to look also at each of these, but because the hidden and the formal curricula are the dominant spaces for *all* student learning, it is these which I will concentrate on. The first section of this chapter looks at selected aspects of the hidden curriculum with respect to fostering an inclusive environment, and the hidden curriculum is picked up again, along with some aspects of the informal curriculum in Section 4 when we look at broader institution practices. Sections 2 and 3 deal principally with the formal curriculum. First, with its content and design, and second with how learning experiences are framed to 'deliver' and assess the content. In these spaces, too, the hidden curriculum exerts its power-full influence. Almost everything proposed in this chapter is currently accepted good practice in higher education learning and teaching theory, but has not found its way into much of the literature on internationalization. The questions presented here, then, put a specific focus on how that good practice might be shaped to enable our students to work across socio-cultural boundaries within and beyond their disciplinary confines to experience learning in ways which might develop their global selves.

The model of internationalization presented here views it as the responsibility of each of us individually and institutionally to enable all our students to move beyond the comforts of the 'uniform environments' which they might otherwise envelope themselves within; to do so requires the security to be willing to struggle with 'the (forever risky) two-way translations between distinct universes of meaning' (Bauman 2008: Loc 731). As will be emphasized through much of the discussion in this chapter, 'celebrations' of cultural differences which are a common feature of many attempts to internationalize our campuses are (in isolation at least) inadequate and possible counter-productive responses. The dangers have been acknowledged for decades, as indicated by citations in Case (1993: 319), though such activities continue to feature: 'Exposing students to ethnic dishes and strange holiday practices is unlikely to promote an enlightened perspective on the lives and concerns of these "foreign" cultures' (Zachariah 1989), and 'attending to limited, and to some extent trivial, cultural dimensions, global educators may actually reinforce stereotypical perceptions' (Schuncke 1984). As counterbalance, Caruana and Ploner (2010: 100) suggest that we should consider, 'complementing celebratory events with others that promote greater informal interactional diversity based on common identities and aspirations'.

As is increasingly the case in the wider discourse of internationalization, we find ourselves considering diversity issues which extend beyond those raised by international students on campus or by the global context as framed by foreign frontiers, even though these will most frequently provide a focal point for our discussions in this chapter. Largely because of differences in first language, the most visible and cited cultural divide on campus often lies between what we commonly refer to as 'home' or 'domestic' students and their international peers (further complicated in the UK context, where, because of differential funding regulations, international students are often presented and treated as distinct from European Union students). In conflating 'international' with language ability, the most striking anomaly is that, of course, some international students speak English as their first language, while some domestic student do not. Much of the literature (including that presented throughout this volume) on cultural difference, acculturation, and culture shock also focuses upon sojourners crossing national borders or geo-cultural regions. The first section of this chapter will include questions of English language ability, and I will most frequently frame the discussions around international students, but all the practice issues we examine have relevance across our entire student body because 'experience of any kind of otherness can be seen as intercultural experience' (Alred *et al.* 2003: 6). Significant work undertaken in mainland Europe around *internationalization at home* (IAH) (Beelen 2007; Crowther *et al.* 2000; Nilsson 2003) has sought to draw upon local communities and cultures as sources for intercultural learning. Research into student contact and interactions across *local* diversity boundaries, largely in the USA, point to outcomes which are supportive of students as *global selves* (Denson and Bowman 2013; Denson and Zhang 2010; Gurin *et al.* 2002). Olson *et al.* (2007) advocate for 'bridging the gap' between internationalization and multicultural education. I endorse all of these, but note also that encounters with alterity arise beyond even the boundaries of traditional diversity demarcations and the concerns of multicultural educationalists. The disjunctures associated with cultural immersion and acculturation explored in Chapter 2, and the associated learning opportunities explored in Chapter 4, may also apply when, for example, a student finds himself for the first time interacting significantly across genders, or sexualities, or with peers whose attitudes and habits towards alcohol or religion (not necessarily a specific religion) are substantively different from, perhaps even diametrically opposed to his own. Global relevance and inclusivity are not restricted either to distant horizons or to local ethnicity divides. So, while Mestenhauser (2002: 15) exhorts his readers to 'commiserate' with him that the presence of international students is 'undervalued, under-appreciated, neglected, and conceptually underdeveloped', we should also look critically at how we frame our responses to other forms of diversity. For what in the UK are termed, for example, *BME* (black and minority ethnic) students or *LGBT* (lesbian, gay, bi-sexual and transgender) students, exclusion and issues such as stereotyping and identification through tokenistic and un-problematized acts of 'celebration' may be at least as salient as they are for international students.

As was referred to in Chapter 1, in many cases it may be only a minority of your domestic students or your international students who have constructed their biographies in truly multicultural contexts, and many may have no experience of contexts where, for example, sexuality is as openly expressed or gender relationships as openly enacted as on our campuses. Research by Denson and Bowman (2013: 563) identified that, 'the greater the differences in the cultural composition between high school and university, the less confident students feel in interacting with people from different cultures and in their enjoyment of such interactions'.

They also identified that such differential levels in confidence are ameliorated as students are exposed to the diversity which a university environment might offer, and conclude, therefore, that their findings 'highlight the importance of encouraging all students to engage in university diversity experiences'. However, I suggest that, notwithstanding this encouraging finding, in our efforts to build inclusive environments we need to be alert to the fact that in this respect, also, our domestic and our international students are diverse; some individuals will need more support in building their identity security than do others. Jarvis (2006: 125), in his discussion on the role of self-efficacy in learning, reminds us that, 'we rarely act unless we believe that we have the ability to perform successfully, and this belief is something that we have learned as a result of both past successful acts and by watching other people behave.'

We cannot really expect students with limited experience of successful behaviour in multicultural spaces or intercultural interactions to have a sense of self-efficacy or the 'ontological security' (Brooks and Everett 2008) to go against peer trends when faced with unsupported and somewhat nebulous 'opportunities'. If this is not part of their cultural capital when they enter our university spaces, it is not to be wondered at that many 'rarely act' spontaneously to expose themselves to the vulnerabilities such spaces may expose. Therefore, how we *structure* the environment and the formalized interactions within learning contexts needs to support and scaffold individuals in their forays among others.

Encouragingly for our enterprise, learning has been shown to transfer across aspects of difference; Zhai and Scheer, for example, cite further research which supports their own findings that 'students with a higher level of global perspective tended to have a more positive attitude toward diversity' (2004: 48), while King and Magolda note that

> the developmental complexity that allows a learner to understand and accept the general idea of difference from self without feeling threat to self enables a person to offer positive regard to others across many types of difference, such as race, ethnicity, social class, gender, sexual orientation, and religion.
>
> (King, P. M. and Baxter Magolda 2005: 572–573)

Unfortunately, I would suggest that learning (or not unlearning) that it is acceptable and normal to other another, in order to bolster our established in-group identity, is likely also to transfer. How complicit is the hidden curriculum in maintaining these boundaries; how can the formal curriculum help erode them?

Where the previous chapters have included a set of reflective questions at the end of each section, these are interspersed more regularly in this final chapter and include some reflective tasks as well as questions. Undertaking some of these with colleagues might provide useful exercises for course/programme development.

Section 1: Shaping the environment – inclusivity and the hidden curriculum

> Education, especially teaching and learning, is one manifestation of human relationships and consequently the concern for the other should underlie all relationships. Whist ideally, this concern for the other should be manifest from teacher to student and also from student to teacher, it is maintained here that teachers are the initiators of the relationship.
>
> (Jarvis 2009a: 14)

The new language which is rapidly ousting the language of Shakespeare as the world's lingua franca is English itself – English in its new global form ... this is not English as we have known it, and have taught it in the past as a foreign language. It is a new phenomenon, and if it represents any kind of triumph it is probably not a cause of celebration by native speakers.

(Graddol 2006: 11)

Kwame Appiah's model of cosmopolitanism, as referred to in Chapter 1 (Appiah 2005, 2006), is one of 'conversation – and in particular, conversation between people from different ways of life'. Conversation is the entrée to learning about other people's situations, establishing the basis for using 'our imaginations to walk in their moccasins'. In such conversations and imaginings the aim is not that we should find agreement but, more fundamentally, they hold the potential to enable us simply to 'get used to one another' (Appiah 2006: xxi, 63 and 78). Robert Putnam's study (2002) into the role of social capital in American society identified the importance of social interaction focused around a range of communal activities to community building; such interaction must start with some level of conversation. Social interactions within communities of practice were presented in Chapter 4 as important sites for learning, and engaging in conversation within these is probably the most significant act for both conscious and subconscious/incidental learning.

The threats to our students' self-identities explored in the opening chapters of this book were both political and social, including those of deterritorialization, detraditionalization, the loss of grand narratives in which to locate their lives, the continuum construction and destruction of temporary, avatar identities through advancing consumerism, and the commodification of nothing. In Chapter 2 we looked also at various features of and underpinnings for tendencies to avoid engaging in conversations with people dissimilar to ourselves. Among these, also, identity threat serves as a strong psychological force:

The more an individual experiences or cultivates an optimal level of identity security and stability, the more she or he is likely to be open to constructive identity change. The more an individual experiences identity threats ... the more he or she is likely to cling to identity stability.

(Ting-Toomey 1999: 44)

Developing our practice and associated learning environments to enable our students to *get used to each other* and establishing a focus on *community building* are proposed here as fundamental to reducing identity threat and building the kind of personal security amongst alterity from within which more transformative learning might take place. Experiencing inclusive university environments and equitable academic spaces are proposed to be *prerequisites* for conversations among diverse students. As discussed, the first of Allport's (1954/1979) requirements for intercultural encounters to reduce prejudice is for participants to have equal status, and De Vita emphasizes the necessity of making this explicit to all students from the outset:

> ... in the multicultural classroom, no successful pedagogy based on student participation can take place unless at the start of the course the tutor sends an unambiguous message of equality to students, a message that promotes an environment which embraces cultural diversity and within which all students feel they have something significant to contribute.
>
> (De Vita 2000: 175)

Reflective questions

- How equitable do you consider your university spaces to be?
- In what ways does your student induction programme make equality issues explicit in student interactions?

I suggest that messages carried through our hidden curricula are, in many cases, ones which *undermine* equality of status. This section illustrates in particular how stereotyping, categorization and attitudes to language frame our campuses as learning spaces, and how these need to be challenged and reframed if they are not to contribute to identity threat, bolster prejudice, and diminish academic equity. These spaces are the oxygen of the hidden curriculum, and the pervasive environment for the kind of *incidental learning* which I suggested in Chapter 4 to be worthy of more significant attention. Much of this territory has been explored in critical approaches to multicultural education (May 1999), but largely neglected in the discourse surrounding internationalization. We will begin with some observations on stereotyping.

Stereotyping and identification

The stereotyping of international students is not limited to the assumptions concerning their English language capabilities noted in the Introduction to this chapter. Ward (2001b: 14) observes that, as 'the international student population is composed of such a diverse group of individuals, it is somewhat surprising that domestic students share consensual beliefs about them'.

True though this is, we must also reflect upon the degree to which we all, academic, administrative and managerial colleagues, contribute to that consensus. I have certainly, and on several occasions, heard stereotypes from colleagues along the lines that *international students*: 'never ask questions in lectures', 'are always trying to speak to me outside class', 'expect me to change the rules for them', 'walk around campus in groups', are 'unsociable/stand-offish', or are 'hardworking'; less anecdotal research suggests these are not unusual cases (see examples in Barron *et al.* 2010).

Whether or not these are true of some international students is not the point, they are certainly not true of all international students, nor are they true only of international students. These, and other concerns, contribute to what is referred to as the 'deficit' model of the international student (Ippolito 2007; Leask 2009).

Of course, international students are not the only groups to be stereotyped (indeed, Ward's observation above is itself guilty of stereotyping domestic students). Wherever directed, stereotyping and deficit models are not conducive to establishing or maintaining an inclusive environment (they are also, of course, completely at odds with notions such as independent and critical thinking which are frequently espoused as core objectives of higher education). Our university environments will not be inclusive, secure places within which to learn from diverse others and grapple with fragility unless:

(i) stereotyping of any kind is challenged whenever it is encountered among colleagues or students; and
(ii) our students are empowered through their learning experiences to recognize it and to challenge it in themselves and in others.

Reflective questions

- Have you encountered colleagues or students engaging in stereotyping international students or other groups? How did you respond/how would you challenge them?
- Do you see any examples of stereotyping in the images, literature, cultural festivals, or other artefacts and events within your university campus spaces?

In the more formal spaces of our lecture theatres and seminar rooms, there is a related 'identification' issue which adds messages to the hidden curriculum. We need to take care to strike a balance between *including* a student because her perspective might be valuable/different, and expecting or suggesting that she might be a representative for her gender, ethnicity, or nationality (for example). I have been fortunate to live, work and travel in several countries and can attest to how often a foreigner is expected to know about, have an opinion about, and be able to represent the views of his nation about any and every aspect of his home country/culture. The interest of others can be very pleasing (and, of course a great place to start a conversation), but being cast in the role of national ambassador and cultural informant can be wearisome and constraining – and is ultimately an act of othering rather than one of inclusion. In identifying individuals in our learning spaces by an aspect of their difference we risk confining them within that identity, in their own eyes and in the eyes of their peers. It is unlikely (I hope) that a gay student (regardless of how open they might be about their sexuality) would be asked to comment in a lecture about 'how gays think about this'. Yet I have witnessed many similar identifications taking place for international students, including, for example, a Malaysian student wearing a headscarf being asked to comment 'from an Islamic perspective' and another student being asked 'and how do you do this in China?' This second might not have been so unreasonable, were it not for the fact that the student was from South Korea. In such cases, as in other institutional acts of identification which we will explore in Section 4, we find echoes of discussions in Chapter 2 concerning cultural caricaturing and Nussbaum's (1997) notion of descriptive romanticism. An inclusive environment is a space for airing, sharing and critiquing diverse perspectives; this must include building awareness and acceptance that gays, women, Muslims, and Chinese or South Korean students also hold diverse perspectives, and have a right to recognition and a voice as individuals. We need to engage 'with difference within difference' (Luke 2010) and to enable, indeed to *require*, our students to do the same. As I said, there is a balance to be struck here between genuine inclusion, valuing the diverse perspectives which others have to bring, and seeing/ identifying students *as* their otherness. Related excluding acts of identification surround aspects of broader university practices, as briefly explored in Section 4.

Reflective question

- How would you formulate questions which seek to encourage/be inclusive of diverse student perspectives in ways which minimize the risk of reducing a student to being a representative of her nationality, ethnicity, gender, and so forth?

Language matters

As noted, it is often on the basis of judgements on capabilities in English language that distinctions are drawn across the student body. When language is cited in these contexts, what is generally being referred to is a student's command of the grammar, vocabulary, and/or pronunciation of a particular variety of English. The fact that language is so much more than even the sum of these parts, or that all varieties of English are only varieties, are rarely reflected on by the fluent native-speaker (the term *native-speaker* is itself not uncontested, but I think it is helpful in this context since it is with many of those for whom English is their mother tongue and often their only tongue that the issues alluded to here apply most critically). Many native-speakers of English have, of course, mastered one or more other languages, and many in the internationalization field argue that foreign language learning is key to intercultural competence. I am not convinced this is either necessary or sufficient, but do recognize its potential contribution. At least one British university, University College London (UCL), has mandated a level of foreign language competence as a prerequisite to undergraduate entry or as a required study component during a student's degree programme. As a very poor linguist myself, I applaud the move; the fact that any university thinks this necessary, though, might be seen as testament to the lamentable attitude towards foreign languages which permeates many Anglophone communities. This attitude, in a rather ironic twist of logic, often then transforms itself into expectations of exceptional degrees of fluency in English for anybody else the English native-speaker might find herself having to deal with: 'How are we supposed to have a good academic discussion when people don't have a basic grasp of the language we will be having it in?' asked a UK student quoted in Bache and Hayton (2012: 417). Linguistic imperialism is rife on our campuses.

I anticipate that many readers will wish to retaliate that as students have elected to undertake their studies on an Anglophone campus, fluency in English is not an unreasonable expectation. However, it is we – the institution, academic department, or specific programme – who set the conditions a student must meet in order to gain entry; we who have determined both the level of English language a student must have *and* the means by which she must evidence this. Having thus set the bar, surely, it is *our* responsibility thereafter to ensure that all the requirements for participating fully in university life can be met by someone who has successfully jumped it. These requirements include, significantly, the capabilities and willingness of their English speaking peers to play their part in the communication process.

Reflective questions

- How is the English language entry bar set for programmes you are associated with?
- Do you know what that bar actually means in terms of required competence – and if so, do *you* use and expect English language at the level set?

Thinking about this, you may elect to consider raising the bar, but if you do not, then I think you have elected for the possibility of a much richer learning space – but only if you are prepared to take quite radical steps to equalize that space. Of course, a proportion of the international students we admit have skills in English as a foreign language which considerably exceed the minimum requirements we set for admissions (apart from those who first language *is* English). This can contribute to the perceived problem, as those students become the benchmark against which their peers come to be judged. It is also worth noting that weak English language competence (real or perceived) is something which it is easy to cite as the cause of a student's difficulties. This may mask from our attention, and from theirs, other personal, social or academic problems – this is particularly concerning when the language 'problem' is more of our making than theirs.

A radical step I suggest we should be taking, both as a move to equalize our learning spaces, but also as an enabler of the global self among the English native-speaker student population, is to challenge the current locus of responsibility for effective communication. Rather than being solely a requirement for students whose first language is not English to learn to meet the expectations of those for whom it is, an equalized, inclusive, and *more globally appropriate* environment should also require English native-speakers to develop and exhibit capabilities to communicate effectively among those for whom English is not a first language. Although usually cited in connection with non-Anglophone campuses with multilingual student populations, I am advocating here a capability to code switch – as appropriate to the other students (or non-students) present – to something akin to what is referred to as English as a Lingua Franca (ELF). Permutations on ELF include *English as an International Language* (EIL) and *Global English* (Graddol 2006), and for our purposes any of these provides a helpful way to envision a form of *intercultural communication in English* (*ICE* – if we need another acronym). It is relevant to reiterate the point made in Chapter 1 that capability in ELF on campuses beyond the Anglophone world is increasingly expected of *everybody* – students, academics and administrators – as a feature of the growth in English-medium delivery. This is not, of course, uncontentious or uncontested (Preisler *et al.* 2011), but it does suggest it to be a feasible aspiration. One multinational project has reported successfully engaging students across continents in online experience of ELF interactions, albeit it with an employability focus rather than any broader global self rationale (for a brief summary, see Goddard and Henry 2013).

It is safe to assume that very few Anglophone universities will follow the UCL example. However, rather than requiring *foreign* language competence, expecting all students to use English appropriately and effectively in multilingual communities and contexts would be a significant learning opportunity for the often monolingual (domestic or international) English native-speaker. Although it is possible that a variety of English will not always be the global *lingua franca*, it is likely to remain so for a considerable time. Paradoxically perhaps, as implied in the opening quote from David Graddol, what for many has been its highly troubling hegemony is now beginning to work increasingly to the detriment of those for whom English is their first language. While once native-speaker competence was the (largely unattainable) goal and gold standard of the learner of English as a foreign language, this is now less commonly the case. After all, *which* native-speaker might be the model? And *why* should anybody need or want that *specific variety* of English in order to do business with, travel among or engage in conversations with the majority of the global population for whom it is a second or foreign language? Whatever we or our English native-speaker students might think of the language skills of our international students, they are likely to communicate more effectively (be more intelligible and less likely to cause offence) among groups of non-native English speakers than when joined by their English native-speaker peers, whose presence 'hinders communication' (Graddol 2006: 115). There is not (as yet at least) any specified model of ELF, but there are millions of cross-cultural interactions taking place every hour and on every continent in a kind of ELF between people for whom English is not their first language; '[a]pproximately 80 per cent of users of English around the world are bi- or multi-lingual and using English as an additional language' (Wicaksono 2013: 243). At the very least, foreign language skills apart, the 20 per cent minority of English native-speakers would serve themselves well to gain some capacity to operate equally effectively in these contexts. Sharing campus spaces and learning activities which are inclusive towards speakers of ELF offers significant potential for the development of communicative competence better suited to a world increasingly favouring less native-speaker variants of English as a *lingua franca*. It also advances the rather important *disposition* for the global self that in conversations, as in communities, we each hold responsibilities for building communication and supporting the other.

Equally importantly for our concern here is that shifting the onus of responsibility for effective communication towards the dominant group is an act of academic equity, as language dominance impacts considerably on the balance of power within the curriculum (Henderson 2009). Advancing everyone's capabilities in intercultural communicative competence (in English) and redressing some of the current power imbalances wrought by the privileging of native-speaker varieties

Figure 5.1 Some characteristics which might be evidenced by more effective intercultural communicators (in English)

To enact such a shift more broadly requires interventions in curriculum and its associated learning and assessment experiences, and across the wider functions of the university, as we will explore in subsequent sections. Figure 5.1 provides an indication of some of the characteristics which might be evidenced by more effective intercultural communicators in English; as noted above these include but go far beyond what might be termed the formal systems of the language itself. Underpinning such expectations for students, of course, must be that university colleagues also work on their own capabilities in this regard.

Reflective questions

- Is it reasonable that having set a language competence bar, we create learning activities, spaces and expectations which align to the competencies that bar requires?
- Is it reasonable, or too radical, to expect English native-speaker students on Anglophone campuses to be required to develop and exhibit the capabilities of effective and inclusive intercultural communication – to engage in intercultural communication in English in ways which help equalize the learning spaces they occupy?
- Do you see value for English native-speaker students in developing their capabilities to engage effectively in intercultural communication in English in situations beyond university?

Reflective task

If you are an English native-speaker, or a speaker of English as a second language, refer to Figure 5.1 and create an opportunity to monitor your own use of English (perhaps by recording a seminar or lecture) against the suggested characteristics of a good intercultural communicator in English.

This section has provided examples of stereotyping and categorization which contribute to the hidden curriculum of our campus spaces. These, coupled with (and at times in league with) often highly parochial and chauvinistic attitudes towards non-native-speaker English language use, contribute to non-inclusive learning environments. Inclusive environments are a prerequisite for equitable academic opportunity as well as for intercultural learning. However, additional, more direct, interventions in curriculum design and delivery are also needed to support students (international and domestic) into intercultural conversations and communities, and to ensure we provide 'equably for the learning ambitions of all students, irrespective of their national, ethnic, cultural, social class/caste or gender identities' (Haigh, M. J. 2002: 51).

and outcomes

> It is the mass of accumulated knowledge that has become the contemporary epitome of disorder and chaos. In that mass, all orthodox ordering devices – topics of relevance, assignment of importance, usefulness-determining needs and value-determining authorities – have been progressively shrunk and dissolved ... Assigning importance to various bits of information, and even more assigning to some more importance than to others, is perhaps the most perplexing task and the most difficult decision to take.
>
> (Bauman 2005: 49)

> ... the intercultural experience should be part of the general discourse and should not be marginalised and placed at the edges of disciplines; rather it should be made central to the way in which all disciplines are taught.
>
> (Sen Gupta 2003: 161)

This section is concerned principally with the *design* of the formal curriculum, that which is set down as the content, outcomes, and modes of assessment of a unit of study. Practice in how these are expressed varies across and beyond Anglophone countries; however some underlying principles may not. All students experience their academic life and learning through 'units of study' of various sizes. These can be combined in various ways according to national, institutional, and programme-level traditions and regulations. In any context, though, published course documentation should make clear to students:

(i) what a unit of study is about;
(ii) what they will be expected to be able to do at the end of it;
(iii) how that ability will be assessed; and
(iv) how they are expected to engage with their learning journey, and how they will be supported to do so.

Point (iv) is the focus of the next section on 'Shaping the Delivery' (I use 'delivery' as it is a common term for the way in which learning experiences are constructed and enacted in higher education, but it is not really suitable for the constructivist learning model favoured in this book, in which learning is something constructed by the learner rather than something which is or can be 'delivered' by the teacher). Significant differences exist with regard to how units of study might be combined to construct a programme leading to a named award, with, for example, typically much greater flexibility for students in North American institutions, and much tighter structuring in the UK (where many degree programmes prescribe every unit of study, and most will allow only for choices between a very limited number of electives). What follows refers to what we might call the *core curriculum* – that which is studied by *every* student working towards a specific award. It is absolutely not adequate to our task to relegate/delegate this work to non-mandated *General Education* courses, to elective modules which might be avoided, to generic 'personal and professional skills' modules, or to optional elements within the informal curriculum.

Curriculum content

... the global context surrounding issues in each academic field of study needs to be reflected in the organization of majors, degree programs, and coursework at both undergraduate and graduate levels. Lending a global flavour to these structures not only underscores the significance a university attaches to the globally informed creation and management of knowledge but also makes available increasingly crucial opportunities for students and faculty to center their efforts of knowledge creation and acquisition on issues and skills holding global and collective significance that, in turn, can be applied to a variety of geographic contexts.

(Rhoads and Szelényi 2011b: 281)

One might suggest that a university that hopes to prepare students adequately for supercomplexity and uncertainty would offer an undergraduate program that affords rich opportunities for students to be exposed to conflicting frames of reference.

(Kreber 2009: 16)

The idealized *Renaissance Man* of sixteenth- and seventeenth-century Europe was a polymath able to discourse on any significant current knowledge across all areas of enquiry. What has been uncovered for us to know has grown exponentially since then. Additionally, much twenty-first-century knowledge often becomes quickly outdated, may be rapidly exposed as contested and contestable, and remains always ('radically') incomplete. To the extent to which this is true of our globalizing, consuming, and technologically advancing world, defining curriculum content around a tightly constrained set of knowledge might be interpreted as a restricting and counter-educational task. Counter-educational because the valorization of current (or more likely somewhat less than current) knowledge, and associated requirements to reproduce that knowledge or to work within its confines might be argued to inhibit sceptical inquiry and independent thinking, and to do little to prepare students to make their way in a world where little is certain for long. In that sense, such approaches to curriculum design might also be seen as inefficient even in an education-for-employability paradigm. Of course, we cannot denude our curriculum of content, but we can examine how that content is *selected, presented* and *engaged with*. These are complex and interrelated questions, the first concerns the *sources and contexts* we use to frame the content of our curriculum, the second concerns the degree to which we recognize and explore how others may relate to that knowledge (is it presented as a 'fact' or as a 'truth'; are associated ethical issues considered, for example), and the third concerns the degree to which we require and enable our students to take a critical stance towards that knowledge, including the degree to which we expose, and so enable our students to expose, the friability or 'fragility' (Barnett, R. 2000) of any clear and present truth. This, in and of itself, may represent highly troublesome knowledge (Meyer and Land 2003), but is a learning threshold which must be crossed in any approach to education as freedom in a globalizing world.

Selecting curriculum content from culturally diverse contexts (what Welikala, 2011 refers to as a 'multi-perspective curriculum' in part to acknowledge that such diversity can derive from local as well as more distant contexts, but also in recognition of the *individual* diversity which is to be found within national or other cultural groupings) is not in itself an easy task when we are often ourselves immersed in a particular academic tradition with its associated canon. Consider as one example: 'I have been very conscious of the fact that almost all the data of social psychology comes from individualist cultures. Yet, the overwhelming majority of humans live in collectivist cultures' (Triandis 2001: 37).

Although the validity of any fundamental Western–non-Western differences of this kind have been challenged in this book and elsewhere (Cousin 2011), I think we can recognize that content which derives mostly or exclusively from a single cultural context is likely to be limiting in terms of its:

- relevance/authenticity to a diverse student body;
- capacity to enable students to see their subject area from diverse perspectives; and
- potential to engage students in a critical review of their own values or practices.

As already discussed, relevance/authenticity are important aspects of inclusivity. Most learning theorists would also recognize that '[s]ignificant learning occurs when the learner perceives the relevance of the subject matter' (Rogers 1969: 157), something highlighted as particularly salient in Knowles' (1980) theories of *adult* learning. Sourcing content (including key texts, case studies, graphics, etc.) from globally/locally diverse contexts and 'authored by people from different cultures' (Stone 2006: 412) is, then, proposed to be integral to curriculum internationalization. To be clear, there is no objective here for students to learn about any specific culture; as in the discussions around intercultural competence in Chapter 2, this is *culture-general* learning along the lines of, *there are other cultures, mine is another culture, cultures sometimes do things differently, these differences are interesting and a potential source of learning, for example...*

Reflective question

- Thinking of a unit of study you are familiar with, what proportion of the content do you think derives from/is based within *a global context which differs in significant ways* from that of your institutional and national context?

As noted in Chapter 1, although it is necessary to utilize widely sourced content in your curriculum, this is also argued to be insufficient it itself; characterized as an 'add-on' approach if achieved through a kind of retro-fit to existing curriculum, and an 'infusion' approach if achieved more systematically. Both of these approaches are characterized as continuing to frame the alternative (whether international or inter-cultural) content and contexts through Anglophone or Western paradigms (Bond 2003; De Vita and Case 2003; Mestenhauser 1998). Our *framing* of selected content is in part concerned with whether/how/which related local/global issues are brought to bear in its examination. Doug Bourn, for example, argues the need for university curricula to 'recognise the impact of changing global forces, continuing inequalities in the world, sustainable development and climate change, the fragmentation of communities and the subsequent desire for national and global identities' (Bourn 2011: 563). These issues (and others) may not in themselves be appropriate as direct areas of focus for many disciplines, but *framing* disciplinary knowledge and practice within such considerations where there are relevant linkages would seem entirely appropriate for our global students. This has been more broadly captured in the notion of 'global imagination' (Rizvi n.d.: 5), that is 'the capacity to determine how knowledge is globally linked, no matter how locally specific its uses.' In Chapter 2 I alluded to Rawls' influential metaphor of siting ourselves behind a veil of ignorance in order to make impartial decisions because we are ignorant of where we sit within the society in which those decisions will be enacted. In reality, however, our students, like ourselves and the rest of society, do not see the world from behind such a perfect veil. Rather, they see how they sit in the world largely through the less objectifying veil of their own socio-political and cultural perspectives. Perspectives which are unlikely to be challenged when their disciplinary curriculum is presented through similarly narrowly selected and framed sources.

Such considerations of the way our selected content is presented and framed moves us towards what is referred to as a 'transformative' approach to curriculum internationalization, which 'requires a shift in the ways in which we understand the world'(Bond, op. cit.: 8), and may involve what Caruana (2007: 18) describes as a 'pedagogy of recognition' which 'engages students in a critical relationship with texts and theories, enabling them to deconstruct their own lives and to imagine alternatives'. For Kubow *et al.* (2000: 139) a curriculum for *multidimensional citizenship* similarly requires the provision of 'a deliberative and reflective framework' in order that students are enabled to 'understand their multiple roles at all levels'. The transformative approach can be further advanced if students are enabled and required to engage with curriculum content in ways that involve them not only critically engaging *with* texts and theories, but also taking a critical stance *towards* texts and theories *per se*. When successful, such a transformative approach is argued to enable students to feel comfortable amongst alterity, and capable, even, of shifting their perspectives between differing worldviews. Not because they have achieved an extreme form of relativism, but because they hold, essentially, an equally critical/sceptical stance towards *all* claims to truth. This seems to me to be entirely congruent with notions of what *higher* education is about, and I extract at length below from Brookfield's (1987: 7–9) presentation of the *components of critical thinking* to illustrate how strongly this central notion in higher education reflects the discussion above regarding transformative curriculum internationalization:

1   *Identifying and challenging assumptions is central to critical thinking.*
2   *Challenging the importance of context is crucial to critical thinking.*

When we are aware of how hidden and uncritically assimilated assumptions are important to shaping our habitual perceptions, understandings, and interpretations of the world, and to influencing the behaviors that result from these interpretations, we become aware of how context influences thoughts and actions.

3   *Critical thinkers try to imagine and explore alternatives.*

Central to critical thinking is the capacity to imagine and explore alternatives to existing ways of thinking and living ... Being aware of how context shapes what they consider normal and natural ways of thinking and living, critical thinkers realize that in other contexts entirely different norms ... are considered ordinary. These contexts are scrutinized for assumptions that might be adopted and integrated into their own lives.

4   *Imagining and exploring alternatives leads to reflective scepticism.*

When we realize that alternatives to supposedly fixed belief systems, habitual behaviors, and entrenched social structures always exist, we become sceptical of claims to universal truth or to ultimate explanations.

For our enterprise, I would add that a critical thinking global self also (and perhaps even 'chiefly' as these authors suggest) 'questions the appropriateness or moral relevance of the action' (Papestephenou and Angeli 2007: 608, cited in Walker 2010: 227).

Internationalizing our curriculum, therefore, entails ourselves adopting a critical stance towards the cultural range of its content *per se*, of the ways in which such content is then framed, and of the degree to which we enable and require our students to engage critically with all content as a mechanism to develop their global imagination.

Before we leave this discussion, it is worth noting a few potential objections to relinquishing more locally based content, and a couple of examples of how what may appear/claim to be globally relevant curriculum may not be so. First, is it not reasonable for a (say) British degree in a British university accessed entirely or predominantly by British students to build its content around British contexts, practice, and perspectives? Clearly not if we accept the impacts of globalization on individual identity and social meaning-making, the nature of identity formation, and the requirements for learning dilemmas drawn in the earlier chapters in this book. Even if you never see an international student and remain sceptical about the aims of developing the 'global self', those chapters also point towards more pragmatic rationales for diversifying curriculum content and the complexity of the student's relationship with it. Of course, some British degrees (for example) do require very clear anchoring within British practice, typically where this is mandated by professional, subject or regulatory bodies (PSRBs). Even here, though, there is scope and need for students to draw upon practice elsewhere, to provide a critical perspective *from which* to examine local practice, as a vehicle to build capabilities to apply the practice among locally diverse populations, as a dimension to global graduate employability, and as 'citizens acting on the basis of more informed global understandings' (Rhoads and Szelényi 2011b: 278).

With regard to the second issue – claims for global relevance – I have reviewed and critiqued curriculum content with colleagues across a wide range of disciplines in a number of institutions. A few, but only a few, have argued that their particular curriculum has no need for anything other than local content. Very many, though, have argued that 'of course' global content is necessary, and 'of course' it is present. Closer inspection, though, has often revealed that where it is present it is minimally so (added-in rather than infused) and often far from being truly diverse/international. I give just two examples to illustrate this, both drawn from subject areas which we would probably expect to be inherently international in their orientation. First, an 'International Business' degree. The module titles, aims, and objectives were peppered with 'international', and content areas similarly so. However, 'international' was soon exposed to refer to contexts where *Western* business philosophy and practice abounded and their validity was cited as fact (not truth), so lending support to rather than offering critiques of dominant business models and theories. Indeed, cited examples were further limited to Anglophone companies in Anglophone countries. The second example is a French language degree. How could such a degree not be international? Several modules, as is common in modern foreign language degrees, involved contextualizing the language with authentic examples of its use, and looking at aspects of the social and cultural practices of its speakers. The limiting factors, though, were (i) that the authentic examples and social and cultural practices were all drawn from French contexts *not* from the wider Francophone world, and (ii) even here they focused on mainstream French socio-cultural contexts and practices, ignoring, for example, immigrant varieties of French, minority cultural positionings and practices in France, and so forth. This provided a sanitized and unproblematized construct of French society and culture, did little to prepare students to communicate in anything much removed from standard French, and (I would argue) served to alienate students from the subject by divorcing French life from the complexities of their own socio-cultural experience. All that aside from more significant (in terms of global selves) missed opportunities for 'pedagogic recognition' and reflection upon others' lives and values in order to critique own cultural practices, assumptions, and place in the world, for example.

The brief description of these two examples provides an indication of what a critical examination of curriculum content for any unit of study might reveal. To facilitate such an examination, the reflective task in Table 5.1 sets out questions which might form the basis of a review of curriculum *content* in any discipline area, with the caveats, though, that not all questions will be *equally* relevant in all subjects, and that it will always be necessary to shape generic questions to the particulars of your own subject, students, and broader educational and professional contexts (Leask 2008). Questions refer to the 'unit of study', so can be considered for modules, courses, programmes, etc. – though ideally they should be reviewed from whole programme level down to individual classes and learning resources. The questions are developed from a publication on embedding cross-cultural capability and global perspectives utilized in one institution-wide curriculum review process, now available under a Creative Commons Licence for free adaptation (Killick 2006).

The next part of our discussion on curriculum design, concerns how we articulate what it is that we expect students *to be* and *to be able to do* as a result of their engagement with it. This takes us first into a discussion on *graduate attributes* and how these might be used to frame generic student capabilities, and then into a discussion on the role of and the formulation of *intended learning outcomes* as a mechanism to embed and contextualize those graduate attribute aspirations within a unit of study.

Table 5.1 Reflective task: Curriculum review

Consider the content of a unit of study you are familiar with against these selected questions for curriculum review:

Question	Your response
How does/could the content of the unit of study incorporate the knowledge and understanding brought to it by students from diverse backgrounds?	
How are students/could students be given the opportunity to analyse and recognize the impact of their own tacit knowledge and the influence of their biographies and cultural identity in their responses to the content of the unit of study?	
How does/could the content of the unit of study make students aware of the global impacts of professions/activities related to the subject area?	
How does/could the content of the unit of study enable other perspectives on areas of knowledge to be recognized and valued?	
How does/could the content of the unit of study encourage students to be curious beyond their own cultural boundaries?	

Graduate attributes

> [The] more manageable place to start is with something like graduate attributes. What, we might ask, would cosmopolitan and multiculturally aware graduates be in the second decade of the 21st century? What could we reasonably expect such graduates to be able to do? And what knowledge and expertise would enable them to be what they need to be and to do what they need to do?
>
> (Donald 2007: 296)

> Knowledge remains important, but the focus is no longer knowledge transfer or acquisition. Instead, knowing is understood as created, embodied and enacted. In other words, the question for students would be not only what they know, but also who they are becoming.
>
> (Dall'Alba and Barnacle 2007: 683)

As alluded to in Chapter 1, the aims and objectives of Anglophone higher education have to a large extent been deconstructed into somewhat atomized units of study, each with its prescribed intended learning outcomes. Despite sharing many of the reservations about such outcomes-based approaches, I will spend some time later in this chapter advocating for significant attention to be paid to learning outcomes as drivers of the student learning experience. In more recent times, and perhaps in some cases as an attempt to regain something of a more holistic understanding of graduateness, there have been moves to introduce generic graduate attributes or qualities into university characterizations of their students. Statements of graduate attributes were *required* of Australian universities (Leask 2001), and have since been or are in the process of being voluntarily adopted by some institutions in other countries. Notably, there are related moves in some universities to reformulate atomized programme structures into fewer and larger units of study (molecularization?).

The mandated Australian experience of introducing graduate attribute/outcome statements seems not to have been wholly successful. Simon Barrie's research (2004, 2006, 2007) has revealed a number of issues. The degree to which academic staff understand, associate with, and actively construct learning and assessment experiences to foster the attributes seems the most serious:

> The extent to which the rhetoric of [graduate attribute] statements actually represents a shared understanding of the outcomes of a university education is a matter of conjecture. The extent to which present day university teaching and learning processes actually develop such outcomes in graduates is even more contestable.
>
> (Barrie 2006: 216)

However, the aspirations for the global student envisioned in this book are capabilities which I am proposing to be appropriate for all students across all disciplines, albeit with the need to contextualize them to each specific subject. As such, they represent a form of graduate attribute – and setting out with some clarity what that may look like will help frame student expectations and formulate learning outcomes. The weaknesses identified by Barrie in the Australian experience might derive in large measure from a failure to engage academics in the process of *embedding* generic attributes in their subject-level learning outcomes.

In Chapter 1 I set out a model for the global self founded upon how our students come to see them *selves-in-the-world*, and the capabilities they build to *act-in-the-world*; broadly, identity and agency. I also proposed that learning associated with these might be broken down into learning which is *globally relevant* by being situated in a global context and learning being enacted within and built from the principles and practice of *inclusivity*. As noted, these derive directly from work undertaken in my own institution to define one of three graduate attributes introduced across the undergraduate curriculum. The attribute was articulated as 'having a global outlook' (Jones and Killick 2013; Killick 2011), and billed as: 'Enabling effective and responsible engagement in a multicultural and globalising world' (the other two attributes were being *digitally literate* and *enterprising*). I have no doubt that there is scope for developing and further contextualizing this attribute, and anybody seeking to frame attributes and learning objectives for their own students must, in any case, start from their own contexts. However, it does provide *a* model to illustrate the more general principle that overarching visions of what constitute a graduate need to be articulated *before* formulating subject-level learning outcomes and their associated learning and assessment activities. Whether these are set down as 'graduate attributes' is a lesser issue than that they are set down and articulated clearly to students.

Work to set down the capabilities we might deem appropriate for people who dwell in a culturally complex world is not new, and I would suggest there is much of relevance to the global student in work published over twenty years ago (which acknowledges work from almost twenty years before that (Hanvey 1976)). Case (1993: 321–324) set out five key elements associated with a global perspective as a 'central goal of adult education':

1 *open-mindedness* – 'a willingness to base our beliefs on the impartial consideration of available evidence' and 'a willingness to *assess* our world views';
2 *anticipation of complexity* – 'the inclination to look beyond simplistic explanations of complex ethical and empirical issues and to see global phenomena as part of a constellation of interrelated factors';
3 *resistance to stereotyping* – 'a skepticism about the adequacy of accounts of people, cultures, or nations that either are limited to a narrow range of characteristics … or depict little or no diversity within them' and a resistance to posing 'we–they dualisms';
4 *inclination to empathize* – 'a willingness and capacity to place ourselves in the role or predicament of others or at least to imagine issues from other individuals' or groups' perspectives' requiring also 'suspending … our own feelings'; and
5 *nonchauvinism* – 'the inclination neither to prejudice or other judgements of others because we are not affiliated with them, nor to discount unfairly the interests of others even if, on occasion, they are incompatible with our own interests' including 'presentism' i.e. a focus on current generations to the exclusion of future generations.

We looked at Berry's (1990a, 1994, 2005) model indicating how attitudinal responses influence acculturation patterns in Chapter 2 and explored in Chapter 3 how the power of attitudes and heuristics play out in driving behaviour generally and in our responses to others in particular. Unsurprisingly, then, the preponderance of attitudes is immediately apparent in how Case (and many if not all other global citizenship and related taxonomies) frames expectations regarding student capabilities (notably here – 'willingness' and 'inclination'). With regard to Case's 'inclination to empathize', commentators on both cosmopolitanism and citizenship in a globalizing world (Appadurai 1997, 2001; Appiah 2006; Elliot 2001; Falk 2002; Nussbaum 1997) give some emphasis to the capacity of *imagination*, in terms of imagining the worlds we inhabit/roles we play, imagining ourselves, and imagining others and the world in their eyes. Case (1993: 323) also points out that 'the ability to sensitively imagine another's perspective requires suspending, however temporarily, our own feelings', representing a further affective capability. As has already been noted a number of times in earlier chapters, universities typically focus their attention on cognitive capabilities, but as has also been noted several times, and as is apparent in its principal dimension of *self-in-the-world*, the affective dimension to being is fundamental to the global student and the global self. The essential invisibility of our affective capabilities, at least in terms of formal assessment of student learning (we cannot measure 'willingness' to act, only the capability to carry out the action), excludes the affective dimension from appearing in learning outcomes (see the requirements for these in the next section). However, I think we can articulate aspects of the affective dimension within descriptions of graduate attributes. The process of embedding those graduate attributes at subject level then requires making explicit the observable capabilities which are *consistent with* these affective attributes. I have to admit that this is somewhat messy and the resulting measurement of student achievement will be imperfect, but I have yet to see a better proposal. A messy and imperfect solution seems better than no solution at all, and the more we develop our own capabilities in this, the less messy the process might become.

The proposal for practice here, then, is that an important starting point for the consideration of an internationalized curriculum is the careful articulation of the affective, behavioural and cognitive attributes of our ideal graduate. With this to hand, the work of contextualizing it with subject learning outcomes can begin.

Reflective task

Taking as your starting point the questions in the quote from Donald which opened this section, construct your own graduate attribute statement:

- What would cosmopolitan and multiculturally aware graduates be in the second decade of the twenty-first century?
- What could we reasonably expect such graduates to be able to do?
- And what attitudes, knowledge and skills would enable them to be what they need to be and to do what they need to do?'

Intended learning outcomes

> The vocabulary, the ideas and the conceptualisation of what it is to be a student and to educate for such student being do not live in the same educational universe as inhabited by the outcomes approach.
>
> (Barnett, R. 2007: 5)

Along with others (Hussey and Smith 2002, 2008), I have a good deal of sympathy with Barnett's rejection of outcomes as adequate to the complex task of framing what it is our graduates must be. And my imperfect solution offered in the previous section involved utilizing graduate attribute statements to achieve a more holistic description of our aspirations for our students. However, as indicated earlier, students (and lecturers) need clear guidance on what it is they are expected to be able to *evidence* as a result of a unit of study. This is commonly expressed in the form of module/course learning outcomes. Since learning, in the broadly constructivist model presented in Chapter 4 of this book, is a process of individual lifeworld *construction*, influenced significantly by a learner's prior learning through their unique biographies, and by incidental learning through, for example, the hidden curriculum, it is more accurate to describe these as the *intended* learning outcomes – some learners may not achieve them, and all learners will gain some other learning from their engagement in the learning activities and their journeying through university life more broadly. It is, however, measuring the degree to which they have achieved the *intended* learning outcomes which should structure their assessment, and be the basis upon which grade decisions are made. In reality, regardless of any other learning, these are the *required* learning outcomes for a graduate with this award from this institution at this point in time. Through a process of 'constructive alignment' (Biggs 1999; Biggs and Tang 2011), academics responsible for the unit of study then design both the assessment and the learning experiences to support the students in achieving those intended/required outcomes. In this model of curriculum design, it is immediately apparent that the laid down intended learning outcomes of a unit of study are extremely powerful drivers, and as such they require significant attention when being developed. The basic principles, which are extensively rehearsed in the literature on good practice in higher education (for example, Baume 2009; Biggs and Tang 2011; Race 2006; Stefani 2009), can be summarized as below.

Intended learning outcomes should:

- be framed around 'action' verbs describing what a student should be able to *do* as a result of engaging in the unit of study;
- describe outcomes which are visible and measurable;
- describe outcomes which can be 'exhibited' in an assessment situation; and
- describe outcomes which are appropriate to the level of study.

Given how firmly established these principles are in Anglophone higher education and 'more recently also in other OECD countries' (Nusche 2008: 8), it is surprisingly common to find learning outcomes which do not correspond to some or all of the criteria. A most common fault is to find outcomes which set out capabilities which cannot be observed (and, therefore, not measured), such as:

> At the end of this module, students will be able to *understand* or *value* [concept *x*].

Since neither understanding nor valuing are directly visible, then depending on the level of study, examples of more appropriate verbs would be:

> *describe, present, contrast, analyse, delineate, synthesize, evaluate, critically assess, (etc.)*

The literature on good practice in curriculum design, for example within the much cited SOLO taxonomy (Biggs and Collins 1982), also has a lot to say about 'levelness', and in many cases national subject benchmark statements will set out detailed discipline-specific taxonomies (see, for example, QAA 2013). As noted in earlier chapters, as with Bloom's seminal work (1956), these taxonomies are largely structured around cognitive capabilities, and sometimes around behavioural skills, such as *be able to present* in the list above (though with little reference to the related taxonomy of the psychomotor (behavioural) domain (Simpson 1972). Perhaps for reasons noted in the previous section, the third taxonomy (Krathwohl *et al.* 1964) and a later work by Kaplan (1978), covering the *affective domain* are also rather less frequently referenced:

> A considerable part of the hesitation in the use of affective measures for grading purposes stems from the inadequacy of the appraisal techniques and the ease with which the student may exploit his ability to detect the response which will be rewarded and the response which will be penalised.
>
> (Krathwohl *et al.* 1964: 17)

As these authors go on to explore, however, there may be more fundamental reasons for resisting the incorporation of intended affective outcomes in our university curricula:

> A much more serious reason for the hesitation in the use of affective measures for grading purposes comes from somewhat deeper philosophical and cultural values. Achievement, competence, productivity, etc., are regarded as public matters ... In contrast, one's beliefs, attitudes, values, and personality characteristics are more likely to be regarded as private; I may reveal them if I wish, but no one can force me to do so.
>
> (Krathwohl *et al.*, op. cit.: 17–18)

Krathwohl *et al.*'s affective taxonomy was developed in part through consideration of some previous unsuccessful attempts to encapsulate affective attitudes (for example, looking at the attitude of *being interested in*, they cite a range of vague and/or vaguely qualified outcomes leading from *being aware of* a subject, through *avidly seeking* information about it, and *feeling positive* towards it, to *being fairly enamoured* by it). Their own taxonomy is based upon the importance which the particular phenomenon plays in an individual's life, which they characterize as 'internalization'. Table 5.2 takes one example which might be relevant to a curriculum for the global student from each of their levels. This does not at all do justice to the full taxonomy and the thoughtful work underpinning it. However, it does illustrate that, in the main, even this work does not present us directly with a tool for the development of intended learning outcomes which meet the criteria set out above. However, it does provide a tool for considering what kind of observable and measurable outcomes within the cognitive and/or behavioural domains might *be commensurate with* the kinds of affective learning required for the global student, including in 4.1, some degree of concern for future generations.

The reflective task in Table 5.3 offers some illustrative examples of generic learning outcomes which could be observable and measurable in an assessment situation, set aside the affective outcomes listed in Table 5.2. These intended outcomes are not discipline-specific, and, as previously emphasized, to truly embed them in a module, course, or programme requires constructing subject-specific outcomes in such a way that aspects of a global outlook are tied into disciplinary requirements. The reflective task, therefore, asks you to modify these to fit a specific subject area which you are familiar with. The principle for practice here, based upon the notion of incidental learning discussed in

Table 5.2 Selected examples from the taxonomy of the affective domain

1.1	Awareness of the feelings of others whose activities are of little interest to ourselves.
1.2	Accepts as associates and co-helpers, in everyday undertakings, other human beings without regard to race, religion, or national origin.
1.3	Alertness toward human values and judgements on life as they are recorded in literature.
2.1	Willingness to force oneself to participate with others.
2.2	Participates actively and thoughtfully in group discussions, with growing awareness of audience.
2.3	Takes pleasure in conversing with many different types of people.
3.1	Grows in his sense of kinship with human beings of all nations.
3.2	Interest in enabling other persons to attain satisfaction of basic common needs.
3.3	Loyalty to the social goals of a free society and a world community.
4.1	Forms judgements as to the responsibility of society for conserving human and material resources.
4.2	Judges people of various races, cultures, national origins, and occupations in terms of their behaviours as individuals.
5.3	Readiness to revise judgements and to change behaviour in the light of evidence.
5.4	Develops a conscience.

Source: Krathwohl *et al.*, 1964.

Selected examples from Krathwohl et al.	Indicative generic observable intended outcome. At the end of this unit of study, you will be able to...
1.1 Awareness of the feelings of others whose activities are of little interest to ourselves.	describe situations in which the lives of people of other cultures and geographical contexts are negatively impacted by decisions taken elsewhere.
Modification:[a]	
1.2 Accepts as associates and co-helpers, in everyday undertakings, other human beings without regard to race, religion, or national origin.	identify how the contributions of diverse others have enhanced the outcomes of your group work.
Modification:	
1.3 Alertness toward human values and judgements on life as they are recorded in literature.	identify values and judgements on life in media from a variety of contexts.
Modification:	
2.1 Willingness to force oneself to participate with others.	engage with co-researchers from diverse socio-cultural backgrounds to complete a research project.
Modification:	
2.2 Participates actively and thoughtfully in group discussions, with growing awareness of audience.	present your own ideas effectively for contexts involving speakers of English as a second or foreign language.
Modification:	

(Continued)

Selected examples from Krathwohl et al.	Indicative generic observable intended outcome. At the end of this unit of study, you will be able to…
2.3 Takes pleasure in conversing with many different types of people.	participate in debate, demonstrating mindfulness and respect for the ideas of others.
Modification:	
3.1 Grows in his sense of kinship with human beings of all nations.	identify commonalities and differences in aspects of your own life and values with those of peers living in a significantly different global context.
Modification:	
3.2 Interest in enabling other persons to attain satisfaction of basic common needs.	identify and analyse examples of actions related to your discipline impact negatively on the lives of those on another continent.
Modification:	
3.3 Loyalty to the social goals of a free society and a world community.	evaluate how aspects of your own freedoms would be impacted by living in another society.
Modification:	
4.1 Forms judgements as to the responsibility of society for conserving human and material resources.	analyse the impact on energy consumption over the next fifty years if all human beings matched the average in your own society.
Modification:	

4.2 Judges people of various races, cultures, national origins, and occupations in terms of their behaviours as individuals.	critically deconstruct the practice of stereotyping and present etic and emic interpretations of your own and others' cultural practices.
Modification:	
5.3 Readiness to revise judgements and to change behaviour in the light of evidence.	present alternative solutions to a given problem based upon contrasting human priorities.
Modification:	
5.4 Develops a conscience.	develop a reasoned and ethical argument to support a proposed course of action.
Modification:	

Note: a Where relevant and appropriate, modify the generic examples of observable intended learning outcomes which may contribute to affective development through related incidental learning, by contextualising them to a specific area of study you are familiar with.

Table 5.4 Examples of intended learning outcome modifications to embed aspects of the graduate attribute of having a global outlook

Original learning outcome Students will be able to…	Modified learning outcome Students will be able to…	Comment

To illustrate the point that a global outlook is not limited to 'international' knowledge, the first example is adapted from a single subject which is already international in its focus:

analyse market opportunities in the international business environment.	analyse market opportunities in two contrasting international business environments.	There is scope in the original learning outcome (LO) to assume homogeneity across international business environments, and no requirement to seek out differences which might set markets apart. In this case, we have limited it to two environments to encourage 'deeper' engagement, but of course it might be that a broad range would be more appropriate for the module/cohort/level.

(Continued)

Table 5.4 (Continued)

Original learning outcome Students will be able to…	Modified learning outcome Students will be able to…	Comment
The following are examples where multicultural/international dimensions are very likely to be assumed/inherent/understood/deeply embedded in the discipline/profession – and which are here modified only to make this explicit and transparent to all stakeholders:		
debate the ethical responsibilities of science in society with reference to current issues.	debate the ethical responsibilities of science with reference to current issues in a multicultural society.	The location of ethical issues in a multicultural society might be implicit, but making it explicit directs students' attention and makes it less likely to be overlooked when devising content/assessment.
consider how different kinds of bodies (for example, fat, thin, old, impaired, sporty, 'fit'), and their various meanings, are socially constructed.	consider how different kinds of bodies (for example, fat, thin, old, impaired, sporty, 'fit'), and their various meanings, are socially constructed by different communities.	This is an example of how this LO might be altered to explicitly take into account different local or global communities and their socio-cultural constructions of the body, perhaps helping develop greater critical awareness of own culture 'norms'.
The following is from a highly UK-centric subject area, where students are focusing on UK/English practice. The modification can be seen to enhance skills and/or critical understanding of the core subject through the 'external' element:		
identify and describe key issues which have been created and debated due to changes in the modern British education system since 1988.	identify and describe key issues which have been created and debated due to changes in the modern British education system since 1988 with reference to contrasting practice in one other national context.	This change has moved the depth of engagement required, and may have thereby lost a breadth which is required within the module. It has, though, brought students to engage with British issues/debates/ changes from a more informed perspective – perhaps enabling them to view established norms from a more critical stance.

Chapter 4, is that by structuring experiences and assessments around appropriate cognitive and behavioural outcomes, the *likelihood* of associated affective learning taking place is enhanced. Note that 2.2 in the table is an example of how learning outcomes can be drafted to embed the development and performance of intercultural communication in English competences as discussed in Section 1 of this chapter.

As an extension to this reflective task, you might find it interesting to review the set of illustrative verbs with related examples of activities linked to each level of the affective domain developed at Indiana University (Centre for the Study of Global Change n.d.).

In more general terms, curriculum internationalization requires a deliberate process of examining all learning outcomes to ensure that the capabilities/attributes of the global student (such as those you set out in the attribute statement task previously) become embedded throughout a programme of study.

Table 5.4 is adapted from a guidance document (Killick 2011) for curriculum review to embed the global outlook attribute described earlier, with its dimensions of inclusivity and global relevance, (a more detailed discussion this institution-wide project is provided by Jones and Killick 2013). It provides illustrations of modifications to subject learning outcomes which retain the subject focus but add or enhance inclusivity and global relevance dimensions.

There are also more generic approaches to the design of learning outcomes which embed attributes of the global student. For example, as in 2.2 in Table 5.3, with respect to students being able to communicate more effectively across cultures and among users of English as a second or foreign language, requirements concerning this can be added to many learning outcomes which require the use of English. Further examples would be: *Students will be able to...*

- *present an analysis of* [subject specific topic] *appropriately for an audience of diverse cultures and first languages.*
- *respectfully engage in critical debate concerning* [subject specific topic] *with others from diverse cultural backgrounds.*
- *conduct primary research involving participants from a range of cultural backgrounds.*

Reflective task

Consider the learning outcomes associated with one unit of study which you are familiar with. Setting these beside the aspirations for the global student set out in this book (or beside the graduate attribute statement you produced earlier) can you make modifications to any of them which will retain their subject focus while embedding aspects of inclusivity or global relevance?

Having looked at the content and the ways in which we define the aims and outcomes of an internationalized curriculum, the next section considers our practice in providing learning experiences to support those outcomes.

Section 3: Shaping the delivery – learning experiences and communities

While the presence of international students on campus is welcomed ... their presence in the classroom does not contribute to the internationalization of the course or the teaching pedagogies. The presence of foreign students does not even make a positive impact on the education of domestic students except in limited situations where the pedagogic approach enables students to share their individual knowledge and experience.

(Bond 2003: 14)

Research has shown that the presence of international students, even in large numbers, is insufficient in itself to promote intercultural interactions, to develop intercultural friendships and to result in international understanding. Rather, situations must be structured to foster these processes.

(Ward 2001b: 5)

The research suggests that despite increasingly diverse student bodies, and despite newly initiated curricular requirements for diversity classes (primarily on race and ethnicity), students are not actually learning about and from diversity.

(Barnett, P. E. 2011: 671)

In looking at practice so far I have suggested:

- a need to equalize university environments by addressing stereotyping and categorization within the hidden curriculum, and by establishing the principle that everyone in a university community carries communication responsibility within an ELF situation;
- that defining the generic capabilities and attributes which constitute graduate-ness in a globalizing world should inform the aims and objectives for students on any programme of study;
- that the content of the formal curriculum should draw upon more diverse global and local sources; and
- that the learning outcomes should be designed to require and enable critical stances towards that content – including recognition that it sits alongside alternative truths, and has qualities of friability in a world of rapid change.

This section focuses on the ways in which we might structure learning experiences both to strengthen inclusivity and to facilitate the development of our intended outcomes with regard to the global self. We return especially to the notions of experience, community and reflection which were seen as fundamental contributions to learning in Chapter 4, and to 'conversation' as a powerful space for enhancing comfort among diverse others. Much of what is discussed finds echoes in a 'pedagogy of encounter' (Welikala 2011).

Student-centred learning

As explored, a constructivist view of the learning process resonates well with the ways in which the experiences which make up our students' biographies, including very significantly the people who make up their socio-cultural world, both help them shape their (arbitrary) lifeworlds and simultaneously form the boundaries of their lifeworld horizons. We have also noted that the process of *education* is one in which they are given opportunities to engage with ideas, behaviours, and emotions beyond those boundaries in ways which would not happen if left to their own devices. This can make it a challenging experience, and a discomforting one at times. In such a view of learning, educators are not merely subject experts in the sense of being containers of knowledge for transfer to the learner. An educator's role is significantly more important, and more difficult. It is for us to *create the situations* in which transformative learning can occur as students engage with, experience, challenge, and *accommodate* new truths about the world and their place within it – reformulate their lifeworlds. In such situations the educator or a student's peers may be the more-knowing other to scaffold her across her ZPD (Vygotsky's (1962, 1978) 'zone of proximal development' as discussed in Chapter 4), but it is the student alone who can make that journey (in models of prefigurative culture as discussed in Chapter 3, of course, it is the student also who may often be the one to guide the educator across unfamiliar terrain). This is, in essence, what is referred to as *student-centred learning* – and is as relevant to the teaching of business studies as it is to art, physics, or health care. Contrary to some rather common misconceptions, student-centred leaning is not about giving students what they *want* as part of a *students-as-customers* model linked to marketization. Rather, it is an educational approach broadly grounded in the constructivist learning paradigm. Student-centred approaches, therefore, privilege student *experience, encounter* and *reflection* as mechanisms to support the process of lifeworld change, while recognizing the differential biographies, perspectives and emotional responses which diverse students will bring to each. I pick up each of these in this section with specific regard to how they might be enacted in an education for the global student. Perhaps because student-centred approaches *require* students to be active rather than passive participants in their learning (Gibbs 1995), students do not always respond positively when expected to engage with related learning activities, and are very likely to need support in developing an understanding of the rationale behind them and support in engaging with the associated learning activities. In the terminology employed in some of the opening sections to this book, this requires students to *re-envisage* what it is to be a learner, and who they are as learners. Others have identified how closely students' conceptions of learning correlate to their approaches to learning – and by extension to their respect for/engagement in learning activities (Entwistle and Peterson 2004; Herrmann 2013). Student-centred learning approaches are often not congruent with a student's experience of learning from school education, and may be seen as unfocused, unproductive, an abdication of the teacher's responsibility, and so forth. The following have been identified as common aspects of a student-centred approach, and it is noteworthy that student responsibility, autonomy and relationships of mutual respect feature:

1   the reliance on active rather than passive learning;
2   an emphasis on deep learning and understanding;
3   increased responsibility and accountability on the part of the student;

4   an increased sense of autonomy in the learner;
5   an interdependence between teacher and learner;
6   mutual respect within the learner teacher relationship;
7   and a reflexive approach to the teaching and learning process on the part of
     both teacher and learner.

(Lea *et al.* 2003: 322)

Experiential learning

In Chapter 4 I presented a summary of several principles for experiential learning
which would facilitate significant learning (Rogers 1969), and we have seen how
key educationalists and education psychologists from Dewey to Mezirow place
high value on experience as the key to meaningful or transformative learning.
More specifically in relation to the global student, '[r]esearchers from the fields
of cross-cultural psychology and intercultural training consistently emphasize
the important role experience plays in culture learning' (Cushner and Mahon
2002: 45), while most advocates of study abroad and international schooling
place a particular emphasis on their experiential nature in the development of
various aspects of interculturality:

> ... it is through the experience of confronting oneself in a cross-cultural
> situation ... that the individual learns what culture is: learns both some-
> thing of his or her native culture, something of a second culture and
> something of the concept of culture in the abstract.

And:

> It is the shock of cross-cultural contact, the crisis of engagement, that stimu-
> lates the learning necessary for intercultural literacy ... Without cross-cultural
> contact, the learning can only ever be about another culture.

(Heyward 2002: 15 and 18)

Extending experiential learning activities is widely advocated as worthwhile
work in any review of course delivery, and there are a wide range of approaches
and techniques available to enhance the experiential nature of campus-based
learning. These include, among many others, simulations, case studies,
students as researchers, debates, flipped lectures in which students study the
content in advance and use the lecture time to discuss, question and deepen
their understanding, and many types of in-class and out-of-class group work.
Some of these will be more relevant and/or more familiar to some disciplines
than others.

Where any experiential learning approach is employed in the context of a culturally or otherwise diverse student population, and especially with objectives
which concern enabling global student development, Allport's (1954/1979)
Contact Hypothesis discussed in previous chapters needs to be considered in both

the construction of the activities and in how students are guided to engage with them. By way of a reminder, here is one contextualization of Allport's requirements to intercultural student encounters at university:

- *Equality*: in this case, is the contact taking place in a situation where the different groups of students have equal status and feel equal to each other?
- *Common goals*: do the groups of students have a meaningful shared purpose that they are working towards?
- *Intergroup cooperation*: to what extent does the university context encourage cooperation between different groups of students?
- *Authority support*: do the perceived authorities – in this case, administrators and the teaching staff at the university in particular – explicitly encourage positive intercultural contact?

(Schweisfurth and Gu 2009: 465)

In Chapter 4 I cited the 'learning partnerships' model (Baxter Magolda 2009; Baxter Magolda and King 2004) for supporting students in their journeys to self-authorship. The three underpinning principles can now be clearly seen to echo Allport's requirements:

- Validate learners as knowers;
- Situate learning in learners' experience;
- Define learning as mutually constructing meaning.

(Baxter Magolda 2001: 191)

Reflective questions

- When you employ experiential learning activities which involve students working together, how much consideration do you give to factors such as those presented by Allport?
- How much time do you dedicate to supporting students in 'feeling equal to each other', gaining a sense of 'shared purpose' or coming to understand that learning is a process of mutually constructing meaning, for example?

Experiencing learning is also to experience oneself in the experience. As we explored in Chapter 4, a student's developing schemata includes those which relate to who they are, and how they behave and feel and proceed within the experiences they have – their 'scripts of the self' - including those experiences which involve other people. Virtuous learning circles, learning which crosses dimensions, indicate the importance of involving our global students in intercultural learning experiences in which they successfully negotiate their interactions with others and build schemata to take them forward into further successes and stronger self-identification. Furthermore, the extended contact theory (Wright *et al.* 1997) suggests that even through only seeing peers from within one's in-group holding positive relations with 'others' outside that in-group can enhance how those others are perceived, perhaps opening up the potential for one's own interactions with them.

This leads us, then, into considerations of the role of community in the effective construction of learning experiences for the global student.

Communities of practice and group work learning

> Men live in a community in virtue of the things which they have in common; and communication is the way in which they come to possess things in common.
>
> (Dewey 1916/2012: Loc 116)

> ... groups live by communication, dialogue, exchange of experience. Groups are constituted by sharing memories, not by holding them back and barring access to strangers.
>
> (Bauman 2008: Loc 990–991)

> Over the years, it has become clear that unless inter-cultural contact is engineered as part of formal study, social cohesion will not happen and all students will miss out on critical learning opportunities.
>
> (Volet and Ang 1998: 9)

Looking at communities of practice as the locus for human learning in Chapter 4, I proposed that within an effective learning community, 'peers or near-peers can play a powerful role as knowledge circulation among these (near) equals "spreads exceedingly rapidly and effectively"' (Lave and Wenger 1998: 93). The conditions for bringing diverse students together as true peers are highlighted in the reflective question above, and have been discussed at length in earlier chapters, and in this chapter with particular regard to inclusive environments. However, the point is worth labouring further because I believe considerations around constructing and guiding students within their communal learning activities are frequently neglected and the cause of much failure. With regard to the 'payback' for time invested in this, it is worth noting that although achieving successful intercultural interactions in communities of peers is being presented here because of its value to the global student, research has indicated that it also contributes to broader academic gains and well-being more generally. For example, various findings indicate that cross-national peer-support increases international student retention, grades, and satisfaction, while more limited contact relates to loneliness, depression, stress and negative perceptions of their own cultural and academic adjustment (Trice 2007: 108; Ward 2001b: 4; Zhou *et al.* 2008: 70). More broadly, Tadmor *et al.* (2009: 105) report that 'researchers now agree that immersion in different cultures can ... have a positive effect on psychological functioning and well-being' and has been shown to 'foster flexibility, innovation, creativity and decision quality'. More generically, '[g]ood dialogue elicits those activities that shape, elaborate and deepen understanding' (Biggs and Tang 2011: 23).

In constructivist and student-centred learning perspective, it is in group work that we might establish the most solid communities of practice (Lave and Wenger 1998) and stimulate the co-construction of knowledge as more-knowing peers scaffold others across their ZPD (Vygotsky 1978). Advocates of cooperative learning approaches (Johnson and Johnson 1998), recently finding their way into higher education, seek to strengthen outcomes for all by integrating an explicit responsibility for supporting peer as well as personal learning.

The use of group work learning is common in higher education, and there is much written already about good practice in establishing teams and groups to work effectively. However, it is group work, particularly when it is directly linked to assessment, which often causes students to voice their concerns about working across cultures. As happens in stereotyping more generally, when a peer who is not identifiably 'other' fails to contribute fully to a group work task the fault is likely to be attributed to the individual, but when an international student does so, the fault is often attributed to her national or even her generic *international-student* identity. The dangers of misattribution discussed in Chapter 2 are also relevant here as, for example, more limited eye contact made by a student from one culture may be misinterpreted to indicate lack of social engagement or a level of dishonesty (similarly, attribution to type or group can also occur across genders, ethnicities, and so forth). As illustrated in Section 1, a major cause of complaint concerns international students' language ability and/or norms of social interaction, even though (or because) the domestic student voicing these concerns may be unaware of her own social interaction patterns and may have little will or capability to play her own part in speaking a less parochial variety of English in order to bridge any communication gaps. Although a small-scale investigation, research in Australia suggested that negative attitudes to diverse group work might be reinforced when working in more mono-cultural groups, rather than through any actual negative experience in mixed groups, with non-diverse groups being 'significantly less positive towards mixing at the end of the particular group assignment' (Kimmel and Volet 2012: 162).

In looking at intercultural dialogue as the basis for enabling participation in European society, Anderson (2010: 15 and 17) emphasizes the importance not only of free participation by all within their communities, but also of full and equal participation. Full participation is about 'ensuring that the forms of participation freely accessible to all are not watered-down, marginal forms of participation but rather the robust, genuine article'. Equal participation is 'seen as applying to equal status with regard to the activities and processes that determine people's life chances' since 'the social and cultural world one faces as a subordinated participant is one in which one cannot be fully at home, cannot see fully as one own (sic)'. While this work is set in a broader context of the socio-political community of (European) society, the principles have applicability when we conceptualize the student group as a community of practice. Anderson (2010) sets six conditions for intercultural dialogue which is to contribute to free, full and equal participation in society: focus, bindingness, openness, reciprocity, reflexivity, and recognition. Of these we have already, in one way or another, considered focus, openness, reflexivity and recognition in our discussions on inclusive environments. These apply also, perhaps especially, when setting up group work (whether specifically intercultural or not). In Chapter 2 we noted briefly McGregor's (2004) call for 'recognition and reciprocity' as fundamental to inclusive deliberative processes, and this seems to be strongly echoed in Anderson's notions of *bindingness*:

> ... you can't seriously take yourself to be engaged in genuine dialogue if you persist in manipulating the exchange, excluding participants arbitrarily, misrepresenting one's own views (or those of others), and so on. Genuine dialogue makes its own demands on participants because it essentially involves interdependence; like the two halves of an arching bridge, dialogue exists only by virtue of mutual, supporting commitment to it.

And, 'perhaps the most striking demand', *reciprocity*:

> ... the idea that the roles of speaker and listener are not fixed but interchangeable; indeed, it is true for each and every participant that she can be a speaker only if the others are listeners, and vice versa. The key idea of dialogue is thus that no perspective is assumed to be automatically authoritative.

(Anderson 2010: 21)

Anderson (2010, op. cit.: 27–28) identifies a (provisional) set of competencies which he associates with engaging in 'fruitful' intercultural dialogue. In terms of our practice, I suggest that enabling students to develop such competencies should be at least as much *a focus of our planning and design* as the actual content or subject outcomes we might envisage:

- competence in listening and role-taking, including a willingness to hear the perspective and see the reality of one's partners in dialogue;
- competence in self-expression, including the ability to express confidently and convincingly one's own perspective and values, without unduly provoking others;
- competence in non-defensively appreciating and recognizing the accomplishments of other groups;
- competence in 'endurance', including an understanding that dialogue is not about getting one's way, as well as a willingness to accept that concessions and reasonable accommodation will have to be made;

- competence in disagreeing, including the willingness and ability to raise points of dispute and to critique the current terms of the dialogue;
- competence in conflict resolution, including the ability to temper one's formulations, as well as the ability to stick with the dialogue through the strong emotions and painful accusations that are often generated in intercultural dialogue.

Anderson recognizes that intercultural dialogue in the context of the wider society is frightening for participants, and we also need to acknowledge this for our students. It is likely that the level of fear will rise as the stakes are raised; hence, perhaps, the emergence of more voiced complaints when group work is assessed. Several of Anderson's competencies relate back to the need for dimensions of emotional intelligence, including emotion recognition and regulation, as discussed in Chapter 2. So group work in which relevant competencies, including emotional competencies, are *explicitly developed* needs to be experienced before (but not instead of) group work in which those competencies which can be assessed are assessed. It is worth noting, in that respect, that Anderson's list includes quite a number of items which could be redrafted as (assessable) learning outcomes.

Reflective question

- Review Anderson's list of competences for fruitful dialogue above. Can you see how any of these could be explicitly *developed* through adjustments to group work activities which you currently set up for your students?

We should not leave this discussion without reminding ourselves that in any group work context, successful participation is founded upon trust. Establishing mutual trust is made more complex for our students when they are among diverse others, and the anxiety and uncertainty stresses associated with cultural immersion alluded to in Chapter 2 are more salient. Discussing diversity education, Pamela Barnett (2011: 674) suggests that '[T]rusting other students enough to speak real feelings and perhaps even confront them, is to engage in an act of vulnerability'. Such an act is argued to be a catalyst for 'powerful change' because students can learn more 'when they risk exposing what they know or think they know, what they believe in or hope for, what they fear and wonder about', but if trust is needed, it is likely that it first needs to be built. Barnett cites work on combating racism (Rojzman 1999) as identifying a psychological principle that

> people must become aware of their own distrust, fears and needs in ways that lead them to change themselves. They might decide to protect themselves or to deliberately trust others not to take advantage of their vulnerability. This

principle can find expression in strategies that are not only appropriate for diversity classes, but necessary. One way to promote that awareness is to ask people to consider their own fears, and even voice them to the group.

(Barnett, P. E. 2011: 675)

This 'mobilization of risk and vulnerability' is proposed as necessary for the emergence of a functioning group. Perspectives on group working such as this offer far more insight into how we should approach the significant problem of developing communities of practice and learning sites of intercultural encounter, I suggest, than do more commonly used, and more simplistic, exercises along the lines of 'forming, storming, norming and performing' (Tuckman 1965) or looking at the roles and working styles which might characterize high performance teams (Belbin 2010).

Reflective questions

- Do you recognize participation in (intercultural) group work to be an act of vulnerability which is necessary for the emergence of a working group identity?
- What balance do you tend to give to the process of building and supporting groups to work comfortably and inclusively compared to the attention given to the completion of a group task?

Problematizing with our students the issues and concerns they have within intercultural group contexts is difficult work, and requires that we take care to establish the learning environment as a safe space for all concerned. The kind of process involved also requires that we enable students to engage in personal reflection, in order to 'become aware of their own distrust, fears and needs' and 'consider their own fears', for example. Reflective learning (as you will know by now even if you did not know at the start of this book) is also fundamentally implicated in an experiential approach to learning, while Archer asserts the internal conversations of reflexion to be fundamental to 'the means by which we make our way' in a rapidly changing world more generally (Archer 2007: 4).

Reflection/reflexion

The key to learning from experience is focussed reflection … . Often learners will engage in reflection spontaneously as a reaction to the confusion and emotional arousal generated by the experience. However, effective reflection is a skill that can be learned, and focused reflection, as a pattern of thought, is more likely to yield positive gains than is unstructured rumination.

(Savicki 2008: 76)

Thinking ... is the intentional endeavor to discover specific connections between something which we do and the consequences which result, so that the two become continuous.

(Dewey 1916/2012: Loc 2700)

In engaging with themselves as cultural beings at the same time as meeting what is strange and not yet understood in others, [students] are forced to be reflexive – to acknowledge their role in understanding others.

(Roberts, C. 2003: 115)

Reflection is characterized as 'the element that transforms simple experience to a learning experience' (National Society for Experiential Education 2013). Reflexion involves the reflective process, but with greater focus on how *I*, the individual, and my social contexts are dialogically implicated in all experience. Reflection and/or reflexion in-action and on-action is fundamental in some professions and discipline areas, such as the Health Sciences and Education, and quite absent in others. Many readers will be very familiar with much of what I say below, therefore, while others may be less so.

In learning and teaching theory, within Anglophone higher education at least, there has been significant attention given over to reflection both within learning theory and as a professional approach to the enhancement of learning and teaching practice. David Kolb's reflective cycle and related work on learning styles (Kolb 1976, 1981, 1984) has been a particularly influential, if also contested, model. In the full reflective cycle, we set out consciously to examine an experience in order to understand what it means to us, and then employ our fresh understanding to change the way in which we might enact the same/related experience in the future, and then return to our starting position by examining the change itself. By showing a cycle which includes also acting and then examining the outcomes of the action, Kolb is encapsulating the essence of *praxis* (Freire 1970), though Freire would further require that the action seeks to transform the world with particular regard for the quality of human existence. Kolb proposed a 'perception continuum' between *feeling* and *thinking,* and a 'processing continuum' between *watching* and *doing.* His learning styles model associates different combinations of these with each stage in the cycle, and proposes, therefore, that people with strengths in different combinations would be better able at performing related stages in the cycle. However, since effective experiential learning requires engagement with the full cycle/all combinations, successful learners should be helped to develop beyond any preferred learning style. They must be (become) able to

involve themselves fully, openly, and without bias in new experiences ... observe and reflect on these experiences from many perspectives ... create concepts that integrate their observations into logically sound theories ... use these theories to make decisions and solve problems.

(Kolb 1981: 236)

I do not intend to discuss the extensive literature on learning styles here, suffice to say there are a number of inventories which purport to help students identify their preferred style, but the theoretical modelling of learning styles is not strongly supported by empirical evidence of its validity (Coffield *et al.* 2004). In general terms, it seems likely that we can say that learning is stimulated by a range of activities (for example, observing, analysing, evaluating, creating), that most of us probably do some of these things better than others, and that (with education) each of us could probably do any of them better than we do. A central tenet of the constructive alignment process (Biggs 1999; Biggs and Tang 2011) is that learning activities should support students in gaining the skills required of them in the learning outcomes – so, for example, where a learning outcome calls for students to '*analyse* the impact of x on y', the learning activities within the unit of study should involve students in experiencing and reflecting upon the process of *analysis*. A good spread of learning outcomes across a programme of study should lead academics, therefore, to provide students with diverse learning style preferences with a good spread of supportive and developmental learning activities. The processes set out in the reflective learning cycle suggest that this is necessary not only with regard to meeting specific learning outcomes, but also in order to build more generic capabilities to learn through experience of any kind. Since global selves are suggested in this book to be in need of capabilities to respond to and to learn from/within rapidly changing circumstances, I suggest the learning experiences we provide also need to develop their capabilities to engage with all stages of the reflective cycle within conditions of change and uncertainty.

Reflective task

Review some of the learning outcomes you considered modifying in the earlier reflective task, or others from a unit of study you are familiar with. To what extent do they require students to exhibit a range of capabilities which relate to stages in the reflective cycle such as those identified in the quotation from Kolb above (1981: 236)? Do the learning experiences you create for your students provide them with experience of engaging with a similar range of perceiving and processing activities?

As noted, reflexion is *a form of reflection* in which we give particular emphasis to considering *ourselves* in relation to our social context and to considering our social contexts in relation to *ourselves*, 'a process which includes the self being able to consider itself as an object' (Archer 2007: 4 and 72). Although Archer claims the experience of conducting the internal conversation of reflexive thinking is common to all, it is not equally so, as she also proposes four 'modes of reflexivity'(op. cit.: 93). Among these, *communicative reflexives* require 'completion and confirmation by others' for their internal conversations before taking any action; *fractured reflexives* take no action as their conversation brings only distress and disorientation; the internal conversations of *autonomous reflexives* lead them to take direct action; while *meta-reflexives* are also critically reflexive about their internal conversations and about social actions. In these terms, meta-reflexivity would seem to me to be akin to critical thinking, but with a particular emphasis upon critical thinking about self and self-initiated action. Such a stance is implicit with regard to several qualities and actions of the intercultural communicator and global self highlighted in this book, including *mindfulness, etic perspectives, perspective transformation*, and *isomorphic attributions*. Each of these requires the individual to be reflecting upon her own established modes of being, acting, valuing (etc.) and those of another/others she has encountered or is encountering. Echoing Heidegger's (1962/1998) notion of our unexamined flow among the ready-to-hand, Archer notes that for Mead and Dewey, reflexive conversation is triggered when routine is blocked and she proposes that 'contextual incongruity' is a significant factor for facilitating meta-reflexivity (Archer 2007: 38 and 315); the other significant factor being the degree to which the individual cares about the particular issue in question. In Chapter 4 I highlighted the central relationship between experiencing the unready-to-hand and the disorienting dilemmas required for learning to take place, while *caring about* the issues is implied when we noted the need for relevant and authenticity curriculum content. The importance of 'contextual incongruity' to this discussion on practice is the implication that the learning activities/spaces we create in order to deliver the curriculum need to challenge our students' ready-to-hand assumptions, modes of being, values, and so forth. However, an important implication of Archer's differing modes of reflexivity is that a student's preferred or accustomed mode will impact upon their approach to engaging with the issues. As discussed with regard to identity threat and with regard to culture shock, too much incongruity may lead to defensiveness or impotence to act, and in Archer's terms, perhaps, to *fractured reflexives*.

As in our discussions for group work, this implies that we would do well to focus as much (or perhaps even more) of our attention on developing students' capabilities and securities with the *process* of reflection/reflexion than with the content. Again, bringing to the fore a concern for student *being* rather than simply their *knowing*. Dewey significantly, I think, helps us think about how we might structure our learning activities to minimize the risks of too much incongruity:

> ... reflective thinking, in distinction from other operations to which we apply the name of thought, involves (1) a state of doubt, hesitancy, perplexity, mental difficulty, in which thinking originates, and (2) an act of searching, hunting, inquiring, to find material that will resolve doubt, settle and dispose of the perplexity.
>
> (Dewey 1933: 12)

Perhaps it is obvious, but this seems to call for us to build learning activities which are designed not only to engage students in the processes of searching, hunting and inquiring, but which are also designed to ensure that students are able to pursue the issue to a point where perplexity is, at least to some degree, resolved.

Reflexive questions

- Do any of the activities you create for students require a degree of reflective/reflexive thinking, as described above?
- Are the issues you pose in any such activities sufficiently 'perplexing' to engage your students in a 'hunting' process?
- (How) could students undertaking a unit of study you are familiar with be required to engage in reflective/reflexive thinking concerning their own (cultural) norms of thinking or behaving?

Assessment

> The highest quality learning experiences will emerge out of collaborative assignments that pair Canadian and international students in linked assignments.
>
> (Whalley *et al.* 1997: 6)

Assessment, many argue, is *the* most important driver of student engagement and learning:

> Assessment makes more difference to the way that students spend their time, focus their effort, and perform, than any other aspect of the courses they study, including the teaching. If teachers want to make their course work better, then there is more leverage through changing aspects of the assessment than anywhere else.
>
> (Gibbs 2010: 1)

As we have seen already, the process of constructive alignment requires that assessment tasks, like learning tasks, must be designed to reflect the intended learning outcomes.

If we combine the perspectives on assessment above, it is clear that if a course has successfully embedded the capabilities of the global self within the intended learning outcomes, then these must also be embedded in the tasks for the assessment of those capabilities, and that in doing so, the curriculum creates important drivers for students to engage in related learning.

There is a problem, as has been noted, in so far as we are not able to assess how our students *feel* about, say, respecting the opinions of others. I have already acknowledged that I have only a somewhat messy answer to this dilemma – which is that we define intended learning outcomes and engage our students in learning activities and experiences which are *commensurate with* the affective attributes associated with the global self. This, then, carries through to assessment. Roberts, researching transformative learning with regard to student value orientations towards sustainability, concluded that it was 'difficult to envisage ways in which transformations themselves could be captured within outcomes-based academic frameworks' (Roberts, J. 2008: 126). By extension, I would suggest that it is difficult to imagine how the affective dimension to transformative learning can be *measured,* which is the purpose of assessment, in *any* academic framework. However, the likelihood that we cannot reliably assess students' feelings or transformative change to their values, should not deter us from seeking to assess their capabilities to think and act as global selves.

Reflective task

Review Table 5.4 and devise assessment tasks which require students to evidence their ability with regard to some of the modified learning outcomes. If you have modified or devised intended learning outcomes to embed attributes of the global student for your own course, what assessment tasks (would) require students to evidence their abilities with regard to those?

Deardorff (2005: 28) presents a series of questions concerning the assessment of the outcomes of internationalization. Many of these are concerned with assessing institutional outcomes, but among those which relate to the assessment of students, one question directs our attention again to issues of equity: 'Have students' diverse backgrounds and experiences been taken into account when assessing outcomes?' Given the influence of biography in shaping the schemata which constitute a student's lifeworld, and the impacts which this has upon their learning, equitable assessment tasks, and the criteria which are used for judging how successfully they have been applied seem a critical question to consider here. One obvious factor arising from earlier considerations in this chapter is the requirements concerning the use of English. Where a course has not adopted a policy of introducing capabilities in effective intercultural communication to their expectations of all students, assessment criteria which require competence in English must ensure that the competence needed is not set above that which is required for admissions, (or that which could reasonably be expected of a student *who has be adequately supported* since arrival to develop their entry level competencies). Assessment criteria which make no explicit reference to performance in English should, of course, not reward or penalize any student for their use of language. Beyond the particular example of English language, however, is the much broader set of considerations regarding the extent to which a given piece of assessment requires background/tacit knowledge which may be differentially developed through a student's biography prior to university. If we take as an example the pre-modified learning outcome from Table 5.4, 'Students will be able to identify and describe key issues which have been created and debated due to changes in the modern British education system since 1988, it becomes clear that the addition of 'with reference to contrasting practice in one other national context' not only provides a critical perspective from which to examine those key issues, but also partially redresses a cultural bias by enabling international students to draw upon their tacit knowledge of their own national context. Once again, though, this is not a matter of concern exclusively for international students. The differential embodied capital (Bourdieu 1986/2006) brought by students who are the first in family to attend higher education compared to those who are the sons and daughters of professors would be another example, as might the socio-cultural reference points of many first or second generation immigrants. To be clear, the issue here is not about assessing the capabilities designed into and developed through a unit of study, but about being mindful in the formulation of assessment tasks and associated marking criteria not to advantage or disadvantage students because of their differentially situated biographies.

Reflective task

Review a selection of assessment tasks for a unit of study you are familiar with for any examples which:

- advantage students whose specific socio-cultural background would give them tacit knowledge of the subject;
- involve the use of culture-specific references or examples which might not be transparent to students from non-dominant cultural groups;
- require a writing style/approach which is likely to be familiar to those educated through the local (national) school system but which has not been made explicit or developed within the unit of study.

Section 4: Shaping broader institutional practice

I don't think that the West is radically changing their views on the educational process but I do think that China is Westernising. Trying to understand.
(Professor from Hong Kong, quoted in Ryan 2013: 286)

Institutional messages

The gap between institutional rhetoric on internationalization, as evidenced by mission statements and other institutional proclamations, and its realization in institutional practices, policies, and culture is striking on many campuses.
(Green 2002: 15)

Policy must be supported by services and resources that nurture student and staff engagement with cultural diversity on and off campus and develop understanding of the way in which the discipline itself is culturally constructed. Intercultural engagement is challenging and effortful for both staff and students.

(Leask 2009: 66)

We noted in the Introduction to this chapter that many universities tend to categorize international students on the basis of their fee status. In some cases, this can be associated with (most likely well-intentioned) differential treatment – for example, international students in some institutions may have a separate series of induction events when they join the university, might be assigned mentors through the international office, might have free access to English language support, might have targeted social events arranged through the year, might be asked to complete a separate student feedback questionnaire (with incentives for doing so). In Anglophone contexts, at least, even where some international events are opened up to all students, many institutions will lament that barely any domestic students turn up. Since our institutions separately identify international students in these ways, and by their financial status, and in many cases also allocate them separate living accommodation, it is not surprising that domestic students do not necessarily recognize an *international evening*, for example, as a space for them. With regard to student accommodation, some research has indicated that living in the same residence can 'significantly influence' domestic students' 'level of intercultural acceptance and cross-cultural knowledge and openness' (Nesdale and Todd 2000: 25). Institutional identifications also have academic implications for international students. Habu (2000), for example, found it an 'irony of globalization' that any benefits the Japanese women in his study gained through intercultural contact opportunities while attending British universities were reversed as they recognized how they were being identified by their institution principally as income generators. Looking more broadly, might widening participation students, BAME (Black, Asian, Minority Ethnic, a categorization used in the UK) students, students with disabilities, or female students in STEM (science, technology, engineering and mathematics) subjects (for example) feel similarly demeaned because they are part of recruitment targets and diversity celebrations, rather than valued for their individual contribution to the university community? We might similarly question whether or not some academics are also at times paraded in public (in some cases literally, more commonly through conspicuous appearances in prospectus photos or course publicity information) on the basis of some visible otherness. Of course, I understand that displaying role models for low participation groups has some legitimacy, but it is a complex matter, and being mindful about messages which might undermine the inclusivity we are seeking to promote is a responsibility for each of us.

As well as critiquing institutional categorizations, there may also be a need to review the degree to which all students (and employees) are equally subject to and/or protected by institutional regulations, policies and procedures. By way of one example, I have attended many panels to consider student submissions for mitigation on the grounds of a range of extenuating circumstances. In the main, these have been fair and decisions made in the best interest of the student as long as independent evidence supports the submission. I have, though, witnessed panels accepting as mitigation the death of a quite distant family member on the grounds that 'we know that extended family is more important in that student's culture'. The cases were not, then, dealt with as individual submissions on the basis of independent evidence, but on the basis of *inferred* circumstance about a typified cultural 'truth'. Had the same cases been submitted by a student from another culture, they would not have been accepted as the independent evidence was not adequate to support claims of stress and disruption. This is not to suggest that academic regulations and their implementation should not be able to respond flexibly to individual circumstances, or even to group circumstances, where these are legitimately identified. I believe that it is reasonable, for example, that a student with an identified learning disability might have additional time to complete an examination, or that a PhD viva for an Islamic student should be arranged, if requested, to take place in the morning if it happens to fall within Ramadan. I would expect a secular PhD student to be similarly flexible for her Islamic examiner, and an Islamic student in the UK not to expect tutorial support on a Sunday. These are (I assume) quite clear-cut cases, but other situations are less so.

Reflective question

- Should a whole cohort examination be schedule for the morning during Ramadan? What if all the students in the cohort are Islamic? What if only one is?

I do not pretend these are easy matters; an inclusive environment within a university is subject to the same problems we face when seeking to create an inclusive environment in society as a whole. My point here, though, is that all areas of the university need to adopt a constantly critical stance to their work, and not to assume that either current practice or some proposed change to that practice is equitable. I suggest, importantly, that it is appropriate to engage our students in the conversations around these complex issues. Asmar (2005: 295) asks 'whether making difference invisible is really in the overall interests of a student body whose members will graduate into a globalised and multicultural world'. I suggest that it is not, and nor is it in anybody's interest to avoid engaging with the difficult questions which diversity raises. Interrogating the equity of regulations, policies and procedures are necessary in terms of 'educational justice' (Peel and Frank 2008: 101), of providing an inclusive environment and of creating an institutional culture which supports the development of the global student. Engaging students 'of difference' in our interrogations would seem both sensible and equitable.

An additional significant feature of institutional practice concerns the accessibility of institutional documentation to those who speak English as a foreign or second language; whether or not they are from another country. In Section 1 I suggested shifting the balance of communication responsibility within intercultural interactions on our campuses by introducing expectations concerning capabilities for students and staff in intercultural communication (in English). Three of the characteristics cited in Figure 5.1 were:

- using fewer idiomatic, metaphoric, and jargonistic expressions;
- citing fewer own-culture reference points; and
- using shorter and less complex syntax.

Reviewing our published materials against similar guidelines would also contribute to more effective and inclusive written communications, and should be undertaken across institutional documentation from academic regulations to marketing leaflets.

More broadly, we should also note the requirement for a university's aspirations for its graduates to be reflected in the way it conducts its own relations with the world – the 'university as a global citizen' (Shiel and Takeda 2008: 7). This would include, for example, its contributions to the local community, its approaches to (global) corporate social responsibility, the equitability within its relationships with global partner institutions, the openness with which it shares its knowledge and resources, and the fairness of its employment practices. Ryan's quotation from the professor in Hong Kong which opens this section indicates also, perhaps, how little Western universities identify that the wider world may have something to teach them. The most obvious learning space here could – should – be through our transnational partnerships.

Reflective questions

- (How) does your own institution differently identify its international and its domestic students in terms of policies, regulations, or the provision of services? Do any of these serve to set the two groups apart?
- If your institution is involved in transnational partnerships, how much learning flows into the institution? What is the balance in expectations regarding your partner's need to change/adopt practice and your own institution's need to do the same?

The informal curriculum

I focused the discussions in Section 2 of this chapter on the formal and hidden curricula in our learning and teaching practices because these are experienced by all our students. The informal curriculum is available, sometimes to all and sometimes only to a few students, and so might not directly or significantly constitute part of a student's university experience. The provision of optional activities such as international film evenings, Malaysian student societies (for example), an international guest lecturer series, global food festivals, and the like have the potential to contribute to messages concerning the value of others and the values of others even for those who do not directly participate in them. But as noted above, acts of identification can be interpreted as acts of 'othering', perhaps even of segregation – and informal curricular activities also need critical scrutiny.

Probably the greatest informal curriculum opportunity associated with internationalization is the provision of international experience opportunities for the domestic student population, and a few comments on this seem necessary here. A great deal of literature and often significant institutional resources are devoted to researching, extolling the benefits of, advocating for, and organizing periods of international experience within or additional to a student's credit-bearing programme of study. Most commonly these take the form of international 'exchanges' or study tours, but also, and increasingly, international volunteering (Jones 2010), work placements (internships), and service learning (Annette 2000, 2002; Killick 2007) experiences are being developed. Although not all of these involve 'study', the common catch-all term of 'study abroad' covers them all. It may be surprising to readers outside North America that several very large and successful businesses thrive on providing such opportunities for students across the USA, mostly with credit-bearing articulations to multiple universities. Much of this industry seems (to this author at least) to compete more on how exotic their destinations are than upon the educational validity of the experience, and as noted in Chapter 2, to risk exacerbating any tendencies of the touring student to claim rights over the toured. Nonetheless, there is a plethora of small- and large-scale research which (in the overwhelming majority of cases) identifies a range of significant positive outcomes of study abroad, including the development of several characteristics which would support the development of more global selves. There are a few more critical voices, but they remain by far a minority (see, for example, Brockington and Wiedenhoeft 2009; Coleman 1999; Gmelch 1997; Heyward 2002). I am personally convinced that many of these experiences have great potential, and often are as 'life-changing' as students and international educators claim. I was responsible for establishing and managing one university's international exchange programme and have, like most international educators, witnessed the euphoria of many returning students. Other volumes in this series pay significant attention to study abroad outcomes, and to characteristics of well-designed and implemented programmes. In this book, though, our focus is what can be done on our home campuses rather than through study abroad, and I believe that diverting a portion of study abroad resources (including the research effort) to the home campus experience would be a positive move. With the exception of a few subject areas such as modern languages and ethnography, in the vast majority of cases study abroad sits within the optional informal curriculum, and my main concern around the attention it receives is with participation patterns. Although percentages vary widely across institutions and somewhat between countries, participation can be below 1 per

cent and only rarely exceeds 10 per cent of students; for example, research involving 109 UK institutions indicated the average participation in experiences abroad
to be around 0.95 per cent (King, R. *et al.* 2010). Institutional claims for much
higher percentages are rarely based upon what might be considered a significant
period or form of international experience. Moreover, the demographics of participants in general are heavily biased towards white, middle class, and female
students. Study abroad usually costs the individual student financially (including giving up any part-time job), requires an amount of self-confidence at the
outset, is more attractive to those whose cultural capital includes familial experience of international travel, and is generally much more difficult to access for
students with caring responsibilities or disabilities. Unless institutions are able
and willing to resource levelling the playing field, study abroad is likely to remain
a game largely restricted to the already relatively advantaged. Equity issues aside,
with average participation rates so low, study abroad is, in the foreseeable future,
unlikely to offer transformational learning for a majority of our students. My
second reason for believing that the home campus is the better focal point for
the internationalization objectives set out here is that among the participating
students, there is a serious danger that what happens in Vegas by-and-large stays
in Vegas. Intercultural experience on study abroad is often characterized by the
participants themselves as taking place in 'fantastic' locations among 'amazing'
people (the adjectives are interchangeable); by implication, it is not 'normal',
home-spun, or mainstream. I rather suspect that John Urry's caution (2000: 38)
that much tourism 'involves an ecstatic spiralling search for further and even more
bizarre inauthentic simulations produced by, and within, safe modern environments of global networks' applies also to much study abroad. Of course, good
programme design, perhaps most importantly how the study abroad experience is
embedded in pre- and post-experience learning on campus and made an explicit
focus of attention during the experience (Behrnd and Porzelt 2012), can help
with this, and several individual practitioners are developing and delivering inno-
vative projects to achieve this. The Australian Learning and Teaching Council has
also recently sponsored a 'Bringing the learning home' project to enhance the
outcomes of study abroad across the sector (Australian Learning and Teaching
Council 2010). However, such embedding remains a comparatively rare feature
of study abroad programmes, and is unlikely to feature significantly when they
do not contribute directly to the formal curriculum. In my own research into
students on a range of study abroad experiences (Killick 2012, 2013) I was struck
by just how much of the students' reported transformational learning derived
from interactions and individuals who were incidental to any structured components of their study abroad programme. Indeed, the 'significant others' in their
transformational learning were individuals or groups which the outbound students had not anticipated, wanted, or deliberately sought out. In principle, any
of their 'amazing' encounters could have taken place on their home campus, had
the conditions there been more conducive to intercultural boundary crossing.
I most certainly do not wish to prevent students from benefitting from study

abroad opportunities, but do suggest that changes to our mainstream curricula and learning experiences such as those set out in this chapter will have a more significant impact on a much greater number of our students, and offer a more equitable arena in which to focus scarce institutional resources.

Reflective questions

- What are the participation patterns in study abroad experiences like in your own institution? Is there a dedicated office/resource to enable students to engage in study abroad activities? Is there a similar resource dedicated to curriculum and campus change to facilitate global/intercultural learning?
- Should there be?

Human resources

One important barrier in teaching intercultural awareness stems from faculty who are likely to be more culturally and linguistically encapsulated than their students. Further, most instructors are not prepared to teach in multicultural settings and, in some instances, their belief systems make them resistant to doing so.

(Gordon and Newburry 2007: 244)

Any failure/reluctance on the part of faculty members to fully accept responsibility for internationalization will alter, possibly fundamentally, our understanding of what an internationalized curriculum is and how we will go about participating in curricular reform.

(Bond 2003: 6)

A fundamental assumption of this book is that the academic has a professional responsibility to offer her students the best learning experience she can. This implies a continuing need to engage with professional development in best practices in learning, teaching and assessment. With respect to the contexts and aspirations outlined in this book, we as teachers, no less than our students, need to be open to new and different forms of knowledge and new ways of working (Clifford, V. A. 2011: 556), to be 'reflexive and able to critically question [our] own teaching and learning orientations' (Welikala 2011: 16) and to reflect upon our own cultural values, attitudes and behaviours, and how they manifest themselves in our own 'ethnocentric tendencies', 'transcultural stress' (Gabb 2006: 362 and 365) and 'intercultural sophistication' (Yershova *et al.* 2000: 67). Gabb itemizes specific areas for the development of academic staff working with culturally diverse students:

- cross-cultural communication;
- production of teaching materials appropriate to a culturally diverse audience;

- additions or modifications to curricula that include examples or case studies from other cultures;
- the use of language that is not based on local metaphor, slang, or colloquialisms;
- the provision of clear explanations of such language when required; and
- knowledge of cultural dimensions represented in multicultural classrooms.

(Gabb 2006: 362)

Others have detailed the characteristics of those teaching in intercultural settings (Teekens 2001, 2003), and Van der Werf (2012) has built from this work a comprehensive *International Competencies Matrix* 'to stimulate the awareness of the need for specific or additional competences for working as a teacher in an internationalized environment and to foster the discussion on how to acquire or improve these competences' (Van der Werf, op. cit.: 101), noting that a version of the matrix had actually been utilized in annual appraisals in one university.

Reflective question

- To what extent do you think 'international competencies' (or similar) should feature as expectations for academics?

This chapter has pointed to changes in practice which imply competence in each of these. However, as we have explored in previous chapters with regard to our students, significant change is rarely a painless process; it involves stepping outside the ready-to-hand and can threaten our identities. Significant learning extends beyond competencies into values, attitudes, notions of self-efficacy to constitute ways of *being* just as much for academic staff as it does for students. This may account for conclusions by Schuerholz-Lehr (2007) that there is little evidence to confirm that attributes such as intercultural sensitivity and world-mindedness among academic staff translate into classroom practice. As far as this discussion on wider institutional practice is concerned, individual change (learning) requires support (education) if it is to be effective in terms of its application. In a study of faculty and staff in one US university, Olson and Kroeger noted a need for 'global, intercultural, and professional development ... that is ongoing, substantial, and inclusive of work in another language and culture' (Olson and Kroeger 2001: 116). For some colleagues, particularly as universities extend their overseas campuses and/or franchised delivery, the opportunities for substantial and inclusive work in another culture are very real (see, for example, Hamza 2010), though the educational development support for them to do so seems generally to be very limited. For most of us, though, the opportunities for substantial and inclusive work lie within our daily practice on our home campuses. I have identified communities of practice and engagement in reflection as key to how our students might learn from their experiences in general, and the capacity to be mindful and take emic and etic perspectives as of particular importance within their intercultural encounters. The same would apply to the intercultural learning of all university employees. Institutional support to guide academic staff specifically to develop confidence in their own diverse communities and the habits of professional reflection, whether that be regarding curriculum internationalization or other change processes, predominantly lies with a university's educational development unit. If we have educational aspirations such as those set out in this book, it is the responsibility of the institution to ensure that those charged with supporting and developing assessment, learning and teaching practices have, themselves, a clear understanding of the aspirations for (global) students, of the implications this has for the hidden, formal, and informal curricula, and of the capabilities this demands of academic staff.

Several institutions actively seek to extend the cultural diversity of their academic staff, though many do not achieve very wide cultural representation, and in some cases the efforts are visibly tokenistic. However, the point I wish to make here is that appointing academic colleagues from diverse global and cultural backgrounds, like recruiting international students, should not be expected to contribute to successful internationalization of the student experience unless those colleagues are also supported, respected and given equitable spaces in which to practice. While research activity might be supported through international disciplinary communities, the same may not be true of the local learning and teaching communities, where 'the day-to-day reality of teaching and learning in UK HE, such as administration of courses, curriculum design, assessment and approaches to teaching styles which reflect local practices, will probably be unfamiliar to academics from another educational culture' (Luxon and Peelo 2009: 651).

Clifford *et al.* (2012) saw evidence of international colleagues undergoing experiences of culture shock as they transitioned into one British university, and a subsequent work points to evidence that these colleagues were experiencing on-going shifts in their identities. These were perhaps driven by the ways in which colleagues identified them by the otherness, which 'generated thinking about the university's induction processes for staff and students alike' (Haigh, M. 2013: 205). In Luxon and Peelo's research, international academics identified a range of 'complex linguistic and cultural challenges' specific to their integration to the teaching community of their institutions which led the researchers to question the extent to which participants' 'prior acculturation as teachers is valued, or whether, in reality, it is seen as problematic' (Luxon and Peelo, op. cit.: 657). They go on to identify the importance of educational development programmes for these colleagues, too. However, while I agree entirely that, as responsible employers if nothing else, universities must make proper provision for supporting these colleagues through transition to their new academic environments, ensuring that we as their colleagues practice the inclusivity with them which we preach for our students is perhaps an even more important lesson here – do we equalize participation in academic working spaces? How often, for example, are those colleagues with international backgrounds or experience, or those colleagues from diverse local cultures and communities actively encouraged 'to contribute to the development of high quality internationally-oriented curricula' (EU General Secretariat 2013), and how often, instead, is this activity principally left to those with most experience of the processes of the institution and the established canon of the discipline?

Reflective questions

- How inclusive/equalized do you think and feel your own academic communities are for those who come from other cultures, nationalities and first language groups?
- What (more) positive contributions could you make to make those communities more inclusive and equitable?

This chapter started with a folk tale about descriptions of an elephant based upon restricted experiences of the animal. Within the chapter I have presented separately aspects of the practice of higher education, but, as with our elephant, none of the issues and suggestions raised should be seen or enacted in isolation; they come together in a 'dynamic interplay'(Leask 2009: 208) as our students undertake their sojourns through higher education. A university education will only effectively contribute to our students' development as global selves if we attend to all aspects of the complexity which constitute their lived-experience and give shape to who they are.

Seeking to achieve this is the complexity of processes which collectively constitute internationalization.

Afterword

> Our hope of salvation lies in our being surprised by the Other. Let us learn always to receive further surprises.
>
> (Illich 1973)

In this book, I have suggested that important aspects of the (super) complexity which characterizes the worlds in which our students must make their way are:

- the impacts of globalization upon:
    - the social, cultural and geo-political contexts which shape their becoming;
    - interpretations of and relationships with knowledge and truth;
    - their personal biographies which shape their conceptualizations of themselves and their world(s);
    - the shaping of higher education policy and practice;
    - the shaping of our campus and learning spaces;
    - the construction of our disciplines and their enactment in a complex and rapidly changing world;
- the impacts of the psychology of the individual student upon the shaping of her lifeworld, including:
    - the formulations of her norms, truths, and procedures for acting in the world;
    - her relationships towards others who are similar and others who are different;
    - the processes which underpin her three-dimensional learning;
    - the challenges of her lifeworld (re)formation; her self-identity in particular;
    - the responses she makes, and which make her, when faced with inequitable learning spaces.

I have presented a characterization of the global student as one whose *self-in-the-world* identity primarily and *act-in-the-world* agency secondarily constitute the capabilities which will enable him to make his way in the globalizing world on the basis of those things he has reason to value (Sen 1993, 1999), alert to his own entanglement in global issues and actions and their impacts on global others. However, for this to happen, his university experience needs to enable lifeworld change through holistic, significant learning and perspective transformation.

And I have suggested, therefore, that each of us in higher education with opportunities to influence the student experience has a responsibility to review and reshape our practice to better support such lifeworld change. In terms of our practice, I have proposed in particular a need to enable students to build and to experience themselves engaging within conversations and communities with diverse others, and that facilitating this requires us to:

- provide equitable and inclusive university environments through attention to the informal curriculum, including:

  o examining and challenging the stereotyping of others;
  o being alert to the dangers of acts of identification;
  o requiring and exhibiting capabilities in intercultural communication (in English);

- construct a formal curriculum which:

  o draws upon and critically engages with diverse sources for its content;
  o articulates clearly the attributes of the global student, suggested to encompass the dimensions of global relevance and inclusivity;
  o embeds relevant aspects of these attributes directly within the *subject curriculum* through explicit intended learning outcomes at course/ module and programme levels;

- deliver a formal curriculum which:

  o adopts a student-centred philosophy/constructivist approach;
  o reflects in its learning activities and in its assessment requirements the capabilities expressed in its intended learning outcomes;
  o requires and supports students in their engagement with other peoples and perspectives in ways which are commensurate with the development of affective attributes of the global self;
  o is built around equitable experiential learning within diverse communities of practice;
  o focuses on *process* to foster conversation and community among all students;
  o places emphasis on supporting the development of capabilities to engage in critical reflection/reflexion;

- formulate institutional policies and practices which:

  o situate the university as global citizen;
  o treat all students as individuals and avoid differential recognition based upon fee status, first language, or other group identifications;

- o involve equitable international partnerships which recognize alternative approaches and perspectives as contributing to its own learning and development;
- o articulate clear internationalization aspirations and directions as the basis for supporting the development of academic practices and practitioners; and
- o create equitable cross-cultural spaces for the development and sharing of educational approaches within inclusive communities of academic practitioners.

The capabilities to converse and form communities across cultures are fundamental to our getting along together, to seeing each other as equally human. If we can develop our practice to better offer university experiences which enable our students to go on to make their way in the world as global selves, their capacity for being *surprised* rather than shocked or alienated by Others will be a good defence against identity threat and the fundamentalisms it can generate, and a strong bolster for their own, unfinalizable (Bakhtin 1984), agency in the complex, turbulent times which characterize their radically incomplete globalizing world.

All this, I suggest, characterizes a higher education fit for a global era.

Selected resources and links to support practice

There are several freely available resources to support the higher education sector in the process of internationalizing our curricular and our learning and teaching practices. The following are particularly recommended (some have been cited elsewhere in the book):

- This *Themed Resource Bank for Internationalisation* provides an extensive annotated bibliography with links to original sources where available: http://www.leedsmet.ac.uk/world-widehorizons/index_resource_bank.htm
- This extensive set of resources on the *International Student Lifecycle* covers teaching contexts and approaches, learning, curriculum, and international competencies: http://www.heacademy.ac.uk/international-student-life-cycle
- This booklet provides curriculum review teams with a series of questions regarding how their course brings in *cross-cultural capability and global perspectives*, with examples of possible responses: http://repository-intralibrary.leedsmet.ac.uk/open_virtual_file_path/i2346n81341t/Cross-Cultural%20Capability%20&%20Global%20Perspectives.pdf
- This staff development resources reviews issues faced in the task of *integrating home and international students* and suggests mechanisms for doing so through learning and teaching practices: http://repository.leedsmet.ac.uk/main/view_record.php?identifier=6965&SearchGroup=Open+Educational+Resources
- This resource also provides a guide for academics wishing to enhance *interaction between domestic and international students*: http://www.cshe.unimelb.edu.au/research/experience/enhancing_interact.html
- This site provides a *conceptual framework* and guidance on *process* for curriculum internationalization along with a number of supporting resources: http://www.ioc.net.au/main/course/view.php?id=2
- This site provides a comprehensive global people/ intercultural *competency framework* and related publications through its own resource bank: http://www2.warwick.ac.uk/fac/cross_fac/globalpeople/

- This site provides practical resources on course design, pedagogy, global issues in specific world areas, and more related to curriculum internationalization: http://www.indiana.edu/~global/icab/resources.php
- This resource contains a series of case studies illustrating how international students can be integrated/engaged to enhance internationalization on their host campuses/courses: http://www.bccie.bc.ca/sites/bccie_society/files/intcontrib.pdf

Glossary

The following terms are used in specific ways in this book, and may deviate from meanings they denote in specific disciplinary contexts or may be unfamiliar to the reader because of their use within specific disciplinary contexts.

Alterity   Used here to refer to the identification of people from different socio-cultural backgrounds. It is quite common in literature on intercultural and cross-cultural encounters to refer to 'the Other' or 'Others' with a capital O to denote this kind of difference. Apart from the confusions this can lead to in when to capitalize and when not, there seems to me to be an implicit idea in this usage that only Others are other. Alterity better captures the idea that we are all different – I am as Other as the next Other.

Capability   I spend some time exploring the complexity of this term in Chapter 3. I draw in particular upon the work of Amartya Sen (1993, 1999, 2003) in the meaning of capability as the factors in an individual's life which make it possible for her to lead a life she has reason to value. I categorize these capabilities broadly as 'objective' capabilities – factors in the environment (social, political, philosophical, geographical, economic, etc.) – and 'subjective' capabilities – factors in the individual (skills, knowledge, emotional intelligence, personality, self-efficacy, etc.). Universities hold responsibilities to build environments which (equitably) maximize the objective capabilities of their students to enhance their subjective capabilities.

Course and Module   These are often used interchangeably in the text to refer to a unit of study which is independently assessed and combines in a structured way with other courses or modules to form a programme of study which leads to an award (say a Bachelor of Arts). The possible confusion here is that 'course' is used in the UK generally to refer to the whole programme of study, whereas it is used in the USA to refer to what in the UK is called a 'module'.

Globalization   I do not set out to condemn or to valorize this process. As with most of human activity, I suppose there to be those who contribute to the process intent only on personal gain and others who are more civic-minded. The outcomes of the on-going process (or sets of processes) seem to have devastating impact on some communities and environments and to open up great opportunities and freedoms elsewhere. My interest in this book, broadly, is to look at how this complex of processes, inextricably tied up with the emergence of postmodern interpretations of being, is impacting/will impact on the identities and human relationships of our students.

Internationalization   I use this to refer to the processes which universities are undergoing as a response to some of the changes brought about by globalization. I take some time in Chapter 1 to explore various perspectives on internationalization, and seek to dismiss those which are dominated by marketization, monetization or the enhancement of global reputation. My interpretation of the term is focused on processes to transform the educational work of the university to better meet the needs of its students in a globalizing world.

Lifeworld   This refers to the way in which the world is understood by the individual. It assumes that the world and how I 'know' the world are never one and the same thing. I carry only an individual interpretation of that world. The lifeworld is every aspect of how I believe, feel, understand, anticipate (etc.) the world – including how I see myself in that world. This means that in interactions with others, we are always speaking from different worlds to some extent. I propose, strongly, throughout the book that the degree to which our lifeworld representations of the world differ has a significant impact on the degree to which we are inclined to seek out closer connections with each other. Learning is presented as a process which brings about change to the lifeworld.

Lived-experience   This is used to denote the idea that while two people may share an experience, their *experiencing* of it will be unique to each of them. Lived-experience refers to how the activity in which they both engage is represented in their lifeworld, what it *means* to them and for them. Lived-experience might differ in its emotional impact, in its import, in its influence on worldview, in its impact on confidence, or values, and so forth.

References

Allport, G. 1935. Attitudes. In *A Handbook of Social Psychology*, ed. Murchison, C. Worcester, MA: Clark University Press. 789–844.

Allport, G. 1954/1979. *The Nature of Prejudice*. Cambridge, MA: Perseus Books.

Alred, G., Byram, M. and Fleming, M. 2003. Introduction. In *Intercultural Experience and Education*, eds. Alred, G., Byram, M. and Fleming, M. Clevedon: Multilingual Matters. 1–13.

Altbach, P.G. and Teichler, U. 2001. Internationalization and exchanges in a globalized university. *Journal of Studies in International Education* 5 (1): 5–25.

Anderson, J. 2010. Intercultural dialogue and free, full and equal participation: Towards a new agenda for an intercultural Europe. In *Intercultural Dialogue. Enabling Free, Full and Equal Participation*, eds. Anderson, J. and Kaur-Stubbs, S. London: Platform for Intercultural Europe/Alliance Publishing Trust. 4–35.

Annette, J. 2000. Citizenship studies, community service learning and Higher Education. In *Education for Values*, eds. Gardner, R., Cairns, J. and Lawton, D. London: Kogan Page. 109–123.

Annette, J. 2002. Service learning in an international context. *Frontiers: The Interdisciplinary Journal of Study Abroad* 8 (Winter): 83–93.

Appadurai, A. 1997. *Modernity at Large: Cultural Dimensions of Globalisation*. Minneapolis, MN: University of Minnesota Press.

Appadurai, A. 2001. Grassroots globalization and the research imagination. In *Globalization*, ed. Appadurai, A. Durham, NC: Duke University. 1–21.

Appadurai, A. 1966/2006. Disjuncture and difference in the global cultural economy. In *Education, Globalisation and Social Change*, eds. Lauder, H., Brown, P., Dillabough, J.-A. and Halsey, A.H. Oxford: Oxford University Press. 179–188.

Appiah, K.A. 2005. *The Ethics of Identity*. Woodstock, UK: Princeton University Press. Kindle e-book edition.

Appiah, K.A. 2006. *Cosmopolitanism: Ethics in a World of Strangers*. New York: Norton.

Archer, M.S. 2007. *Making Our Way through the World: Human Reflexivity and Social Mobility*. Cambridge: Cambridge University Press.

Arthur, J. 2005. Student character in the British university. In *Citizenship and Higher Education: The Role of Universities in Communities and Society*, ed. Arthur, J. Abingdon, UK: Routledge Falmer. 8–32.

Ashworth, P. 2003. The phenomenology of the lifeworld and social psychology. *Social Psychology Review* 5 (1): 18–34.

Asmar, C. 2005. Internationalising students: Reassessing diasporic and local student difference. *Studies in Higher Education* 30 (3): 291–309.

Australian Learning and Teaching Council. 2010. Bringing the learning home. Accessed: December 2013 at http://www.tlc.murdoch.edu.au/project/btlh/projectinfo.html

Bache, I. and Hayton, R. 2012. Inquiry-based learning and the international student. *Teaching in Higher Education* 17 (4): 411–423.

Bakhtin, M.M. 1984. *Problems of Dostoyevsky's Poetics*. Trans. Emerson, C. Minneapolis, MN: University of Minnesota Press.

Bakhtin, M.M. 1986. *Speech Genres and Other Late Essays*. Trans. McGee, V. Austin, TX: University of Texas Press.

Ball, S.J. 2003. The teacher's soul and the terrors of performativity. *Journal of Education Policy* 18 (2): 215–228.

Bamber, P. 2008. The impact of student participation in international service-learning programs. In *Education for Sustainable Development: Graduates as Global Citizens*, eds. Shiel, C. and Takeda, S. Bournemouth: Bournemouth University Press. 9–22.

Bandura, A. 1997. *Self-Efficacy: The Exercise of Control*. New York: Freeman.

Barnett, P.E. 2011. Discussions across difference: Addressing the affective dimensions of teaching diverse students about diversity. *Teaching in Higher Education* 16 (6): 669–679.

Barnett, R. 1997. A knowledge strategy for universities. In *The End of Knowledge in Higher Education*, eds. Barnett, R. and Griffin, A. London: Cassell. 166–179.

Barnett, R. 2000. *Realizing the University in an Age of Supercomplexity*. Buckingham: Society for Research into Higher Education and Open University Press.

Barnett, R. 2007. *A Will to Learn: Being a Student in an Age of Uncertainty*. Maidenhead: Society for Research into Higher Education and Open University Press.

Barrie, S.C. 2004. A research-based approach to generic graduate attributes policy. *Higher Education Research & Development* 23 (3): 261–275.

Barrie, S.C. 2006. Understanding what we mean by the generic attributes of graduates. *Higher Education* 51: 215–241.

Barrie, S.C. 2007. A conceptual framework for the teaching and learning of generic graduate attributes. *Studies in Higher Education* 34 (2): 439–458.

Barron, P., Gourlay, L.J. and Gannon-Leary, P. 2010. International students in the higher education classroom: Initial findings from staff at two post-92 universities in the UK. *Journal of Further and Higher Education* 34 (4): 475–489.

Bartlett, F.C. 1932. *Remembering: An Experimental and Social Study*. Cambridge: Cambridge University Press.

Bauman, Z. 1996. From pilgrim to tourist – or a short history of identity. In *Questions of Cultural Identity*, eds. Hall, S. and Du Gay, P. London: Sage. 18–36.

Bauman, Z. 1998. *Globalization. The Human Consequences*. Cambridge: Polity Press.

Bauman, Z. 2000. *Liquid Modernity*. Cambridge: Polity Press.

Bauman, Z. 2005. The liquid-modern challenges to education. In *Values in Higher Education*, eds. Robinson, S. and Katulushi, C. St Bride's Major: Aureus/University of Leeds. 36–50.

Bauman, Z. 2008. *Does Ethics Have a Chance in a World of Consumers?* Cambridge, MA: Harvard University Press. Kindle e-book edition.

Bauman, Z. 2012. Times of interregnum. *Ethics and Global Politics* 5 (1): 49–56.

Baume, D. 2009. *Writing and Using Good Learning Outcomes*. Leeds: Leeds Metropolitan Press. Accessed: December 2013 at http://repository-intralibrary.leeds-met.ac.uk/open_virtual_file_path/i3128n162822t/Writing%20and%20using%20good%20learning%20outcomes.pdf

Baxter Magolda, M. 2001. *Making Their Own Way: Narratives for Transforming Higher Education to Promote Self-development*. Sterling, VA: Stylus.

Baxter Magolda, M. 2009. Educating students for self-authorship. Learning partnerships to achieve complex outcomes. In *The University and its Disciplines: Teaching and Learning Within and Beyond Disciplinary Boundaries*, ed. Kreber, C. London: Routledge. 143–156.

Baxter Magolda, M. and King, P.M., eds. 2004. *Learning Partnerships: Theory and Models of Practice to Educate for Self-authorship*. Sterling, VA: Stylus.

Beck, U. 1994. The reinvention of politics: Towards a theory of reflexive modernization. In *Reflexive Modernization*, eds. Beck, U., Giddens, A. and Lash, S. Cambridge: Polity. 1–55.

Beelen, J., ed. 2007. *Implementing Internationalisation at Home, EAIE Professional Development Series for International Educators*. Amsterdam: European Association for International Education (EAIE).

Beerkens, E. 2003. Globalisation and higher education research. *Journal of Studies in International Education* 7: 128–148.

Behrnd, V. and Porzelt, S. 2012. Intercultural competence and training outcomes of students with experience abroad. *International Journal of Intercultural Relations* 36 (2): 15–17.

Belbin, R.M. 2010. *Team Roles at Work*. 2nd ed. Oxford: Elsevier.

Bennett, M.J. 1986. A developmental approach to training for intercultural sensitivity. *International Journal of Intercultural Relations* 10 (2): 179–195.

Bennett, M.J. 1993. Towards ethnorelativism: A developmental model of intercultural sensitivity. In *Education for the Intercultural Experience*, ed. Paige, R.M. Yarmouth, ME: Intercultural Press. 21–71.

Bennett, M.J. 2008. On becoming a global soul. In *Developing Intercultural Competence and Transformation: A Path to Engagement During Study Abroad*, ed. Savicki, V. Sterling, VA: Stylus. 13–31.

Bennett, M.J. 2009. Defining, measuring, and facilitating intercultural learning: A conceptual introduction to the Intercultural Education double supplement. *Intercultural Education* 20 (Supplement): S1–13.

Berry, J.W. 1990a. Psychology of acculturation. In *Cross-cultural Perspectives*, ed. Berman, J. Lincoln, NE: University of Nebraska Press. 201–234.

Berry, J.W. 1990b. Psychology of acculturation: Understanding individuals moving between cultures. In *Applied Cross-cultural Psychology*, ed. Brislin, R.W. London: Sage. 232–253.

Berry, J.W. 1994. Acculturation and psychological adaptation. In *Journeys into Cross-cultural Psychology*, eds. Bouvy, A.-M., van de Vijver, F.J.R., Boski, P. and Schmitz, P. Lisse, The Netherlands: Swets and Zeitlinger. 129–141.

Berry, J.W. 2005. Acculturation. In *Culture and Human Development*, eds. Friedlmeier, W., Chakkarath, P. and Schwarz, B. New York: Psychology Press. 291–302.

Biggs, J. 1999. *Teaching for Quality Learning at University*. Buckingham: Society for Research into Higher Education/Open University Press.

Biggs, J. and Collins, K.F. 1982. *Evaluating the Quality of Learning: The SOLO Taxonomy*. New York: Academic Press.

Biggs, J. and Tang, C. 2011. *Teaching for Quality Learning at University*. 4th ed. Maidenhead: Open University /Mc-Graw-Hill Education.

Bindé, J. 2001. Toward an ethics of the future. In *Globalization*, ed. Appadurai, A. Durham, NC: Duke University. 90–113.

Bloom, B.S. 1956. *Taxonomy of Educational Objectives. Handbook I: The Cognitive Domain*. New York: David McKay.

Boden, R. and Nedeva, M. 2010. Employing discourse: Universities and graduate 'employability'. *Journal of Education Policy* 25 (1): 37–54.

Bohner, G. and Wänke, M. 2002. *Attitudes and Attitude Change*. Hove: Psychology Press.

Bond, S.L. 2003. *Untapped Resources. Internationalization of the Curriculum and Classroom Experience: A Selected Literature Review*. Ottawa: Canadian Bureau for International Education.

Bourdieu, P. 1984. *Distinction: A Social Critique of the Judgement of Taste*. Trans. Nice, R. London: Routledge & Kegan Paul.

Bourdieu, P. 1986/2006. The forms of capital. In *Education, Globalization and Social Change*, eds. Lauder, H., Brown, P., Dillabough, J.-A. and Halsey, A.H. Oxford: Oxford University Press. 105–118.

Bourn, D. 2011. From internationalisation to global perspectives. *Higher Education Research & Development* 30 (5): 559–571.

Bowe, H. and Martin, K. 2007. *Communicating across Cultures: Mutual Understanding in a Global World*. Cambridge: Cambridge University Press.

Brighouse, H. 2010. Globalization and professional ethic of the professoriat. In *Global Inequalities and Higher Education: Whose Interests Are We Serving?*, ed. Unterhalter, E. Basingstoke: Palgrave Macmillan. 287–311.

Brockington, J.L. and Wiedenhoeft, M.D. 2009. The liberal arts and global citizenship: Fostering intercultural engagement through integrative experiences and structured reflection. In *The Handbook of Practice and Research in Study Abroad: Higher Education and the Quest for Global Citizenship*, ed. Lewin, R. London: Routledge. 117–132.

Brookfield, S.D. 1987. *Developing Critical Thinkers*. Milton Keynes: Open University Press.

Brooks, R. and Everett, G. 2008. The prevalence of 'life planning': Evidence from UK graduates. *British Journal of Sociology of Education* 29 (3): 325–338.

Bruner, J. 1966. *Towards a Theory of Instruction*. Cambridge, MA: Harvard University Press.

Bruner, J. 2009. Culture, mind, and education. In *Contemporary Theories of Learning. Learning Theorists…in Their Own Words*, ed. Illeris, K. London: Routledge.

Carroll, L. 2005. *Alice's Adventures in Wonderland and Through the Looking Glass*. Stilwell: Digireads.com Publishing.

Caruana, V. 2007. Internationalisation of HE in the UK: 'Where are we now and where might we go?'. Presented at the Education in a Changing Environment Conference, Salford.

Caruana, V. and Ploner, J. 2010. *Internationalisation and Equality and Diversity: Merging Identities, a Case Study of Policy and Practice at Six Universities*. London: Equality Challenge Unit.

Case, R. 1993. Key elements of a global perspective. *Social Education* 57 (6): 318–352.

Centre for the Study of Global Change. n.d. Learning taxonomy – Krathwohl's affective domain. Indiana University. Accessed: September 2013 at http://www.indiana.edu/~global/icab/notebook/LearningTaxonomy_Affective.pdf

Clifford, V.A. 2011. Internationalising the home student (Editorial). *Higher Education Research & Development* 30 (5): 555–557.

Clifford, V.A., Adetunji, H. and Haigh, M. 2012. *Fostering Interculturality and Global Perspectives at Brookes through Dialogue with Staff.* Oxford: Oxford Centre for Staff and Learning Development.

Coelen, R.J. 2013. The internationalisation of Higher Education, 2.0. Inaugural Lecture. Stenden University of Applied Science. Accessed: March 2014 at http://www.stenden.com/nl/bedrijven/lectoraten/Internationalisation%20of%20Higher%20Education/Documents/DEF%20Lectorale%20Rede%20Robert%20J%20Coelen%20%20DIGI.pdf

Coffield, F., Moseley, D., Hall, E. and Ecclestone, K. 2004. *Learning Styles and Pedagogy in Post-16 Learning: A Systematic and Critical Review.* London: Learning and Skills Research Centre.

Cogan, J.J. 2000. Citizenship education for the 21st century: Setting the context. In *Citizenship for the 21st Century: An International Perspective on Education,* eds. Cogan, J.J. and Derricott, R. London: Kogan Page. 1–21.

Coleman, J.A. 1999. Language learner attitudes and student residence abroad: New qualitative and qualitative insights. In *Poetics and Praxis of Language and Intercultural Communication,* eds. Killick, D., Parry, M. and Phipps, A. Leeds Metropolitan University: Glasgow University Press/Leeds Metropolitan University. 75–95.

Cormeraie, S. 1998. From theoretical insights to best practice for successful inter-cultural education: The crucial transmission. In *Cross-cultural Capability Conference Proceedings,* eds. Killick, D. and Parry, M. Leeds: Leeds Metropolitan University. 46–55.

Cousin, G. 2011. Rethinking the concept of 'western'. *Higher Education Research & Development* 30 (5): 585–594.

Craib, I. 1998. *Experiencing Identity.* London: Sage.

Crick, B. 1998. *Education for Citizenship and the Teaching of Democracy in Schools.* London: Qualifications and Curriculum Authority.

Crossley, N. 2001. Citizenship, intersubjectivity and the lifeworld. In *Culture and Citizenship,* ed. Stevenson, N. London: Sage. 33–46.

Crowther, P., Joris, M., Otten, M., Nilsson, B., Teekens, H. and Wächter, B. 2000. *Internationalisation at Home: A Position Paper.* Amsterdam: European Association for International Education.

Cushner, K. and Mahon, J. 2002. Overseas student teaching: Affecting personal, professional, and global competencies in an age of globalization. *Journal of Studies in International Education* 6 (1): 44–58.

Dall'Alba, G. and Barnacle, R. 2007. An ontological turn for higher education. *Studies in Higher Education* 32 (6): 679–691.

Davies, L. 2003/2006. Education for positive conflict and interruptive democracy. In *Education, Globalization and Social Change,* eds. Lauder, H., Brown, P., Dillabough, J.-A. and Halsey, A.H. Oxford: Oxford University Press. 1029–1037.

de Jong, H. and Teekens, H. 2003. The case of the University of Twente: Internationalisation as education policy. *Journal of Studies in International Education* 7: 41–51.

De Vita, G. 2000. Inclusive approaches to effective communication and active participation in the multicultural classroom: An international business management context. *Active Learning in Higher Education* 1 (2): 168–180.

De Vita, G. and Case, P. 2003. Rethinking the internationalisation agenda in UK higher education. *Journal of Further and Higher Education* 27 (4): 383–398.

De Wit, H. 2012. Internationalisation of Higher Education: Nine misconceptions. In *Internationalisation Revisited: New Dimensions in the Internationalisation of Higher Education*, eds. Beelen, J. and De Wit, H. Amsterdam: CAREM. 5–21.

Deardorff, D.K. 2005. A matter of logic? Using a programs logic model, institutions of higher education can determine outcomes of internationalization efforts in a meaningful way. *International Educator* May/June: 26–31.

Dearing, R. (Chairman) The National Committee of Inquiry into Higher Education. 1997. *Higher Education in the Learning Society.* Norwich: HMSO.

DEEWR. 2013. About civics and citizenship education. Department of Education, Employment and Workplace Relations. Accessed: December 2013 at http://www. civicsandcitizenship.edu.au/cce/about_civics_and_citizenship_education,9625. html

Denson, N. and Zhang, S. 2010. The impact of student experiences with diversity on developing graduate attributes. *Studies in Higher Education* 25 (5): 529–543.

Denson, N. and Bowman, N. 2013. University diversity and preparation for a global society: The role of diversity in shaping intergroup attitudes and civic outcomes. *Studies in Higher Education* 38 (4): 555–570.

Dewey, J. 1916/1966. *Democracy and Education.* Toronto: Collier-Macmillan.

Dewey, J. 1916/2012. *Democracy and Education.* New York: Start Publishing LLC. Kindle e-book edition.

Dewey, J. 1933. *How We Think.* Boston: D.C. Heath & Co.

Dewey, J. 1934. *Arts as Experience.* New York: Perigee Books.

Dewey, J. 1938/1963. *Experience and Education.* New York: Collier Books.

Di Napoli, R. and Barnett, R. 2008. Introduction. In *Changing Identities in Higher Education. Voicing Perspectives*, eds. Barnett, R. and Di Napoli, R. London: Routledge. 1–8.

Donald, J. 2007. Internationalisation, diversity and the humanities curriculum: Cosmopolitanism and multiculturalism revisited. *Journal of Philosophy of Education* 41 (3): 207–308.

Dower, N. 2003. *An Introduction to Global Citizenship.* Edinburgh: Edinburgh University Press.

Dunne, C. 2009. Host students' perspectives of intercultural contact in an Irish university. *Journal of Studies in International Education* 13 (2): 222–239.

Early, P.C. and Ang, S. 2003. *Cultural Intelligence: Individual Interactions across Cultures.* Stanford, CA: Stanford Business Books.

Easthope, H. 2009. Fixed identities in a mobile world? The relationship between mobility, place, and identity. *Identities: Global Studies in Culture and Power* 16: 61–82.

Elkjaer, B. 2009. Pragmatism: A learning theory for the future. In *Contemporary Theories of Learning: Learning Theorists...in Their Own Words*, ed. Illeris, K. London: Routledge. 74–89.

Elliot, A. 2001. The reinvention of citizenship. In *Culture and Citizenship*, ed. Stevenson, N. London: Sage. 47–61.

Engeström, Y. 2009. Towards an activity-theoretical reconceptualization. In *Contemporary Theories of Learning. Learning Theorists...in Their Own Words*, ed. Illeris, K. London: Routledge. 53–73.

Entwistle, N.J. and Peterson, E.R. 2004. Conceptions of learning and knowledge in higher education: Relationships with study behaviour and influences of learning environments. *International Journal of Educational Research* 41: 407–428.

EU General Secretariat. 2013. Council conclusions on the global dimension of European higher education. EDUC 401 SOC 847 RECH 469 JEUN 98 RELEX 942. Brussels: Council of the European Union.

Falk, R. 2002. An emergent matrix of citizenship: Complex, uneven, and fluid. In *Global Citizenship: A Critical Reader*, eds. Dower, N. and Williams, J. Edinburgh: Edinburgh University Press. 15–29.

Fantini, A.E. 2000. A central concern: Developing intercultural competence. *SIT Occasional Papers Series* 1 (Spring): 25–42.

Featherstone, M. 1995. *Undoing Culture*. London: Sage.

Fleming, F. 2001. *Killing Dragons: The Conquest of the Alps*. London: Granta Books.

Foucault, M. 1977. *Discipline and Punish: The Birth of the Prison*. London: Penguin.

Freire, P. 1970. *Pedagogy of the Oppressed*. New York: Continuum.

Freire, P. 1972. *Cultural Action for Freedom*. Hammondsworth: Penguin.

Friedman, J. 1994. *Cultural Identity and Global Process*. London: Sage.

Fromm, E. 1984. *The Fear of Freedom*. London: Ark.

Furedi, F. 2011. Introduction to the marketisation of higher education and the student as consumer. In *The Marketisation of Higher Education and the Student as Consumer*, eds. Molesworth, M., Scullion, R. and Nixon, E. Abingdon, UK: Routledge. 1–8.

Gabb, D. 2006. Transcultural dynamics in the classroom. *Journal of Studies in International Education* 10 (4): 357–368.

Gacel-Ávila, J. 2005. The internationalisation of higher education: A paradigm for global citizenry. *Journal of Studies in International Education* 9 (2): 121–136.

Gardner, G.H. 1962. Cross-cultural communication. *Journal of Social Psychology* 58: 241–256.

Gardner, H. 1985. *Frames of Mind: The Theory of Multiple Intelligences*. London: Paladin.

Gergen, K.J. 1994. *Toward Transformation in Social Knowledge*. Thousand Oaks, CA: Sage.

Gergen, K.J. 1999. *An Invitation to Social Construction*. London: Sage.

Gibbs, G. 1995. *Assessing Student Centered Courses*. Oxford: Oxford Centre for Staff and Learning Development.

Gibbs, G. 2010. *Using Assessment to Support Student Learning*. Leeds: Leeds Metropolitan University Press.

Giddens, A. 1991. *Modernity and Self-identity: Self and Society in the Late Modern Age*. Cambidge: Polity Press.

Giddens, A. 1994. Living in a post-traditional society. In *Reflexive Modernisation*, eds. Beck, U., Giddens, A. and Lash, S. Cambridge: Polity Press. 56–109.

Giddens, A. 2002. *Runaway World: How Globalization is Reshaping our Lives*. London: Profile Books. Kindle e-book edition.

Giroux, A. and Purpel, D. 1983. *The Hidden Curriculum and Moral Education*. Richmond, CA: McCutchan Publishing.

Giroux, A. and McLaren, P. 1989. *Critical Pedagogy, the State, and the Struggle for Culture*. Albany, NY: State University of New York Press.

Gmelch, G. 1997. Crossing cultures: Student travel and personal development. *International Journal of Intercultural Relations* 21 (4): 475–490.

Goddard, A. and Henry, A. 2013. English language learning for international employability. In *For the Love of Learning: Innovations from Outstanding University Teachers*, ed. Bilham, T. Basingstoke: Palgrave Macmillan.

Goffman, E. 1967. *Interaction Ritual: Essays on Face-to-face Behavior*. New York: Pantheon Books.

Goleman, D. 1995. *Emotional Intelligence*. New York: Bantam Books.

Gordon, M.E. and Newburry, W.E. 2007. Students as a resource for introducing intercultural education in business schools. *Intercultural Education* 18 (3): 243–257.

GPI & AAC&U. 2011. *A Crucible Moment: College Learning and Democracy's Future*. Chicago/Washington, DC: The Global Perspectives Institute, Inc. and Association of American Colleges and Universities.

Graddol, D. 2006. English next. London: British Council – Learning. Accessed: December 2013 at http://www.britishcouncil.org/learning-research-english-next.pdf

Green, M.F. 2002. Internationalizing undergraduate education: Challenges and lessons of success. In *Promising Practices: Spotlighting Excellence in Comprehensive Internationalization*, eds. Engberg, D. and Green, M.F. Washington, DC: American Council on Education. 7–20.

Gregersen-Hermans, J. 2012. To ask or not to ask; That is the question. In *Internationalisation Revisited: New Dimensions in the Internationalisation of Higher Education*, eds. Beelen, J. and De Wit, H. Amsterdam: Centre for Applied Research on Economics and Management. 23–36.

Gudykunst, W. 1994. *Bridging Differences: Effective Intergroup Communication*. 2nd ed. London: Sage.

Gudykunst, W. 1995. Anxiety/uncertainty management (AUM) theory. In *Intercultural Communication Theory*, ed. Wiseman, R.L. Thousand Oaks, CA: Sage. 8–58.

Gudykunst, W. and Mody, B. 2002. *Handbook of International and Intercultural Communication*. Thousand Oaks, CA: Sage.

Gudykunst, W. and Kim, Y.Y. 2003. *Communicating with Strangers: An Approach to Intercultural Communication*. 4th ed. New York: McGraw-Hill.

Gurin, P., Dey, E.L., Hurtado, S., Gurin, G. and Gage, K. 2002. Diversity and higher education: Theory and impact on educational outcomes. *Harvard Educational Review* 72: 330–366.

Habu, T. 2000. The irony of globalization: The experience of Japanese women in British higher education. *Higher Education* 39: 43–66.

Haigh, M. 2002. Internationalisation of the curriculum: Designing inclusive education for a small world. *Journal of Geography in Higher Education* 26 (1): 49–66.

Haigh, M. 2013. Towards the intercultural self. Mahatma Gandhi's international education in London. In *Cross-cultural Teaching and Learning for Home and International Students*, ed. Ryan, J. London: Routledge. 196–210.

Haigh, M. and Clifford, V.A. 2011. Integral vision: A multi-perspective approach to the recognition of graduate attributes. *Higher Education Research & Development* 30 (5): 573–584.

Hall, E.T. 1959. *The Silent Language*. New York: Anchor Books.

Hall, E.T. 1966. *The Hidden Dimension*. New York: Doubleday.

Hamza, A. 2010. International experience: An opportunity for professional development in higher education. *Journal of Studies in International Education* 14 (1): 50–69.

Hanvey, R.G. 1976. *An Attainable Global Perspective*. New York: Global Perspectives in Education. Accessed: March 2014 at http://www.globaled.org/an_att_glob_persp_04_11_29.pdf

Harland, T. and Pickering, N. 2011. *Values in Higher Education Teaching*. London: Routledge.

HEA. 2013. UK Professional Standards Framework. York: Higher Education Academy. Accessed: December 2013 at http://www.heacademy.ac.uk/ukpsf

Hee Yoo, S., Matsamoto, D. and LeRoux, J. 2006. The influence of emotion recognition and emotion regulation on intercultural adjustment. *International Journal of Intercultural Relations* 30: 345–363.

Heidegger, M. 1962/1998. *Being and Time*. Trans. Macquarie, J. and Blackwell, B. Oxford: Blackwell.

Henderson, J. 2009. 'It's all about give and take', or is it? Where, when and how do native and non-native uses of English shape UK university students representations of each other and their learning experience? *Journal of Studies in International Education* 13 (3): 398–409.

Herrmann, K.J. 2013. The impact of cooperative learning on student engagement: Results from an intervention. *Active Learning in Higher Education* 14 (3): 175–187.

Heyward, M. 2002. From international to intercultural: Redefining the international school for a globalised world. *Journal of Research in International Education* 1 (1): 9–32.

Hobbes, T. 1651/2004. *Leviathan*. New York: Barnes and Noble.

Hofstede, G.H. 1984. *Culture's Consequences: International Differences in Work Related Issues*. Thousand Oaks,CA: Sage.

Hofstede, G.H. 1991. *Cultures and Organisations: Software of the Mind*. Maidenhead: McGraw Hill.

Hunter, A. 2008. Transformative learning in international education. In *Developing Intercultural Competence and Transformation: Theory, Research and Application in International Education*, ed. Savicki, V. Sterling, VA: Stylus. 92–107.

Husserl, E. 1936/1970. *The Idea of Phenomenology*. The Hague: Martinus Nijoff.

Hussey, T.B. and Smith, P. 2002. The trouble with learning outcomes. *Active Learning in Higher Education* 3 (3): 220–233.

Hussey, T.B. and Smith, P. 2008. Learning outcomes: A conceptual analysis. *Teaching in Higher Education* 13 (1): 107–115.

Illeris, K. 2002. *The Three Dimensions of Learning*. Roskilde, Denmark: Roskilde University Press/Leicester, UK: NIACE.

Illeris, K. 2004. Transformative learning in the perspective of a comprehensive learning theory. *Journal of Transformative Education* 2 (2): 79–89.

Illich, I. 1973. *Celebration of Awareness*. Harmondsworth: Penguin Education.

Ingold, T. 1993. Globes and spheres: The topology of environmentalism. In *Environmentalism*, ed. Milton, K. London: Routledge.

Ippolito, K. 2007. Promoting intercultural learning in a multicultural university: Ideals and realities. *Teaching in Higher Education* 12 (5): 749–763.

Isin, E.F. and Wood, P.K. 1999. *Citizenship and Identity*. London: Sage.

Jackson, J. 2008. *Language, Identity and Study Abroad*. London: Equinox.

Jarvis, P. 2005. Towards a philosophy of human learning: An existentialist perspective. In *Human Learning: An Holistic Approach*, eds. Jarvis, P. and Parker, S. Abingdon, UK: Routledge. 1–15.

Jarvis, P. 2006. *Towards a Comprehensive Theory of Human Learning: Lifelong Learning and the Learning Society*. Vol. 1. London: Routledge.

Jarvis, P. 2008. *Democracy, Lifelong Learning and the Learning Society: Active Citizenship in a Late Modern Age*. Vol. 3. London: Routledge.

Jarvis, P. 2009a. Ethics, values and higher education. The power of globalisation. In *Universities, Ethics and Professions*, eds. Strain, J., Barnett, R. and Jarvis, P. Abingdon, UK: Routledge. 13–28.

Jarvis, P. 2009b. Learning to be a person in society. In *Contemporary Theories of Learning. Learning Theorists…in Their Own Words*, ed. Illeris, K. London: Routledge. 21–34.

Johnson, D.W. and Johnson, R.T. 1998. *Cooperation and Competition: Theory and Research*. Edina, MN: Interaction Book Company.

Johnson, V.C. and Mulholland, J. 2006. Open doors, secure borders: Advantages of education abroad for public policy. *International Educator* May/June: 4–7.

Jones, E. 2010. 'Don't worry about the worries': Transforming lives through international volunteering. In *Internationalisation and the Student Voice: Higher Education Perspectives*, ed. Jones, E. London: Routledge. 83–97.

Jones, E. and Killick, D. 2007. Internationalisation of the curriculum. In *Internationalising Higher Education*, eds. Jones, E. and Brown, S. London: Routledge. 109–119.

Jones, E. and Lee, S. 2008. Perspectives, policy and institutional cultures: World-wide horizons at Leeds Metropolitan University. In *The Global University: The Role of Senior Managers*, eds. Shiel, C. and McKenzie, A. London: DEA. 26–30.

Jones, E. and Killick, D. 2013. Graduate attributes and the internationalised curriculum: Embedding a global outlook in disciplinary learning outcomes. *Journal of Studies in International Education* 17 (2): 165–182.

Kaplan, L. 1978. *Developing Objectives in the Affective Domain*. San Diego, CA: Collegiate Publishing.

Kauffman, N.L., Martin, J.N., Weaver, H.D. and Weaver, J. 1992. *Students Abroad, Strangers at Home: Education for a Global Society*. Yarmouth, ME: Intercultural Press.

Kaur-Stubbs, S. 2010. Engaged Europe: The role of intercultural dialogue in developing full, free and equal participation. In *Intercultural Dialogue: Enabling Free, Full and Equal Participation*, eds. Anderson, J. and Kaur-Stubbs, S. London: Platform for Intercultural Europe/Alliance Publishing Trust. 36–62.

Kiely, R. 2004. A chameleon with a complex: Searching for transformation in international service-learning. *Michigan Journal of Community Service Learning* 10 (2): 5–20.

Killick, D. 2006. *Cross-cultural Capability and Global Perspectives. Guidelines for Curriculum Review*. Leeds: Leeds Metropolitan University. Accessed: December 2013 at http://repository.leedsmet.ac.uk/main/view_record.php?identifier=8134&SearchGroup=Open+Educational+Resources

Killick, D. 2007. Internationalisation and engagement with the wider community. In *Internationalising Higher Education*, eds. Jones, E. and Brown, S. London: Routledge. 135–153.

Killick, D. 2011. *Embedding a Global Outlook as a Graduate Attribute at Leeds Metropolitan University.* Leeds: Leeds Metropolitan University. Accessed: December 2013 at https://www.leedsmet.ac.uk/staff/files/UG_Embedding_Global_Outlook.pdf

Killick, D. 2012. Seeing ourselves-in-the-world. *Journal of Studies in International Education* 16 (4): 372–389.

Killick, D. 2013. Global citizenship and campus community: Lessons from learning theory and the lived-experience of mobile students. In *Cross-cultural Teaching and Learning for Home and International Students*, ed. Ryan, J. London: Routledge. 182–195.

Kim, U. 2001. Culture, science, and indigenous psychologies. In *The Handbook of Culture and Psychology*, ed. Matsumoto, D. Oxford: Oxford University Press. 51–75.

Kimmel, K. and Volet, S. 2012. University students' perceptions of and attitudes towards culturally diverse group work. *Journal of Studies in International Education* 16 (2): 157–181.

King, P.M. and Baxter Magolda, M.B. 2005. A developmental model of intercultural maturity. *Journal of College Development* 46 (6): 571–592.

King, R., Findlay, A. and Aherns, J. 2010. *International Student Mobility Literature Review.* Report to HEFCE, and co-funded by the British Council, UK National Agency for Erasmus. London: HEFCE. Accessed: December 2013 at http://www.britishcouncil.org/hefce_bc_report2010.pdf

Knight, J. 1994. Internationalization: Elements and checkpoints. Research Monograph, No. 7. Ottawa: Canada: Canadian Bureau for International Education.

Knight, J. 2003. Updated internationalization definition. *International Higher Education* 33: 2–3.

Knight, J. 2009. New developments and unitended consequences: Whither thou goest, internationalization? In *Higher Education on the Move: New Developments in Global Mobility*, eds. Bhandari, R. and Laughlin, S. New York: Institute of International Education. 113–123.

Knowles, E.D. and Ames, D.R. 1999. *The Mentalistic Nature of Folk Person Concepts: Individual and Trait Term Differences.* Berkeley, CA: University of California.

Knowles, M. 1980. *The Modern Practice of Adult Education.* Revised ed. Chicago: Associated Press.

Kolb, D.A. 1976. *The Learning Styles Inventory: Technical Manual.* Boston: McBer.

Kolb, D.A. 1981. Learning styles and disciplinary differences. In *Responding to the New Realities of Diverse Students and a Changing Society*, eds. Chickering, A.W. and Associates. San Francisco, CA: Jossey-Bass. 232–255.

Kolb, D.A. 1984. *Experiential Learning: Experience as the Source of Learning and Development.* Englewood Cliffs, NJ: Prentice-Hall.

Krathwohl, D.R., Bloom, B.S. and Masia, B.B. 1964. *Taxonomy of Educational Objectives. The Classification of Educational Goals. Handbook II: Affective Domain.* London: Longman.

Kreber, C. 2009. Supporting student learning in the context of diversity, complexity and uncertainty. In *The University and Its Disciplines. Teaching and Learning Within and Beyond Disciplinary Boundaries*, ed. Kreber, C. London: Routledge. 3–18.

Kubow, P., Grossman, D. and Ninomiya, S. 2000. Multidimensional citizenship: Educational policy for the 21st Century. In *Citizenship for the 21st Century: An International Perspective on Education*, eds. Cogan, J.J. and Derricott, R. London: Kogan Page. 131–150.

Kymlicka, W. 1995. *Multicultural Citizenship*. Oxford: Clarendon Press.

Langer, E. 1989. *Mindfulness*. Reading, MA: Addison-Wesley.

Lapworth, S. 2008. A crisis in identity. The view of a postgraduate student of higher education. In *Changing Identities in Higher Education: Voicing Perspectives*, eds. Barnett, R. and Di Napoli, R. London: Routledge. 163–174.

Lauder, H., Brown, P., Dillabough, J.-A. and Halsey, A.H., eds. 2006. *Education, Globalization and Social Change*. Oxford: Oxford University Press.

Lave, J. and Wenger, E. 1998. *Situated Learning: Legitimate Peripheral Participation*. Cambridge: Cambridge University Press.

Lea, S.J., Stephenson, D. and Troy, J. 2003. Higher education students' attitudes to student-centred learning: Beyond 'educational bulimia'. *Studies in Higher Education* 28 (3): 321–334.

Leask, B. 2001. Bridging the gap: Internationalizing university curricula. *Journal of Studies in International Education* 5 (2): 100–115.

Leask, B. 2003. Beyond the numbers – Levels and layers of internationalisation to utilise and support growth and diversity. Presented at the 17th IDP Australian International Education Conference, Melbourne, Australia.

Leask, B. 2008. A holistic approach to internationalisation – Connecting institutional policy and the curriculum with the everyday reality of student life. In *Education for Sustainable Development: Graduates as Global Citizens*, eds. Shiel, C. and Takeda, S. Bournemouth University: Bournemouth University. 57–66.

Leask, B. 2009. Using formal and informal curricula to improve interactions between home and international students. *Journal of Studies in International Education* 13 (2): 205–221.

Leung, K. and Stephan, W.G. 2001. Social justice from a cultural perspective. In *The Handbook of Culture and Psychology*, ed. Matsumoto, D. Oxford: Oxford University Press. 375–410.

Liu, C.H. and Matthews, R. 2005. Vygotsky's philosophy: Constructivism and its criticisms examined. *International Education Journal* 6 (3): 386–399.

Lucas, J.S. 2003. Intercultural communication for international programs: An experientially-based course design. *Journal of Research in International Education* 2 (3): 301–314.

Luke, A. 2010. Educating the other: Standpoint and theory in the 'internationalization' of higher education. In *Global Inequalities and Higher Education: Whose Interests Are We Serving?*, eds. Unterhalter, E. and Carpenter, V. Basingstoke: Palgrave Macmillan. 43–65.

Luxon, T. and Peelo, M. 2009. Academic sojourners, teaching and internationalisation: The experience of non-UK staff in a British University. *Teaching in Higher Education* 14 (6): 649–659.

McGregor, C. 2004. Care(full) deliberation: A pedagogy for citizenship. *Journal of Transformative Education* 2 (2): 90–106.

McIntosh, P. 2005. Gender perspectives on educating for global citizenship. In *Educating Citizens for Global Awareness*, ed. Noddings, N. New York: Teachers College Press. 22–39.

Major, D. 2005. Learning through work-based learning. In *Enhancing Teaching in Higher Education*, eds. Hartley, P., Woods, A. and Pill, M. Abingdon, UK: Routledge. 16–25.

Marginson, S. 1999. After globalization: Emerging politics of education. *Education Policy* 14 (1): 19–31.

Maslow, A. 1954. *Motivation and Personality.* New York: Harper & Row.

Matsumoto, D. and Juang, L. 2004. *Culture and Psychology.* 3rd ed. Belmont, CA: Wadworth/Thompson Learning.

Matsumoto, D. and Yoo, S.H. 2005. Culture and applied nonverbal communication. In *Applications of Nonverbal Communication,* eds. Riggio, R.E. and Feldman, R.S. Mahwah, NJ: Lawrence Erlbaum Associates. 255–278.

Matsumoto, D., LeRoux, J., Ratzlaff, C., Tatani, H., Uchida, H., Kim, C. and Araki, S. 2001. Development and validation of a measure of intercultural adjustment potential in Japanese sojourners: The Intercultural Adjustment Potential Scale (ICAPS). *International Journal of Intercultural Relations* 25: 483–510.

May, S. 1999. *Critical Multiculturalism: Rethinking Multicultural and Antiracist Education.* London: Falmer Press.

Mead, G.H. 1967. *Mind, Self and Society.* Chicago: University of Chicago Press.

Merleau-Ponty, M. 1962. *Phenomenology of Perception.* London: Routledge & Kegan Paul.

Mestenhauser, J. 1998. Portraits of an international curriculum. An uncommon multidimensional perspective. In *Reforming the Higher Education Curriculum. Internationalizing the Campus,* eds. Mestenhauser, J. and Ellingboe, B. Pheonix, AZ: The American Council on Education and Oryx Press. 3–39.

Mestenhauser, J. 2002. The utilization of foreign students in internationalization of universities. In *Connections and Complexities: The Internationalization of Higher Education in Canada,* eds. Bond, S. and Bowry, C. Winnepeg: Centre for Higher Education Research and Development, The University of Manitoba. 15–27.

Meyer, J. and Land, R. 2003. Threshold concepts and troublesome knowledge: Linkages to ways of thinking and practising within the disciplines. ETL Project, Universities of Edinburgh, Coventry and Durham. Accessed: December 2013 at http://www.tla.ed.ac.uk/etl/docs/ETLreport4.pdf

Meyer, J. and Land, R. 2005. Threshold concepts and troublesome knowledge (2): Epistemological considerations and a conceptual framework for teaching and learning. *Higher Education* 49 (3): 373–388.

Meyer, J., Land, R. and Baillie, C., eds. 2010. *Threshold Concepts and Transformational Learning.* Boston: Sense Publishers.

Mezirow, J. 1978. Perspective transformation. *Adult Education* 28: 100–110.

Mezirow, J. 1991. *Transformative Dimensions of Adult Learning.* San Francisco, CA: Jossey-Bass.

Mezirow, J. 1994. Understanding transformation theory. *Adult Education Quarterly* 44 (4): 222–232.

Mezirow, J. 2000. Learning to think like an adult. Core concepts of Transformational Theory. In *Learning as Transformation,* eds. Mezirow, J. and Associates. San Fransisco, CA: Jossey-Bass. 3–33.

Mezirow, J. and Associates, eds. 2000. *Learning as Transformation: Critical Perspectives on a Theory in Progress.* San Francisco, CA: Jossey-Bass.

Middlehurst, R. and Woodfield, S. 2007. *Responding to the Internationalisation Agenda: Implications for Institutional Strategy.* Research Project Report 05/06. York: Higher Education Academy.

Moon, J.A. 2004. *A Handbook of Reflective and Experiential Learning.* London: Routledge Falmer.

Morley, L. 2001. Producing new workers: Quality, equality and employability in higher education. *Quality in Higher Education* 7 (2): 131–138.

Murphy-Lejeune, E. 2002. *Student Mobility and Narrative in Europe*. London: Routledge.

Naido, R. 2010. Global learning in a neoliberal age: Implications for development. In *Global Inequalities and Higher Education: Whose Interests Are We Serving?*, eds. Unterhalter, E. and Carpenter, V. Basingstoke: Palgrave Macmillan. 66–90.

National Intelligence Council. 2008. *Global Trends 2025: A Transformed World*. Washington, DC: National Intelligence Department.

National Society for Experiential Education. 2013. Eight principles of good practice for all experiential learning activities. Accessed: December 2013 at http://www.nsee.org/standards-and-practice

Nesdale, D. and Todd, P. 2000. Effect of contact on intercultural acceptance: A field study. *International Journal of Intercultural Relations* 24: 341–360.

Nilsson, B. 2003. Internationalisation at home from a Swedish perspective: The case of Malmö. *Journal of Studies in International Education* 7 (1): 27–40.

Nissen, T. 1970. *Indlæring og pædagogik*. Copenhagen: Munksgaard.

Nusche, D. 2008. *Assessment of Learning Outcomes in Higher Education: A Comparative Review of Selected Practices*. OECD Publishing. Accessed: December 2013 at http://www.oecd-ilibrary.org/education/assessment-of-learning-outcomes-in-higher-education_244257272573

Nussbaum, M. 1997. *Cultivating Humanity: A Classical Defense of Reform in Liberal Education*. Cambridge, MA: Harvard University Press.

Nussbaum, M. 2000. *Women and Human Development: The Capabilities Approach*. Cambridge: Cambridge University Press.

Oberg, K. 1960. Culture shock: Adjustment to new cultural environments. *Practical Anthropology* 7: 177–182.

Olson, C.L. and Kroeger, K.R. 2001. Global competency and intercultural sensitivity. *Journal of Studies in International Education* 5 (116): 116–137.

Olson, C.L., Evans, R. and Shoenberg, R.F. 2007. *At Home in the World: Bridging the Gap Between Internationalization and Multicultural Education*. Washington, DC: American Council on Education.

Olssen, M. 2004/2006. Neoliberalism, globalization, democracy: Challenges for education. In *Education, Globalization, and Social Change*, eds. Lauder, H., Brown, P., Dillabough, J.-A. and Halsey, A.H. Oxford: Oxford University Press. 261–287.

Opotow, S. 1990. Moral exclusion and injustice: An introduction. *Journal of Social Issues* 46 (1): 1–20.

Otter, D. 2007. Globalisation and sustainability. Global perspectives and education for sustainable development in higher education. In *Internationalising Higher Education*, eds. Jones, E. and Brown, S. London: Routledge. 42–53.

Papestephenou, M. and Angeli, C. 2007. Critical thinking beyond skill. *Educational Philosophy and Theory* 39 (6): 604–621.

Pedersen, P. 1995. *The Five Stages of Culture Shock: Critical Incidents Around the World*. Westport, CT: Greenwood.

Peel, D. and Frank, A. 2008. The internationalisation of planning education: Issues, perceptions and polarities for action. *Town Planning Review* 79 (1): 87–123.

Peng, K., Ames, D.R. and Knowles, E.D. 2001. Culture and human inference. Perspectives from three traditions. In *The Handbook of Culture and Psychology*, ed. Matsumoto, D. Oxford: Oxford University Press. 245–264.

Philippot, P., Douilliez, C., Pham, T., Foisy, M.-L. and Kornreich, C. 2005. Facial expression decoding deficits in clinical populations with interpersonal relationship dysfunctions. In *Applications of Nonverbal Communication*, eds. Riggio, R.E. and Feldman, R.S. Mahwah, NJ: Lawrence Erbaum Associates.

Piaget, J. 1929. *The Child's Conception of the World*. London: Routledge and Kegan Paul.

Piaget, J. 1954. *The Child's Construction of Reality*. London: Routledge and Kegan Paul.

Piaget, J. 1972. *The Psychology of the Child*. New York: Basic Books.

Piaget, J. 1977. *Equilibration of Cognitive Structures*. New York: Viking.

Pinker, S. 2011. *The Better Angels of our Nature*. London: Penguin.

Preisler, B., Klitgård, A. and Fabricius, A., eds. 2011. *Language and Learning in the International University: Practicing Diversity in the Face of English Language Uniformity*. Cleveland: Multilingual Matters.

Putnam, R.D., ed. 2002. *Democracies in Flux: The Evolution of Social Capital in Contemporary Society*. New York: Oxford University Press.

QAA. 2013. Honours Degree Subject Benchmark Statements. UK Quality Assurance Agency. Accessed: December 2013 at http://www.qaa.ac.uk/AssuringStandardsAndQuality/subject-guidance/Pages/Honours-degree-benchmark-statements.aspx

Qiang, Z. 2003. Internationalization of higher education: Towards a conceptual framework. *Policy Futures in Education* 1 (2): 148–270.

Race, P. 2006. *The Lecturer's Toolkit*. London: Routledge.

Rawls, J. 1971. *A Theory of Justice*. Cambridge, MA: Harvard University Press.

Reimer, T., Mata, R., Katsikopoulos, K. and Opwis, K. 2005. On the interplay between heuristic and systematic processes in persuasion. In *Proceedings of the 27th Annual Conference of the Cognitive Science Society*, eds. Bara, B.G., Barsalou, L. and Bucciarelli, M. Mahwah, NY: Lawrence Erlbaum Associates. 1833–1838.

Rhoads, R.A. and Szelényi, K. 2011a. Globalization, citizenship, and the university. In *Global Citizenship and the University*, eds. Rhoads, R.A. and Szelényi, K. Stanford, CA: Stanford University Press. 1–50.

Rhoads, R.A. and Szelényi, K., eds. 2011b. *Global Citizenship and the University*. Stanford, CA: Stanford University Press.

Ritzer, G. 1993. *The McDonaldization of Society: An Investigation into the Changing Character of Contemporary Social Life*. Thousand Oaks, CA: Pine Forge Press.

Ritzer, G. 2004. *The Globalization of Nothing*. Thousand Oaks, CA: Sage.

Rizvi, F. n.d. Internationalisation of curriculum. Accessed: September 2013 at: http://www.teaching.rmit.edu.au/resources/icpfr.PDF

Roberts, C. 2003. Ethnography and cultural practice: Ways of learning during residence abroad. In *Intercultural Experience and Education*, eds. Alred, G., Byram, M. and Fleming, M. Clevedon: Multilingual Matters. 114–130.

Roberts, J. 2008. Capturing values: A triangulation of academic frameworks, concepts of education and the student experience. In *Education for Sustainable Development: Graduates as Global Citizens*, eds. Shiel, C. and Takeda, S. Bournemouth: Bournemouth University Press. 117–128.

Robins, K. 1996. Interrupting identities: Turkey/Europe. In *Cultural Identity*, eds. Hall, S. and du Gay, P. London: Sage. 61–86.

Robinson, S. and Katulushi, C. 2005. The integrity of the university. In *Values in Higher Education*, eds. Robinson, S. and Katulushi, C. St Bride's Major: Aureus/ University of Leeds. 242–268.

Robinson, S. and Lee, S. 2007. Global ethics on the ascent. In *Internationalising Higher Education*, eds. Jones, E. and Brown, S. London: Routledge. 9–24.

Rogers, C.R. 1959. Significant learning in therapy and in education. *Educational Leadership* 16: 232–224.

Rogers, C.R. 1961. *On Becoming a Person: A Therapist's View of Psychotherapy*. Boston: Houghton-Mifflin.

Rogers, C.R. 1969. *Freedom to Learn: A View of What Education Might Become*. Columbus, OH: Charles E. Merrill.

Rogers, C.R. 1983. *Freedom to Learn for the 80s*. 2nd ed. Columbus, OH: Charles E Merrill.

Rojzman, C. 1999. *How to Live Together: A New Way of Dealing with Racism and Violence*. St Kilda, West Australia: Acland.

Rutherford, J. 2007. *After Identity*. London: Lawrence & Wishart.

Ryan, J. 2013. Listening to 'other' intellectual traditions: Learning in transcultural spaces. In *Cross-cultural Teaching and Learning for Home and International Students*, ed. Ryan, J. London: Routledge. 279–293.

Said, E. 1985. Orientalism reconsidered. *Race and Class* 27 (2): 1–15.

Said, E. 1978/1987. *Orientalism*. New York: Vintage.

Savicki, V. 2008. Experiential and affective education for international educators. In *Developing Intercultural Competence and Transformation: Theory, Research and Application in International Education*, ed. Savicki, V. Sterling, VA: Stylus. 74–107.

Scholte, J.A. 2000. *Globalization: A Critical Introduction*. Basingstoke: Palgrave.

Schön, D.A. 1983. *The Reflective Practitioner*. New York: Basic Books.

Schuerholz-Lehr, S. 2007. Teaching for global literacy in higher education: How prepared are the educators? *Journal of Studies in International Education* 11 (2): 180–204.

Schuncke, G.M. 1984. Global awareness and younger children: Beginning the process. *Social Studies* 75 (Nov/Dec): 248–251.

Schwartz, S.H. 1994. Are there universal aspects in the structure and content of human values? *Journal of Social Issues* 50: 19–45.

Schwartz, S.H. 2013. Rethinking the concept and measurement of societal culture in light of empirical findings. *Journal of Cross-cultural Psychology* (Advance online publication).

Schweisfurth, M. and Gu, Q. 2009. Exploring the experiences of international students in UK higher education: Possibilities and limits of interculturality in university life. *Intercultural Education* 20 (5): 436–473.

Searle, W. and Ward, C. 1990. The prediction of psychological and sociocultural adjustment during crosscultural transition. *International Journal of Intercultural Relations* 14: 449–464.

Sen, A. 1992. *Inequality Reexamined*. Cambridge, MA: Harvard University Press.

Sen, A. 1993. Capability and well-being. In *The Quality of Life*, eds. Nussbaum, M. and Sen, A. Oxford: Clarendon Press. 30–53.

Sen, A. 1999. *Development as Freedom*. Oxford: Oxford University Press.

Sen, A. 2003. Human capital and human capability. In *Readings in Human Development*, eds. Fukudo-Parr, S. and Kumar, A.K. Oxford: Oxford University Press.

Sen, A. 2008. The idea of justice. *Journal of Human Development* 9 (3): 331–342.

Sen Gupta, A. 2003. Changing the focus: A discussion of the dynamics of the intercultural experience. In *Intercultural Experience and Education*, eds. Alred, G., Byram, M. and Fleming, M. Clevedon: Multilingual Matters. 155–173.

Shaull, R. 1972. Foreword. In *Pedagogy of the Oppressed*, ed. Freire, P. Harmondsworth: Penguin Education. 9–14.

Shiel, C. and Takeda, S. 2008. Global vision and global citizenship at Bournemouth University. In *Conference Proceedings of the Education for Sustainable Development: Graduates as Global Citizens, December 2007*, eds. Shiel, C. and Takeda, S. Bournemouth: Bournemouth University Press. 3–8.

Shupe, E.I. 2007. Clashing cultures: A model of international student conflict. *Journal of Cross-Cultural Psychology* 38 (6): 750–771.

Simpson, E.J. 1972. *The Classification of Educational Objectives in the Psychomotor Domain*. Washington, DC: Gryphon House.

Singelis, T. 1994. Nonverbal communication in intercultural interactions. In *Improving Intercultural Interactions: Modules for Cross-cultural Training Programmes*, eds. Brislin, R.W. and Yoshida, T. London: Sage. 268–295.

Skirry, J. 2006. René Descartes: The mind–body distinction. Accessed: December 2013 at http://www.iep.utm.edu/descmind/

Soysal, Y. 1994. *Limits of Citizenship: Migrants and Postnational Membership in Europe*. Chicago: Chicago University Press.

Stefani, L. 2009. Planning teaching and learning: Curriculum design and development. In *A Handbook for Teaching and Learning in Higher Education*, ed. Fry, H. London: Routledge.

Stephenson, J. 1992. Capability and quality in higher education. In *Quality in Learning: A Capability Approach to Higher Education*, eds. Stephenson, J. and Weil, S. London: Kogan Page. 1–9.

Stephenson, J. 1998. The concept of capability and its importance in higher education. In *Capability and Quality in Higher Education*, eds. Stephenson, J. and Yorke, M. London: Kogan Page. 1–13.

Stone, N. 2006. Internationalising the student learning experience: Possible indicators. *Journal of Studies in International Education* 10 (4): 409–413.

Tadmor, C.T., Tetlock, P.E. and Peng, K. 2009. Acculturation strategies and integrative complexity. The cognitive implications of biculturalism. *Journal of Cross-cultural Psychology* 40 (1): 105–139.

Tajfel, H. 1978. *Differentiation between Social Groups: Studies in the Psychology of Intergroup Relations*. London: Academic Press.

Tajfel, H. 1981. *Human Groups and Social Categories*. Cambridge: Cambridge Press.

Tajfel, H. and Turner, J.C. 1986. The social identity theory of intergroup behavior. In *Psychology of intergroup relations*, eds. Worchel, S. and Austin, W.G. Chicago: Nelson-Hall. 33–47.

Taylor, C. 1991. *The Ethics of Authenticity*. Cambridge, MA: Harvard University Press.

Teekens, H. 2001. A desciption of nine clusters of qualifications for lecturers. In *Teaching and Learning in the International Classroom*, ed. Teekens, H. The Hague: Nuffic. 22–39.

Teekens, H. 2003. The requirement to develop specific skills for teaching in an international setting. *Journal of Studies in In International Education* 7 (1): 108–119.

Tennant, M. 2005. *Psychology and Adult Learning*. 3rd ed. London: Routledge.

Tennant, M. 2009. Lifelong learning as a technology of the self. In *Contemporary Theories of Learning. Learning Theorists … in Their Own Words*, ed. Illeris, K. London: Routledge. 147–158.

Ting-Toomey, S. 1999. *Communicating across Cultures*. New York: The Guilford Press.

Triandis, H.C. 1990. Theoretical concepts that are applicable to the analysis of ethnocentrism. In *Applied Cross-cultural Psychology*, ed. Brislin, R.W. London: Sage. 34–55.

Triandis, H.C. 1994. *Culture and Social Behavior*. New York: McGraw-Hill.

Triandis, H.C. 2001. Individualism and collectivism. Past, present, and future. In *The Handbook of Culture and Psychology*, ed. Matsumoto, D. Oxford: Oxford University Press. 35–50.

Trice, A.G. 2007. Faculty perspectives regarding graduate international students' isolation from host national students. *International Education Journal* 8 (1): 108–117.

Tuckman, B. 1965. Developmental sequence in small groups. *Psychological Bulletin* 63 (6): 384–399.

UNESCO. 2004. *Higher Education for a Globalized Society*. UNESCO Education Position Paper. ED-2004/WS/33.

United Nations. 1990 and 2010. Human Development Index. United Nations. Accessed: December 2013 at http://hdr.undp.org/en/statistics/hdi/

United Nations. 2004. *Human Development Report 2004: Cultural Liberty in Today's Diverse World*. New York: United Nations Development Program.

Urry, J. 1995. *Consuming Places*. London: Routledge.

Urry, J. 2000. *Sociology beyond Societies: Mobilities for the Twenty-first Century*. London: Routledge.

US Department of Education. 2012. *Succeeding Globally through International Education and Engagement: US Department of Education International Strategy 2012–16*. Washington, DC: US Department of Education.

Van der Werf, E. 2012. Internationalisation strategies and the development of competent teaching staff. In *Internationalisation Revisited: New Dimensions in the Internationalisation of Higher Education*, eds. Beelen, J. and De Wit, H. Amsterdam: CAREM. 99–106.

Volet, S. and Ang, G. 1998. Culturally mixed groups on international campuses: An opportunity for inter-cultural learning. *Higher Education Research & Development* 17 (1): 5–23.

Vygotsky, L.S. 1962. *Thought and Language*. Cambridge, MA: MIT Press.

Vygotsky, L.S. 1978. *Mind in Society: The Development of Higher Psychological Processes*. Cambridge, MA: Harvard University Press.

Walker, M. 2010. Pedagogy for rich human being-ness in global times. In *Global Inequalities and Higher Education: Whose Interests are We Serving?*, eds. Unterhalter, E. and Carpenter, V. Basingstoke: Palgrave Macmillan. 219–240.

Walker, M. and Unterhalter, E. 2007. The capability approach: Its potential for work in education. In *Amartya Sen's Capability Approach and Social Justice in Education*, eds. Walker, M. and Unterhalter, E. New York: Palgrave Macmillan.

Ward, C. 2001a. The A, B, Cs of acculturation. In *The Handbook of Culture and Psychology*, ed. Matsumoto, D. Oxford: Oxford University Press. 411–445.

Ward, C. 2001b. *The Impact of International Students on Domestic Students and Host Institutions*. Wellington, NZ: Ministry of Education. Accessed: December 2013 at http://www.educationcounts.govt.nz/publications/international/14684

Ward, C., Bochner, S. and Furnham, A. 2001. *The Psychology of Culture Shock*. 2nd ed. London: Routledge.

Webb, J., Schirato, T. and Danaher, G. 2002. *Understanding Bourdieu*. London: Sage.

Welikala, T. 2011. *Rethinking International Higher Education Curriculum: Mapping the Research Landscape.* Nottingham: Universitas 21.

Welsch, W. 1999. Transculturality: The puzzling form of cultures today. In *Spaces of Culture: City, Nation, World*, eds. Featherstone, M. and Lash, S. London: Sage. 194–213.

Wertsch, J.V., ed. 1986. *Culture, Communication and Cognition: Vygotskian Perspectives.* Cambridge: Cambridge University Press.

Whalley, T. 1996. Toward a theory of culture learning: A study based on journals written by Japanese and Canadian young adults in exchange programs (study abroad). Doctoral Disertation, Simon Fraser University. *Dissertation Abstracts International* 57 (03): 988.

Whalley, T., Langley, L. and Villarreal, L. 1997. *Best Practice Guidelines for Internationalizing the Curriculum.* Victoria, BC: Province of British Columbia Ministry of Education, Skills and Training and the Centre for Curriculum, Transfer and Technology.

White House. 2013. Knowledge and skills for the jobs of the future. The White House. Accessed: December 2013 at http://www.whitehouse.gov/issues/education/higher-education

Wicaksono, R. 2013. Raising students' awareness of the construction of communicative (in)competence in international classrooms. In *Cross-cultural Teaching and Learning for Home and International Students*, ed. Ryan, J. London: Routledge.

Woodward, K. 2002. *Understanding Identity.* London: Arnold.

Wright, S.C., Aron, A., McLaughlin-Volpe, T. and Ropp, S.A. 1997. The extended contact effect: Knowledge of cross-group friendships and prejudice. *Journal of Personality and Social Psychology* 73 (1): 73–90.

Yershova, Y., DaJaeghere, J. and Mestenhauser, J. 2000. Thinking not as usual: Adding the intercultural perspective. *Journal of Studies in International Education* 4 (1): 39–78.

Zachariah, M. 1989. Linking global education with multicultural education. *Alberta Teachers' Association Magazine* 69: 48–51.

Zhai, L. and Scheer, S.D. 2004. Global perspectives and attitudes toward cultural diversity among summer agriculture students at Ohio State University. *Journal of Agricultural Education* 45 (2): 39–51.

Zhou, Y., Jindal-Snape, D., Topping, K. and Todman, J. 2008. Theoretical models of culture shock and adaptation in international students in higher education. *Studies in Higher Education* 31 (3): 63–75.

Index

academic equity 131, 136
acculturation 54–5, 57, 93, 107, 127–8, 147, 178
acculturative stress 55; *see also* culture shock
act-in-the-world 31–3, 35, 80–1, 94, 126, 180; *see also self-in-the-world*
agency 2, 4, 17, 32, 36–9, 68, 78, 80, 82, 97, 126, 146, 180, 182
Allport, G. 63–4, 91, 100, 130, 158–9; *see also* Contact Theory
Appadurai, A. 36, 38, 42–4, 78, 147; *see also* scapes
Appiah, K. 31, 44–5, 47, 86, 130, 147
assessment 25, 76, 137–8, 146–8, 150, 154, 161, 168–70, 176, 178, 181
attitudes 53–6, 60, 86, 91–6, 105, 107, 111, 147, 149–50; *see also* heuristics
authentic, authenticity 16–18, 42, 51, 65, 72, 103, 107, 110, 140, 167

Barnett, R. 14–17, 41, 79, 105, 111, 115, 125, 140, 148
Bauman, Z. 7, 36, 40–44, 64, 68, 71, 75, 104, 127, 138, 160
biography 6, 30, 45–6, 54, 68–74, 98–9, 169–70
Bourdieu, P. 37, 47, 75–8, 170

capability 78–83, 125–6, 135; *see also* cross-cultural capability; Sen, A.
capital: cultural 47, 75–6, 78–84, 129, 175; economic 8; embodied 75, 170; human 28; intellectual 8; social 130
Cartesian 67, 97; *see also* Descartes, R.
categorization 48, 50, 90, 131, 137, 156, 171

citizen, citizenship 16–21, 24, 26, 29–32, 34, 37, 62, 79, 85, 141, 147, 173, 181; European 17–18, 20; *see also* global citizen
commodification: of higher education 41; of nothing 41, 130
communities of practice 116, 118–19, 130, 160–1, 164, 177, 181
competence 33, 49, 53–4, 56–7, 60–61, 65, 133, 140
conscientization 101, 114, 126
constructionism, constructivism 4, 76, 97–8, 100, 112, 116, 118, 138, 148, 156–7, 161, 181
constructive alignment 118, 148, 166, 168
consumerism, consumerist, consumption 39–45, 49, 84–5, 104, 130, 152
Contact Theory 63, 65, 91, 160; *see also* Allport, G.; Extended Contact Theory
conversation 5, 31, 130, 136, 156, 172, 181; *see also* dialogue
cosmopolitanism 17, 31, 86, 130, 147
critical pedagogy 19, 126
critical thinking 93, 95–6, 132, 142, 167
cross-cultural capability 82, 126, 144
culture: iceberg 83, 85–6, 126; macro- 54, 57, 60, 69, 93–4; postfigurative 69, 74; prefigurative 70, 74, 157
culture shock 42, 55, 61, 86, 103, 127, 167, 178; *see also* acculturative stress
curriculum: formal 15, 25, 102, 118, 126–7, 129, 138, 175, 181; hidden 58, 79, 84, 114, 126–7, 129, 131–2, 137, 148, 156; informal 126–7, 139, 173–4, 181; *see also* internationalization

Descartes, R. 67; *see also* Cartesian
deterritorialization 9, 36–7, 85, 130
detraditionalization 84, 130
Dewey, J. 4, 17, 26, 30, 63–4, 75, 79,
  98, 112–14, 158, 160, 165, 167
dialogue 32, 39, 44, 47, 108, 160–63;
  see also conversation
disequilibrium, disjuncture,
  disorientation 31, 111–12
diversity 24–5, 27, 49, 70, 73, 77,
  127–9, 140, 146, 156, 163–4,
  171–2, 178
domestic students 8, 73, 127, 161, 174;
  see also international students
domestication 4, 14, 18

emic 117, 119, 153, 177; *see also* etic
emotion: recognition 56, 61, 107;
  regulation 56, 163; *see also* emotional
empathy, empathize 11, 49, 56, 107,
  146–7
employability 8, 14, 16, 40, 78, 135,
  139, 143
English language 21, 128, 131, 133–4,
  137, 169, 171; ELF 20, 135–6, 156
epistemology, epistemological 45,
  112–13, 121–2, 125
ethics, ethical issues 7, 81–2, 139, 154
ethnocentrism 45, 50–52, 119–20
ethnorelativism 50–51, 65, 119, 126
etic 117, 119, 153, 167, 177; *see also*
  emic
Extended Contact Theory 160; *see also*
  Contact Theory

face 59–60
feedback 57, 171
Freire, P. 1, 4, 14, 18–19, 47, 82, 101,
  114, 126, 165
fundamentalism, fundamentalist 14, 36,
  38–9, 42, 85, 125

Gardner, H. 106–8
Giddens, A. 10, 36–7, 39, 71, 82, 84
global citizen, global citizenship 11, 24,
  26, 29–32, 34, 147, 173, 181; types
  of 29
global imagination 141–2
global outlook 27, 146, 150, 153, 155
global perspectives 15, 82, 126, 144
global relevance 25, 27–8, 128, 143,
  155, 181

global self 5–8, 17, 28–36, 39, 44, 49,
  52, 55, 70–72, 91, 98–9, 101–2,
  104–5, 107–8, 110, 112, 120–22,
  127–8, 134–6, 142–3, 146–7, 156,
  166–9, 174, 179, 181–2; *see also*
  global student
global student 2, 5–6, 8, 23, 28, 30–3,
  36, 41, 45, 57, 60, 63, 69, 82, 86,
  88–9, 91, 113, 145–7, 150, 155,
  157–8, 160, 169, 172, 180–1; *see also*
  global self
grand narratives 15, 37–8, 43, 45, 63,
  73, 130
group work 73, 94, 151, 158–64, 167

habitus 75–9, 84, 102, 108, 117, 119
Heidegger, M. 30, 42, 67, 75, 77, 88,
  167
heuristics 68, 91, 94–6, 106, 147; *see*
  also attitudes
high-context cultures 59; *see also*
  low-context cultures
Husserl, E. 30, 71

identification of self, of others 31,
  48–50, 54, 65, 68, 94, 121, 128,
  131–3, 160, 171, 174, 181
identity 10, 15, 20–1, 30–34, 36,
  39–40, 44–9, 52–3, 73–4, 102,
  104, 120–22, 125–6, 129–32,
  142, 146, 167, 180; academic 13;
  commodification of 41; *see also* self
  identity; social identity
Illich, I. 12, 180
imagination 38–9, 53, 68–9, 81, 130,
  141–2, 147
in-groups 48–50, 52–3, 57–8, 65, 90,
  93, 160; *see also* out-groups
inclusive practice, inclusivity 2, 25,
  27–8, 33, 49, 65, 76, 79, 83, 118,
  129–33, 136, 140, 146, 155–6,
  160–62, 171–2, 177–9, 181–2
intelligence: cultural 108; emotional
  56, 107, 110, 122, 163;
  multiple 107
intercultural: communication 24, 54–61,
  84, 114, 135–7, 154, 169, 173, 181;
  encounter 57, 113–14, 164; *see also*
  non-verbal communication
international students 2, 20–21, 25, 73,
  120, 131–2, 143, 160–61; *see also*
  domestic students

internationalization: approaches to 23, 26; of the curriculum 6, 25–8, 104 (add-on approach 26, 141; infusion approach 26, 141); definition of 22, 33; and equality and diversity 27; at home 128; models of 20–22, 28, 127; principles of 23–4; rationale for 21, 24–6
isomorphic attribution 57

Jarvis, P. 14, 42, 73, 82, 9–99, 105, 115–16, 129

learning: approach 5, 126, 157, 158, 161, 164; affective dimension 103, 109, 147, 169; behavioural dimension 22, 50, 89, 108–9; cognitive dimension 106–10, 115, 118, 122, 147; cooperative 161; environment 1, 98, 164; experiential 18, 112, 114–15, 158–9, 165, 181; incidental 42, 64, 113–15, 130–31, 148, 150, 153; life-long 33; partnerships 122, 159; situated 116; social 118; spaces 61, 63–4, 67–8, 76, 84, 93, 126, 131–2, 134, 137, 180; stages 119–23; student-centred 156–7, 161; three-dimensional 22, 106–11, 115, 159, 180; see also significant learning; transformative learning, transformative approach; virtuous learning circles
learning outcomes 25, 32–3, 144–51, 153–6, 163, 166, 168–9, 181
learning thresholds 103–4, 108, 119
lifeworld 30–31, 33, 43–4, 46, 48, 65–96, 98–100, 102, 104, 106, 109, 112, 115, 118–19, 125, 148, 157, 169, 180–81
lived-experience 9, 44, 46, 67–70, 72, 98, 114–15, 179
low-context cultures 59; see also high-context cultures

markets, marketization 13–14, 16, 24, 27, 44, 47, 153, 157
Maslow, A. 48, 122–3
Mead, G.H. 17, 167
meaning perspectives, meaning schemes 101–3, 105, 114; see also schemes
Merleau-Ponty, M. 44, 68, 72
Mezirow, C. 12, 100–2, 107, 111, 123, 158; see also transformative learning

mindful, mindfulness 42, 56, 61, 91, 113, 115, 136, 152, 167, 170–71, 177
motivation 48, 107–8, 113, 122–3
multicultural, multiculturalism 2, 24–5, 36, 54–6, 63, 73, 85, 128–9, 131, 146, 154, 172, 176–7; multicultural education 25, 128, 131

nation state 10–11, 17, 29–30, 36–9, 52
non-verbal communication 58–60, 136; see also intercultural communication
Nussbaum, M. 39, 42, 81, 133, 147

ontology, ontological 45, 64, 67, 112–13, 125, 129; ontological security 129
Orientalism 52, 83; see also Said, E.
out-groups 48–50, 57; see also in-groups

phenomenologist 67
Piaget, J. 48, 87, 97, 99
postmodern, postmodernism 36, 43–4, 63, 72–3, 82, 84, 104, 125
power 8, 10, 14, 25, 32, 36, 63, 65, 78–9, 118, 127, 136; power dynamics 65, 118–19
prejudice 63, 65, 91–2, 109, 123, 130–31
projects 43, 50, 72, 175
prototypes, prototypical 89–90, 94

ready-to-hand 30–31, 42, 48, 75, 77, 79, 83, 85, 88, 167, 177; see also unready-to-hand
reflection 4, 7, 57, 79, 109, 111–15, 119, 156–7, 164–7, 177–8, 181; reflection-in-action 113, 115; see also reflexion, reflexivity
reflexion, reflexivity 71, 79–83, 162, 164–7, 181; fractured reflexives 166–7; see also reflection
relativism 29, 31, 119, 141
Rogers, C. 100, 106–7, 110, 140, 158; see also significant learning

Said, E. 52, 83; see also Orientalism
scapes (ethnoscapes, financescapes, mediascapes, technoscapes) 38–9, 42–5, 49, 55, 63–4, 73, 85, 125; see also Appadurai, A.
sceptical 2, 15–16, 31, 41, 74, 139, 141–3

schemes, schemata 48, 84, 87–91, 93–4, 99–102, 104–5, 107–9, 116–19, 125, 159–60, 169; *see also* meaning perspectives, meaning schemes; scripts
scripts 54, 84, 87, 89, 91, 113, 121, 159; *see also* schemes, schemata
security, personal, sense of 31, 38, 44, 62, 81, 86, 123, 125, 127, 129–30
Selective Exposure Hypothesis 93, 111; *see also* stereotypes
self: -actualization 107, 123; -authorship 33, 121–2; -concept 47, 77, 107–8, 110; -confidence 79, 81, 175; -efficacy 81, 110, 114, 129, 177; -identity 8, 30–31, 43, 48, 68, 71, 79, 92, 95–6, 180
self-in-the-world 31–5, 40, 45, 49–50, 52, 62, 72, 100, 102, 107, 126, 147; *see also act-in-the-world*
Sen, A. 4, 47, 63, 80–81, 83, 114, 138, 181; *see also* capability
significant learning 27, 47, 100, 106–7, 135, 158, 177, 181; *see also* transformative learning
social identity 44–5, 47–9, 52–3, 57, 86; Social Identity Theory 47–9, 57, 86 social identity threat 48–9; *see also* identity
social justice 16, 19, 25, 50
stereotypes, stereotyping 48, 53, 56, 90–91, 93, 96, 111, 128, 131–2, 137, 146, 153, 156, 161, 181; autostereotypes 90; heterostereotypes 90

study abroad 39, 50, 53, 101, 119–20, 158, 174–6

taxonomies (affective, cognitive, psychomotor) 122, 149–50
threshold concept 103
tourism, toured 36, 39, 45–6, 174–5
transculturality 85–6
transformative learning, transformative approach 26, 44, 100–2, 109, 130, 141, 157–8, 169
troublesome knowledge 103, 140
trust 163
truth, truths 39, 67–8, 76, 104, 125–6, 139–43, 156–7, 172, 180

uncertainty 56–7, 73–4, 88, 93, 102, 125, 139, 163, 166
unfinalizability 104
United Nations 4, 30, 80
universalism 31
unready-to-hand 31, 46, 167; *see also* ready-to-hand

values 4–6, 9, 13, 17–19, 22–3, 25, 37–8, 41, 45–6, 54, 56–7, 60–63, 67, 75, 77, 84, 86–7, 119–20, 122–3, 125–6, 140, 143, 162, 167, 169, 174, 176–7
veil of ignorance 62–3, 141
virtuous learning circles 110, 113, 115, 159
Vygotsky, L. 4, 97, 116–19, 157, 161

CPSIA information can be obtained
at www.ICGtesting.com
Printed in the USA
FFOW01n0352300316
22800FF